# Sail to New Zealand

*The Story of Shaw Savill & Co*
*1858-1882*

by

DAVID SAVILL

ROBERT HALE · LONDON

Robert Hale Limited
Clerkenwell House
Clerkenwell Green
London EC1R 0HT


British Library Cataloguing in Publication Data

Savill, David
 Sail to New Zealand : the story of Shaw
 Savill & Co. 1858-82.
 1. Shaw Savill & Co — History — 19th
 century
 387.5'065'41        HE945.S45

ISBN 0-7090-2809-1

Photoset in North Wales by
Derek Doyle & Associates, Mold, Clwyd
Printed in Great Britain by
St Edmundsbury Press, Bury St Edmunds, Suffolk
and bound by Western Bookbinders Ltd.

# Contents

*To my family*

# List of Illustrations

Colour Plates

Black and White Photographs

### Picture Credits

Lawrence and Aitken Ltd., London: 6, 9-15; Avon Fine Prints Ltd., Christchurch, New Zealand: 8; Maritime Museum Association, San Diego, USA: 16, 27; Shaw Savill & Albion Ltd., London: 21, 25, 29-30, 35, 38; National Maritime Museum, London: 22-4, 26; David R. MacGregor: 33; *Illustrated London News* Picture Library, London: 36-7, 40. All other pictures from family sources.

# Acknowledgements

I wish to acknowledge in particular the help and encouragement I have received from the staff serving in the various departments of the National Maritime Museum, Greenwich, including the Old Brass Foundry.

Help was also received from the staff of the Customs and Excise Department, the *Illustrated London News* Picture Library, Furness Withy & Co Ltd (which now owns Shaw Savill & Albion Co Ltd), the Libraries of the Royal Commonwealth Society and New Zealand House, and the Central Reference Library of Westminster City Council. Also searches by port authorities in New Zealand and North America into their archives have been much appreciated.

In writing this book I have naturally consulted many documents, private papers and other books, but I would like to acknowledge particularly the use I have made of Lloyd's Registers of Shipping, Lloyd's Lists, *Flag of the Southern Cross* by F.C. Bowen, *Shaw Savill Line* by S.D. Waters and *White Wings* by Sir Henry Brett, that great chronicler of sailing-ships in New Zealand waters.

I also owe a special thank-you to Kenneth Savill and other members of my family for their advice and the valuable sources of information they have made available to me.

Finally, I should like to record my debt of gratitude to the indefatigable and patient efforts of Janet Dyke, Valerie Tarry and my daughters, Pippa and Caro in deciphering, typing and re-typing my manuscript and generally helping progress to be made, also to Stourie, my wife, for keeping the boiler stoked.

If anyone feels aggrieved because I have failed to acknowledge their help by way of advice, material, copyright or industry, I can only ask them to accept my apology for a discourtesy never intended.

# Foreword
## by Lord Grey of Naunton
### GCMG, GCVO, OBE

New Zealand was fortunate in the quality of the men and women who went there from Great Britain and Ireland during Queen Victoria's long reign to make their homes across thirteen thousand miles of sea. There was great quality of mind and hand – in farming of many kinds, in the learned professions and in the skilled trades. But there was also great quality of spirit. There had to be, if one was to triumph over the physical difficulties of life in a new land and if one was not to be defeated by the trials and tribulations of the voyage to get there. Courage and resolution were needed. There is much romance in the story of the brave beginnings that have led to New Zealand's creditable place among the nations today.

It should not be forgotten that those beginnings had their less agreeable side. Sober chroniclers of today have even called the early New Zealand 'the lawless land' and 'a society in which sinners predominated'. Those of us who have benefited from the successful labours of the early settlers should add to our pride in their endeavours a respectful acknowledgement of all that they necessarily had to endure.

Vision, courage and resolution were needed also by those who made possible the transfer of settlers from the Old World to the New. This book tells the tale of one such, Walter Savill, ship-manager and ship-owner. In his case the romance is increased, rather than diminished, by the fact that although he despatched more than 1,300 ships to New Zealand and was thus responsible for the passage of scores of thousands of emigrants to a land in which he took a great and effective interest, he himself went no farther towards the Antipodes than the end of Brighton Pier.

Air transport and great changes in general economic circumstances have reduced to a matter of hours journeys than in Walter Savill's day took months and have greatly increased the numbers of people able to make those journeys. What is now commonplace was once the adventure of a lifetime or even, for many, an unattainable dream. For those accustomed to the comparative comfort and safety of travel today it is not easy to realize what a voyage to New Zealand required of the early settlers.

My own first voyage across the world, half a century ago, was in the opposite direction to that of the emigrants. I was bound from New Zealand to England. And I travelled, not in one of Shaw Savill's sailing-ships, but in a steamship of a different line. But sailing as a passage-worker in a somewhat aged vessel and in quite considerable discomfort gave me at least some ability and an inclination to respect and admire the men and women who made the hazardous voyages of long ago. They entrusted their lives to the Commanders and crews who conveyed them. The seamen, for their part, risked their own lives on their skill as sailors and the quality of the sailing-ships that they manned. And those who provided the ships, whether chartered or owned, risked their good repute, their money, their homes and possessions and the wellbeing of their families on their drive and energy and trading skill. The oceans were always unpredictable and ready to exact a price. Tragedies such as that of the *Cospatrick*, retold by David Savill in this book, were a constant reminder of the dangers of the sea.

The names and deeds of many on both sides of the world who contributed to the development of Queen Victoria's farthest dominion are well known; others whose work was equally important are less well remembered. Walter Savill and his associates and their ships played an essential part. It is good that David Savill's filial piety and his own fascination with New Zealand have produced for us this account of 'Young Savill' and his doings.

Naunton, Gloucestershire, 1986

# Preface

The purpose of this book is to publish a family account of Shaw Savill & Co in its first twenty-five years – from when two young men in the City of London, Robert Shaw and Walter Savill, formed a precarious business partnership in 1858 to help consolidate the British connection with New Zealand, by populating the country with British stock, largely from families deprived as a result of the Industrial Revolution. In the process, both men helped Britain push out the frontiers of her Empire and formed within it the substance of one of the most enduring and charismatic shipping enterprises of all time, Shaw Savill & Albion Co Ltd, which went on to carry the vital trade between Britain and New Zealand for 125 years.

This account includes the practicalities of running a shipping business in Victorian Britain, the agonies of sea travel and the withering public comments as the business expanded.

In order to make the story hang together, it has been necessary to go lightly over ground already covered in earlier publications, but unnecessary and lengthy repetition of events has been avoided whenever possible. No claim is made for the account to be a definitive work for this period. Instead, emphasis has been given to the strengths and frailties of a great human endeavour by many people concerned, in the belief that that is where the main interest now lies.

Unfortunately the Blitz of 1941 on London destroyed many old records but the evidence of the results of this partnership does not depend entirely on records. It is everywhere to be seen in New Zealand today and is shared with other Victorian entrepreneurs whose services to the young nation were equally important.

With the advantage of more hindsight it is now possible to see this important period for Shaw Savill and New Zealand more objectively – as a partnership wider than the two young men in London could at first have possibly imagined, a partnership that perforce embraced a third partner, New Zealand, whose interest quite rightly came to prevail. It is also easier now to understand more fully the scale of human endeavour and sacrifice involved by all concerned – governments, migrants, Maoris and ship-owners – and at sea by very individual acts of superhuman skill by lonely Commanders and of quiet courage by indomitable passengers. The sailing-ships, however delightful to behold, were merely the necessary appendages to this immense human effort by so many people bent on offering and seeking a better life in New Zealand.

For Walter Savill, who lost his original partner early, it went on to be a lifetime's work of singular tenacity given to New Zealand, a country in whose future he deeply believed but which he never visited. For the muse of history, his efforts might be seen now as an example of Victorian enterprise and service at their best.

# 1. Antipodean Outposts

The first British connection with New Zealand of real consequence began when Colonel William Wakefield, aged thirty-nine, arrived at Port Nicholson (Wellington) on 20 September 1839 on board the *Tory* with the object of buying land from the Maoris and selling it in Britain to suitable intending settlers, the first shipload of whom was due to follow a few months later. He had been sent on ahead to Wellington by his elder brother, Edward, who had recently revived the New Zealand Company to consolidate the British interest in New Zealand by populating it with British stock on a systematic basis.

Edward Gibbon Wakefield had become a leading colonizer in Britain but was troubled by his Quaker conscience. He believed that Utopia did not just evolve: it had to be planned, using whatever non-utopian methods were necessary. He needed a big stage on which to pull it off – and he very nearly did in New Zealand, but he overlooked the weaknesses of human nature.

The money raised from the sale of land in New Zealand was to be used to give free passages to emigrant labourers to build the churches, schools and roads required and to give a fair return to shareholders. His motives and methods were not unacceptable in Victorian Britain, bent on populating other lands overseas in order to dispose of a surplus and somewhat restless labour force at home in a way most likely to bring benefit to all parties concerned, including the emigrants, who otherwise were faced with slum conditions and a life of deprivation as they became victims of the Industrial Revolution.

The British Government's interest in New Zealand had not been particularly visible hitherto, and Wakefield's initiative was not welcome, as it was feared it would complicate reaching a decision on whether or not to proclaim yet another British possession to protect the inhabitants (the Maoris) and the settlers from their worst instincts when the two met, fears that were justified all too soon.

Prior to 1839 and subsequent to Captain Cook's departure from

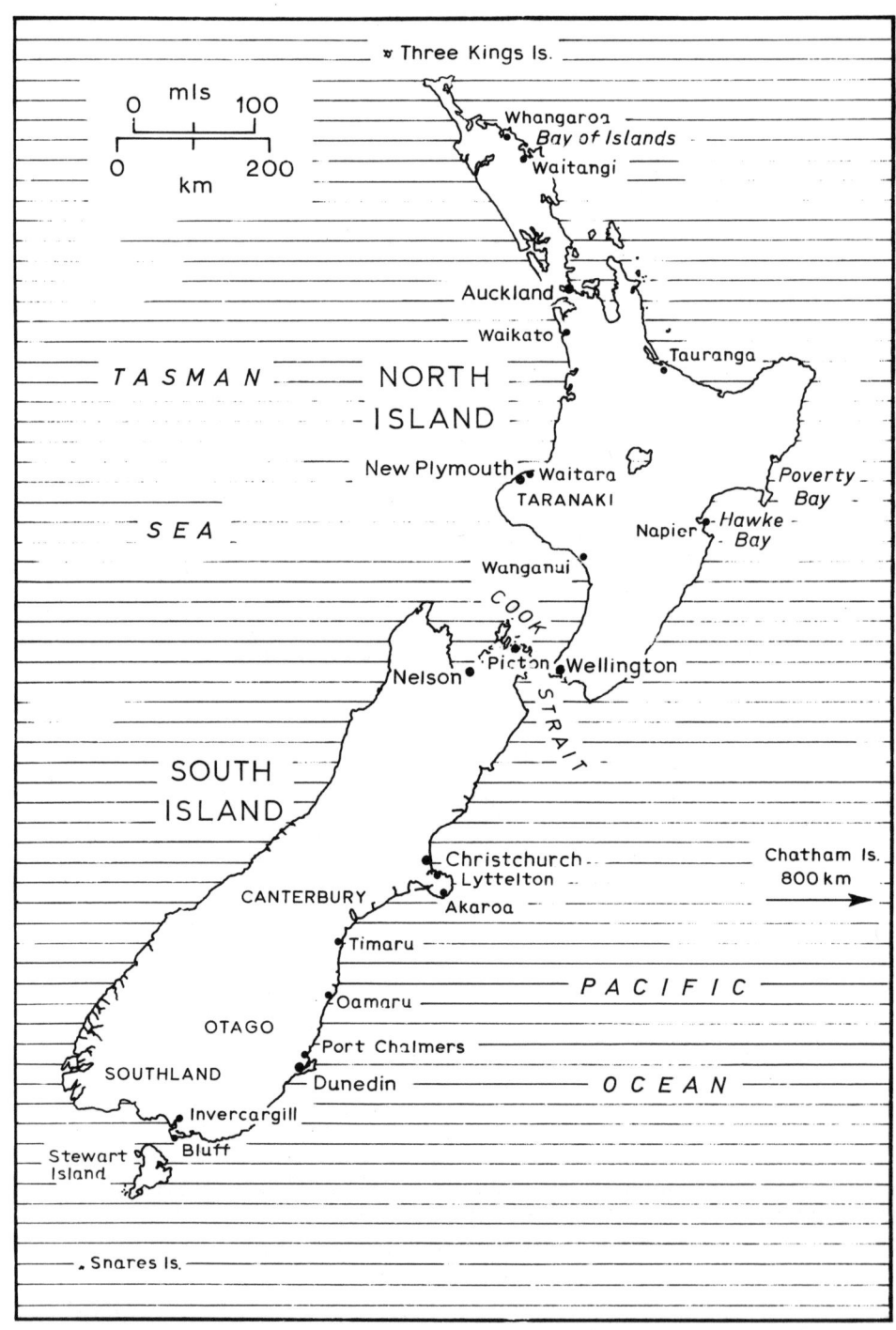

the New Zealand coast in 1777, a sprinkling of European settlers and explorers were already to be found in New Zealand. They were mainly the wrecked or abandoned crews of visiting whaling vessels, merchant adventurers or prosperous rascals pushing their luck, trading in flax and timber, having moved on from Sydney where the frontiersman was becoming subject to too many civilizing restraints for which he did not care. Many were based in or near the Bay of Islands at the extreme north of New Zealand. Most had Maori wives and drowned any sorrows with copious amounts of arrack rum.

French interest was particularly evident in their substantial whaling fleet in New Zealand waters, but the Governor of New South Wales, who watched over the situation in New Zealand on a needs-must basis, found any responsibility he had to assume for the country not too demanding – until 1809, when the crew of a British ship, the *Boyd*, loading timber at Whangaroa in the Bay of Islands, were killed and eaten by the Maoris. The Governor's somewhat tardy reaction was to impose a penalty bond of £1,000 on New Zealand traders to refrain from misconduct with the Maoris. Clearly the *Boyd* crew were seen to be at fault. This was not an auspicious result for promoters of British settlement in New Zealand.

All was reasonably quiet in New Zealand again until 1814, when Samuel Marsden, Senior Chaplain in New South Wales, was given leave to go at his own expense to Whangaroa and explore the vicinity to see if, through religion, trade or education, some accommodation could be reached with the Maoris, some of whom Marsden had made a point of meeting on their visits to Sydney. The upshot of this visit and others was that Marsden proved himself a man of the stamp of David Livingstone or Robert Moffatt of Southern Africa – missionary, trader and patriot, able to turn on the physical wrath of God, as understood by the British, without too much difficulty or squeamishness. He was highly regarded by both Maoris and settlers and soon established the first European settlement at Rangihou in the far north of New Zealand, in 1815. He left twenty-five people there to teach, to build houses and boats, to make fishing lines etc – above all, to teach the Maoris 'how to cultivate their lands and improve their country'. As the missions had to be self-financing, they traded with the Maoris: basic household and farm goods for timber, gum and flax.

The number of missions grew, the Maoris fought one another and the traders profited. In 1825 the first New Zealand Company tried in vain to establish a settlement in the Bay of Islands but not unnaturally took fright at the sight of a Maori *haka* danced for their welcome. Very sensibly they sailed on to Sydney, where the Union flag flying from Government House as they entered harbour must have calmed their shattered nerves. But the continuing French interest in New Zealand was less easily frustrated. A French warship called in 1831, with rumours of a French Roman Catholic bishop to follow. It was enough for the Anglican missionaries, who petitioned London for British protection.

Some people in London also had already begun to think it high time a British presence was formally established in New Zealand to protect the scattered British settlements and assert Britain's assumed right to seek out new peoples, preferably black, to be saved in the British idiom. The more discerning minds must have been thinking equally of the need to protect the right flank of Australia and the trade route from Australia to Britain via the Horn.

By 1833 conditions had come to such a pass that a British Resident, James Busby, a Collector of Inland Revenue in New South Wales, was appointed to watch over the situation and to try to weld the Maoris into a nation of sorts. They were not interested. Even if Busby had had the resources necessary to enforce his actions – he had none – he was hardly an inspiring choice, but he probably suited the arm's-length policy of the British Government. When Charles Darwin, the naturalist, visited the British settlements in the North Island in 1835, he was singularly unimpressed – but then who would not be, having first dallied with the sweet charms of Tahiti?

In 1835 Baron de Thierry proclaimed himself 'King of New Zealand' on the strength of purchasing 40,000 acres in the Bay of Islands from the Maoris. Busby's sense of humour deserted him and he appealed to London for help. He had to wait five years before it arrived, as a sledgehammer.

In 1839, when Colonel Wakefield sailed into Wellington Harbour ready to do business with the Maoris over their land, there were about 2,000 Europeans settled in New Zealand, thankful to have reached land safely from a variety of departure points and having no intention of venturing forth again unless for very compelling reasons. (Forty years later, this population had grown to half a million, which reflects both on the fertility of the settlers and on the prodigious efforts of shipowners to provide tonnage to carry an immense human traffic.)

Colonel Wakefield bought his land, and the immigrants began to arrive at Wellington, still unsure whether they were to step onto British soil. The whole enterprise seemed rather tentative, even to the most committed colonist, but the alternative of widespread unemployment and poverty at home had been a sufficient enducement to them to travel 13,000 miles to New Zealand in small wooden sailing-ships to carve a living out of virgin forest and tussock plains. Britain was in the full surge of the Industrial Revolution, which had begun to mechanize agriculture and displace farm labourers, who were driven to seek jobs in towns, where conditions were grim. At the same time, there were men who were growing rich on the tide of the Revolution and who were interested in investing their profits in overseas enterprises in the Empire. At this time therefore, there were ready supplies of labour and of capital for overseas developments – though New Zealand had to compete for them with other new countries of the Empire, such as Canada, South Africa and Australia.

Once the immigrants were ashore in Wellington and transferred to a better site than their original landing, thanks to a peaceable Maori chief, they set about to order their affairs for the protection of their life and property, as there was no British Government recognition of their action, let alone protection. Two major steps thought necessary were the appointment of a council and a magistrate, and a share-out of essential civic duties. This gave the settlement the appearance of permanence and was re-assuring to the settlers. In effect, it was an organized and carefully thought-out form of local government – which proved to be its undoing.

1839 was also the year when the British Government at last became reluctantly involved in New Zealand. The Company's despatch of emigrants, reports from James Busby of violent tribal wars in New Zealand threatening British lives, petitions from British settlers and the latent French interest in New Zealand had goaded the British Government to bow to the inevitable and despatch a Lieutenant-Governor, Captain William Hobson RN, in a frigate, hard in the wake of the *Tory*. Captain Hobson had, however, first to call at Sydney to get his final orders from his superior, the Governor of New South Wales, and this delay gave Colonel Wakefield four months grace in which to complete more land transactions before the Governor's axe fell on them.

For the next few months, it was 'so far so good' with this first settlement at Wellington – until the French also began to land settlers, at Akaroa, and until the first British Governor began to take a closer look at his territory. Meanwhile the Colonel had been busy buying up land on other parts of the coast of the North and South Islands in a race with land speculators who had begun to arrive from Australia and with the Governor who it was feared had arrived to interfere. The news of Hobson's imminent arrival was a mixed blessing to the Colonel at that moment, as there were shiploads of immigrants at sea expecting to take possession of land he had now to purchase urgently. Later many of these purchases were to prove dubious. The recriminations were to come when the Maoris realized that they had sold their birthright to the Colonel and to others.

Captain Hobson's orders were for New Zealand to be annexed forthwith, subject to the agreement of the Maori chiefs. Only eight days after Hobson's arrival in New Zealand a treaty was signed at Waitangi, on 6 February 1840. It was as quick as that. Hobson and Busby were not prepared to mess about, and they left the Maori chiefs little alternative but to sign.

By the time the French settlers arrived off Akaroa in August 1840, Hobson was well established. He had proclaimed sovereignty over the whole of New Zealand and declared that all claims to land purchased from the Maoris were subject to his confirmation. He had also proclaimed Colonel Wakefield's settlement at Wellington illegal. By design or accident, it had overstepped the mark by arresting a ship's master. Hobson called for its administration to be wound up and the settlers to swear loyalty to the Crown – which of course they were delighted to do now that the British Government had in effect offered them its protection at long last. Another round to the New Zealand Company, and a royal charter to boot followed soon after.

Although Hobson's new authority put a brake on Colonel Wakefield's activities on behalf of the Company, he continued to establish settlements at New Plymouth and Nelson.

What had begun as a trickle of a few pioneering souls possessed of more than their fair share of courage and virtue soon became a steady stream. By 1842, British stock in New Zealand numbered 11,000.

The far-sighted men of the New Zealand Company realized that to persuade the British to emigrate to this territory would require special inducements. For this purpose they ran a newspaper, gave dinners to important citizens in London, Glasgow and Dublin, awarded free passages in return for the purchase of land up to three-quarters of its real value, paid pocket money on the voyage and guaranteed employment on arrival. Posters displayed in bold type the kinds of people sought, and the Company's agents were paid 40 shillings for each married couple they signed up. The Company received a Crown grant of four New Zealand acres for every pound it spent in the cause. Nevertheless, recruitment was very selective initially. There was a premium on fitness, courage, enterprise and adaptability.

At each early settlement established by the Company, a typical English village community was planted, including every branch of village life from the squire to the blacksmith. The emigrants took with them their speech and traditions, their religion and customs and their sturdy independence combined with respect for law and order. The settlement was meant to be self-supporting. The whole concept appealed to Victorian Britain and attracted men and women of a fine type. Later, virtues were less in evidence among the immigrants.

The Company also selected their small wooden ships with great care and usually insisted on dry-docking before putting them on charter. They prescribed rates of victualling and manning. A schoolmaster was provided if there were more than 150 emigrants. A surgeon was always carried and acted as the Company's agent.

On arrival in New Zealand the immigrants found that the glowing picture painted by the Company had little reality. However, they were hardheaded and practical, and most measured up to the challenge of the wild but beautiful country. In the process, many became rather bolshy and outspoken. Early living-conditions were crude and simple, consisting of a reed-and-sod hut with a thatch roof. In spite of the endless difficulties of land tenure, the settlers began to bring wool down to the harbours by 1850 but it was another thirty-two years before sheep carcasses could be carried homeward frozen in ships. Until then, as the small population could not possibly consume the meat available, many carcasses were boiled down into tallow, which commanded only a small price.

In September 1840, seven months after the Waitangi Treaty, the capital was sited and named Auckland. This soon grew into another settlement. In 1848 a settlement was established in Otago and in 1850 one in Canterbury, sponsored respectively by the Free Church of Scotland and the Church of England, but they were still influenced by the Wakefield concept of planned immigration.

The key land-ownership question, however, remained unresolved. In 1843 there had occurred the first serious clash with the Maoris at Wairau, near Nelson. It continued on and off particularly in the North Island, until 1868, frequently as full-scale war.

Depending on your point of view – Maori, pastoralist, speculator or land agent – land tenure in New Zealand was completely out of hand despite various Governors' efforts. The New Zealand Company, for example, thought they had bought two million acres from the Maoris but in fact a Government enquiry later established that they could justly lay claim to only 283,000 acres. Maoris appeared in Sydney, the principal British settlement in the Antipodes, offering to sell the whole of the South Island! The settlers too were not above squatting on land which took their fancy. The Crown monopoly on the purchase of Maori land was everyone's Aunt Sally.

In 1858 the New Zealand Company was formally wound up. It had in fact shot its bolt commercially·by 1850, when its resources could no longer match its activities, but because of the complexity of these its winding-up was a slow process. It had, however, served its purpose well, thanks partly to the soil and climate of the country in which it had invested, its policy of peaceful settlements (on the whole) and the freedom of trade the Government encouraged.

By 1858 the British population in New Zealand was 61,000, of whom the Company had brought out 12,000, and there was some semblance of a society able and willing to support the machinery of a unified and national government, even if the provincial governments wagged its tail. It was hardly a nation state.

New Zealand was still wild and primeval. Much of it was covered by thick bush, forests with huge trees and dense undergrowth, swamps and mountain ranges. The land was divided by swift rivers – swollen currents in winter and shallow creeks in summer – but the climate was agreeable and there was no drought. Land communications, apart from a few bridlepaths, were non-existent. Short coastal sea voyages were, however, possible – even if they meant a wet embarkation and disembarkation.

However, a successful farmer might earn £2,000 a year from wool from an investment of £6,000 on native pastures. If he laid down English grasses his return was even greater. Many returned to Britain with considerable wealth, few failed to do well.

The imperial scene leading up to 1860 was one of tranquillity with the Indian Mutiny and Crimean War behind Britain, Palmerston pursuing a vigorous even aggressive foreign policy, the City young in spirit and optimistic based on the unquestioned stability of the pound sterling, and New Zealand was possessing responsible government. With no major wars in progress, there was also surplus tonnage on the market looking for fresh employment after trooping.

It was as good a time as any to launch an enterprise dependent on all four factors, and Robert Shaw and Walter Savill recognized the fleeting opportunity and seized it in 1858.

They were men of their time, susceptible to the call of the flag, adventurers and wealth-seekers, part merchant, part dreamer and part benefactor – but totally subjects of the Queen Empress and responsive to the heady wine of profitable business in the imperial market-place.

## 2. *Two Lion Cubs*

Little is known about Robert Shaw's forebears. His father, William, was a lace merchant in Edinburgh and came from Protestant Irish stock. He died in 1833, at the comparatively early age of fifty-three, leaving a widow and four children with very little means. Robert's mother, Elizabeth, was the eldest child of a Scots lawyer and possessed a disciplined and cultivated mind supported by her Presbyterian beliefs.

Robert Ewart Shaw, born in 1823, was the third surviving child and ten years of age when his father died.

After her husband's death, Elizabeth Shaw and her little brood travelled to London in search of employment for her sons. She was probably persuaded to do so by a flamboyant young cousin, James Temple, who had a prosperous business (Temple, Low & Co) as a shipping agent and store merchant in Billiter Street in the City of London. It was Temple who is believed to have placed Robert Shaw in employment with Willis, Gann & Co, prominent shipbrokers and merchants in the New Zealand trade, and thereafter he kept an eye on his progress and lent a ready ear to his later plans to branch out on his own. Indeed, without Temple's shipping and business experience and, above all, good will, it is doubtful if Robert Shaw and Walter Savill would have had the necessary resources and self-confidence to form their own business, about twelve years after Shaw came to London.

Robert Shaw was a man of intellect and charm, who inspired confidence, known for his meticulously correct behaviour, his social ease and courtesy. His Irish and Scottish origins had also given him wit and probity.

More is known about the Savills (also Saville, Savile etc). They came originally from the village of Sayville (Sauville today) in the French Vosges, where they were the local landowners. The first record of the Sayville name in England is found at York in 1230, where they were wool traders. More Sayvilles appear in 1335, having sold their French estates to the Duke of Bar.

As England was then still a province of French civilization, with its

Catholic religion, French and Latin language in manor and church and equally feudal social system, the Sayvilles must have found it a home from home and soon integrated into the English establishment basing their livelihood on sheep, wool and cloth. Eventually the family became influential both in the North and in London and were rewarded with honours and titles for their political services, particularly in the seventeenth and eighteenth centuries.

As their business expanded, kin of the family are understood to have moved down to East Anglia, a region also well suited to sheep because of its large areas of poorish soil. The shorter Channel crossing from East Anglia, as opposed to from Yorkshire, added to the profits of the local English wool traders – but eventually the arrival of silk, linen and cotton must have made a big impact on their traditional industry.

In the several small villages and hamlets in the Roding Valley near Chigwell in Essex the family can be traced back to the 1630s, leading quiet rural lives in a modest manner. They were well established in the Dunmow area in particular as farmers and yeoman farmers and country craftsmen – and not above the odd brush with their neighbours, as the tithe records of 1706 for White Roding church report: 'Jon Saville. Philpots £4.00. Jonathan Saville paies me not half ye value for Philpots, which has three score and three acres – I was lied out of it.'

In 1826 there was a Jonathan Savill (local spelling) in Chigwell. He was primarily a builder but also recognized as a land surveyor and valuer. He had spent his youth in the fields and villages of the Roding Valley where his parents had lived and probably knew their lie and value better than many. He had married first, in 1820, a local girl, Ann Bellin, the elder sister of Samuel Bellin, the Victorian painter and engraver. She died three years later, shortly after the birth of the only child of the marriage, a daughter. Ann was twenty-nine when she died and Jonathan thirty-four.

In 1826 Jonathan married for a second time. His bride, Maria Lydall, was only nineteen. She was working as a governess in the vicarage at Chigwell, but her home was at Ipsden in Oxfordshire where her eldest brother occupied the family seat, Uxmore House. Her father, John Lydall, had died young, at thirty-six, only a year after Maria's birth. She was his last child and probably when old enough had to find some genteel occupation to support herself. The marriage at Ipsden to Jonathan Savill may not have been entirely a happy event for the Lydall family because not only was there an eighteen-year difference in age between bride and bridegroom but also the bride had been expected to marry into another county family as befitted her station in life. On the other hand, she was off the hands of her widowed mother and marrying a reputable and established businessman.

Maria was a spirited and handsome girl. She had style, courage, intelligence and grace, not unlike the qualities found in her ancestor who, as a young knight of 'good fame', is alleged to have stepped forward at the Battle of Hastings to hold the Papal Standard when the Hereditary Standard Bearer and another knight were not forthcoming to the request of the Duke of Normandy who had then turned to him, Tostain Fitzrollo le Blanc of Caudebec, to discharge the honour.

As one would expect, Maria was a great help to Jonathan in building up his business, and when she had to take over her husband's firm after his death in 1849, she developed an acute business sense to find the means of supporting the ten children they had reared in their twenty-three years of married life.

In widowhood at forty-two, Maria became a formidable lady, never losing her wit, sparkle and femininity. Samuel Bellin, who remained a close friend of Jonathan after the death of his sister Ann, painted Maria in a thoughtful pose, which was probably how she wanted to be portrayed to match the maturity of her new responsibilities. In many ways she was a hundred years ahead of her time, for her new situation forced unexpected responsibilities upon her which women in the Victorian age rarely saw as their role, either by inclination or by training and education. She took charge of her late husband's building firm, employing twenty men. She committed herself to the protection and education of her children, who were between nineteen years of age and a few months when her husband died. She placed in jobs her sons with sufficient intelligence and resolution to do well. She provided a home for her daughters until they married. She generated a respectable income from her husband's business. Above all, she saw to it that the moral values of Victorian Britain were known and sustained in her home. She was indeed the head of the family in every sense.

Alfred, the eldest son, undoubtedly helped his mother considerably in her widowhood. He supported her in his father's business and helped his brothers into jobs as they completed their grammar school education. The fourth son, and sixth child, Walter, had been born on 5 March 1836, and when he was fourteen Alfred helped to place him in the office of Henry Willis of Willis, Gann & Co of 3 Crosby Square in the City of London. Willis was probably known to the family as a client or had connections with the Lydalls, as it is inconceivable that Alfred, a twenty-one-year-old country youth would have approached a respected figure in the City on spec. In his letter of 14 December 1850, Willis wrote mistakenly about Alfred's 'son': 'Mr Henry H. Willis' compliments to Mr Savill and begs to inform him that he will take his son into his Office as Clerk, the answers to his enquiries being highly satisfactory.'

Walter joined the firm on Monday 16 December for a month on trial. He was placed in their shipping department and paid an allowance of £20 p.a. There he learnt the business of the carriage of goods by sea, shipbroking and ship management for the New Zealand trade. Two years later, when he had reached sixteen, his allowance more than doubled to £50 p.a., plus 'a dinner contribution' of £15 p.a. He was making good progress but because of his age not being very well paid (about £1,700 p.a. at 1986 values according to Bank of England sources). He was now in the freight section of the department under the kindly but watchful eye of his manager, Robert Shaw.

In 1855 Alfred also began work in the City, where, when only twenty-six, he opened an office of his mother's firm at 27 Rood Lane. Here he built up a reputation as a land agent, surveyor and auctioneer, whilst most of the building side of the business prospered under his mother's control at Chigwell. Perhaps he was getting under her feet at Chigwell or she wanted him too to strike out on his own. At any rate, five years later, when she was fifty-three, she had had enough of running the building side of the business and handed it over to him. He went on to found one of the prime firms of land agents, surveyors and valuers in the country, which still bears his name. One of his grandsons would create the Savill Garden in Windsor Great Park.

In the 1850s all Jonathan Savill's sons were working in the City, having had a firm but gentle push from their mother to make their way in the world with the best of any one. One is tempted to speculate as to how much they saw of each other there both in the beginning and later as they became successful, and whether there was ever any link-up between their various enterprises and interests. If there was not a pooling of resources, was there a pooling of advice and consultation, with Maria seated at her rightful place at the head of the table conducting an imaginative but restless orchestra of youthful industry and enterprise as her talented sons exposed their plans, admitted their anxieties and thrashed out their next moves?

Besides Alfred, there was Walter, whose shipping enterprise also bore the family name (for 125 years). There were Ebenezer and Philip who became successful brewers, Savill Brothers, in the Mile End Road in the City and whose brewery is still in use by Charrington's. Then there was young Martin, who did not have his brothers' business acumen and drive but who was sufficiently established in the City in the soft drinks industry at one time to marry the daughter of a Lord Mayor of London, Sir Thomas White. The remaining and youngest brother, Sydney, died in 1861 when only thirteen.

The brothers were to leave between them £2.5 million. In the City, Alfred became known by his contemporaries as 'Save All', Walter as 'Grab All' and Martin as 'Spend All'. One is tempted to speculate on the obvious attribute which could have been laid at the feet of Ebenezer and Philip but none is known. There is a strongly held suspicion that John Galsworthy looked to the burgeoning Savill family for some of his material for his *Forsyte Saga*.

Between 1851 and 1857 Walter had his head down in the heavy ledgers of Willis, Gann when he was not out canvassing for cargo or down at the Docks. He was learning the ropes of shipping practice, making business friends (who were to stand him in good stead later on) and gaining the confidence and trust of Robert Shaw, with whom a year later he would be in business.

It wasn't until 1864, some six years after the formation of Shaw Savill, that Walter considered himself sufficiently secure to marry. Matilda Helen Burness was twenty-one and he twenty-eight. She was the daughter of James Burness, most of whose family still lived near Aberdeen. He had, however, moved south and opened an office in Leadenhall Street, very near Walter, where he operated a business supplying coal to ships in London and exporting it to various coaling stations along the trade routes where sail was giving way to steam. In due course the quiet young girl from Aberdeen and the pushing young businessman in the City met, brought together by a common business interest in the coal that was supplied in modest amounts to the sailing ships on charter to Shaw Savill for use in their galleys.

Matilda could trace her family back to Walter Campbell of Bogjorgan Farm in Glenbervie, Kincardineshire, as could a celebrated son of Scotland.

Although the Burness family came from Kincardineshire they were in fact a sept of the Campbells of Argyll having fled in the seventeenth century from a small estate (Burn House) on Loch Etive after the Civil War when they had supported the losing party, the King and the Marquess of Montrose, against the wishes of their clan chief, the Marquess of Argyll, a Covenanter.

In exile in Kincardineshire, the family changed their name from Campbell to Burnhouse (after their Argyllshire estate). This was later modified to Burnes. One particular Burnes son, William, later

moved south, first to Edinburgh and then to Ayrshire. When the
Ayrshire people were faced with the name Burnes as written they
took it to be pronounced as one syllable – Burns. The Ayrshire
branch of the family let it be but the Kincardineshire family ensured
the perpetuation of the two syllable name by adding an 's' to make
it Burness. One of William's sons, Robert, was to bring fame and
honour to the family through his verse to become Scotland's
national poet.

In the next fourteen years, Matilda bore Walter five sons and five
daughters. He took her to live first at Leytonstone in Essex, then at
Wanstead Hall, Wanstead and finally at Finches, a well-propor-
tioned and fine pile of Victorian neo-Gothic at Lindfield in Sussex,
which he bought lock, stock and barrel. He was in too much of a
hurry to employ Norman Shaw, architect.

For holidays, the family went to Moffat in Dumfriesshire where
Matilda's father had bought a house. She thereby retained the link
with Scotland and with the other branch of her family living in the
area. Increasingly, however, the delights of fishing and a scramble
over the moors gave way to the temptations of Brighton where
most of them, both sons and daughters, attended their first schools
and where Walter's brother, Ebenezer, lived at No. 6 Eastern
Terrace with his large family of thirteen children. So impressed
were Matilda and Walter with the effects of the bracing sea air and
bathing on their own children that they eventually established a
second home there on the sea front, at No. 9 Queen's Gardens at
the foot of Grand Avenue. Brighton came to suit Walter for other
reasons also. If he wanted to, he could travel there in his own ships
from London. Indeed that is as far as he ever went in them: on the
few occasions he took to the sea, usually in the *Lady Jocelyn*, his
favourite ship, a boatman used to meet the ship off the chain pier
and take him off. Brighton was also gay, fashionable, female and
amusing, and a great place for casting cares aside.

But back in 1857, he had none. He was still a young clerk in the
offices of Willis, Gann in the heart of the City, earning a modest
consideration which did nothing to quench the bright fire of
youthful energy, ambition and expectation burning in his belly as
he walked hurriedly along the City lanes deep in thought.

# 3. Private Enterprise

Willis, Gann were the leading shipping firm in London for passengers and cargoes in the New Zealand trade. Their main competitors operated from Glasgow under the name of P. Henderson & Co ('Paddy Henderson' to all). Business had been good for Willis, Gann since 1840, following the signing of the Treaty of Waitangi between the British Sovereign and the Maoris, which led to the first organized major shiploads of settlers being despatched to New Zealand by the New Zealand Company. Willis, Gann considered themselves to be in a strong position and not surprisingly had become complacent. At least, this was how the head of their freight section, Robert Shaw, and his principal clerk, Walter Savill, saw it in the late 1850s.

By 1858 both Shaw and Savill had decided that they could do better on their own, even though it meant that they would be in competition with their former employers. The times were also ripe for new enterprises.

The break came in January, after Shaw had had a major disagreement with his employers as a result of which they reduced his salary. The exact cause of the break is unknown but for some time both Shaw and Savill had been finding it difficult to defend their employers' policy of providing ships on the New Zealand berth spasmodically, no more than as the occasion demanded. In their view, the trade had developed sufficiently to justify a regular service of sailings to the main ports and fewer transhipments for the smaller ports. A direct service was needed by some of them. Shaw had found himself unable to meet shippers' demands whilst he was in the employ of Willis, Gann in 1857. Given this situation, there was ample opportunity for friction, misunderstanding and bad blood between them and their shippers, shipbrokers and principals, when things went wrong.

Shaw left Willis, Gann almost immediately following his disagreement, and Savill went with him. Within two months, having formed a partnership, they were sufficiently organized to be able to advertise a ship for New Zealand on their own berth in

London. It was not bad going in the circumstances.

The sudden and simultaneous departure of two top men from the key freight section of Willis, Gann (to be followed by others who went to join Shaw & Savill) must have come as a severe shock to the firm, without the additional fact that they knew they were to be faced with vigorous competition from men steeped in trade and with the closest contacts with shippers. Indeed, within five years they had surrendered the trade and their shipping business to their two former employees with, it is fair to say, good grace and good will – and probably some pride in the achievements of the two young men they had trained in the business, though it was many years before they could better the passage time of the nippy *Spray of the Ocean* which Willis, Gann sent to Auckland in 1859 in only eighty-seven days.

The partnership was established in offices at 24 Billiter Street (a few doors from Temple, Low & Co) in the City, in February 1858. Walter Savill was almost twenty-two years of age, had virtually no money and had nothing to lose by this venture. He borrowed from his mother to help him get going. Robert Shaw was better placed. He had a little capital – but he had a wife and home to maintain. He was thirty-five years old.

The situation facing them both in that early spring of 1858 was daunting. They had experience and were able in matters of ship management and broking and cargo handling in the New Zealand trade, but they were not men of means. They had many business contacts and friends, but they lacked influence. They had youth, energy, vision and will, but the main competition – their previous employers, the New Zealand Line of Packet Ships of John Morrison & Co, with sailings from London, and Henderson's Line of Packets with sailings from Glasgow – was well dug in. Others in the London trade included John Lidgett, Young & Co and W. Rufus Powell. All offered services in fanciful advertisements that would be seen as criminally misleading and false today. There were only occasional direct New Zealand sailings from Liverpool at that date, by James Baines' Black Ball Line of British and Australian Royal Mail Packets, and Pilkington & Wilson's White Star Lines; most passengers to New Zealand had to tranship at Melbourne or Sydney, making it a prolonged voyage for them.

Of all the competitors in the New Zealand trade at that time, Paddy Henderson in Glasgow was the only one to survive. The others, in London, faded quite quickly under the commercial doggedness of Shaw and Savill as they increased the pressure of competition with each turn of the screw of their new enterprise.

Paddy Henderson had been founded in Glasgow in 1834 by

First public notice in *The Times*, 15 March 1858

merchants specializing in Italian imports. They then began building
ships for the Mediterranean and Australian trades. They even had a
steamship mail contract between Suez and Melbourne. They first
began sailing to New Zealand, to Otago, in 1848 and soon
established strong links between the Clyde and the South Island.
Their first owned ship, the *Lady Douglas*, sailed for New Zealand in
1856. They found homeward cargoes in Burma of teak and rice.
Henderson's was a vigorous and likeable organization and soon
became friendly with the two young brokers in London, whom
they saw as no threat initially because their own Glasgow-Otago
trade was pretty well sewn up. The London brokers were seen to
have more catholic interests in New Zealand (although in fact
between 1858 and 1863 twenty-three per cent of their sailings
from London called also at Otago). Apart from some later
devilment with an emigration contract to Otago, Shaw Savill
always left departures from Scotland to Paddy Henderson (except
for one rare occasion in 1872 when they despatched the *Helen
Denny* from Glasgow to Auckland and Canterbury on 2 August.
This was a special arrangement agreed with the Glasgow firm from
which they had just bought her).

In those early days of 1858, Paddy Henderson were seen in London to be too far away in Glasgow to bother the Partners at all. It was a different trade up there. The Partners had a more pressing problem than speculating on the unique Scottish affair of the heart with Otago. They had yet to find their first ship to put on the berth in London on terms they could afford.

As a new business, the Partners lacked an office organization, credibility, finance and ships. They were publicly committed by their well-known views in the trade to assume enormous responsibilities including the life or death of members of the public travelling thousands of miles by sea in dangerous conditions, saddling themselves with huge debts, with their houses and families as surety in the event of failure. They had no means of knowing for at least six to seven months whether or not all was well and profitable with their first despatch, assuming that is that such proved feasible.

First, they had needed to set up an organization, an office and staff. This had not been too difficult as some good staff had joined them from Willis, Gann, both from the office and docks, and suitable but modest premises had soon been found in Billiter Street. In September they moved to 34, Leadenhall Street (where the firm was to stay for eighty-three years, until 1941 when the building was bombed).

The administrative and organizational requirements were manifold. There were no telephones, typewriters, electricity, biro pens or adding-machines in offices, yet a number of comprehensive and expensive shipping conventions and practices had to be observed as part of the back-up to any ship on the berth. The shore side to the business had therefore to be grotesquely labour intensive.

Having set up the organization, there still remained the major questions of credibility, finance and ships. These three key constituents were interwoven and could best be settled at a stroke by the efficient selection and programming of suitable tonnage and a word in the ear of a friendly banker who appreciated good collateral – a promised fistful of bills of lading for cargo about to be shipped. As for credibility, this had to be acquired with those involved in the New Zealand trade. This was not too difficult for the Partners in view of the years they had spent with, and their reputation in, Willis, Gann. But as new loading brokers and charterers they were assuming responsibilities which they had previously been able to avoid and for which now they had a direct public accountability.

They could not escape, either legally or morally, from the

Maria and Jonathan, Walter Savill's parents

Matilda Burness – wife of Walter Savill

*Electra* – oil painting by G. Dell

responsibility to safeguard cargoes and passengers placed in their care on board their ships, whether merely loaded or chartered. They could not therefore afford to load or charter other than the best ships available for the trade registered A1 at Lloyd's, not too old, staunch and the right size for the hazardous long voyage. They had to show care and honesty of purpose, and exude confidence to the timid. They had to declare not just a commercial interest in New Zealand but total commitment to its young life as a new colony. They had to quote competitive rates for freight and passengers and to build up an office and docks organization that worked smoothly together. To succeed, they had to offer a better service than anyone else and to justify their public position that the trade had grown sufficiently to support regular sailings.

One means of acquiring credibility was to assume you already had it – but proof of services helped. With this in mind, the Partners boldly decided to seek the earliest moment when they could write to the British Government and its agencies offering new services to New Zealand able to discharge satisfactorily any mail or emigrant contract available. They had also concluded that the only hope they, as newcomers, had of obtaining a mail contract was to put a steamship on the berth, regardless of fears about the voyage's out-turn. At the very least, they argued, the new firm would have been brought to the attention of the Government, which was important, and the out-turn on one voyage was not all that critical, seeing that they were committed to several because of the immense distance involved and sparsity of communications.

As to their delicate financial position, they could not afford to buy any ship or any part of one – cash and credit were in very short supply. (The first purchase of a ship, the *Cossipore*, 707 registered tons, was not until some seven years later, in 1865, by which time profits on the chartered vessels had begun to accumulate.) They had assumed from the start that they could afford to set themselves up as loading brokers for other people's ships primarily for cargoes, but within a matter of a few weeks they realized that they could also afford to charter under their own name if their organization and credit were sound and respectable. Soon they managed to act effectively in both capacities – with a little bit of luck and with backing from the bank.

One can almost hear the persuasive Scottish tongue of the quiet Robert Shaw as he sat, a figure of probity and sobriety, in the quietness of the banker's parlour while his partner was out in the bustle and noise of the City's lanes visiting the cavernous halls of the great merchant houses and the small attic offices of agents of manufacturing industry in the Midlands, and accosting his shipping friends on the pavements in efforts to lay his hands on the promise of any piece of cargo offering for New Zealand, especially for the unproven goldfields at Nelson, the latest news on which was always worth a round of drinks in the pubs where in particular so much canvassing for cargo was done. A scribble on the back of a sailing-card was sufficient and acceptable evidence of a promise of cargo or of a bargain freight rate struck – after several further rounds of drinks. Then, hurrying on to the next shipper, and the next, until Walter Savill was able to place in Robert Shaw's hands an offer of business, the necessary credit for which could not be easily refused by the careful man at the bank.

The Partners realized early that they could never expect the banks to put up all the money they still needed, even after taking into account the prospect of an immediate and helpful cash-flow from bills of lading and passengers' tickets. With their very limited personal resources available as a mortgage, they found they could not offer adequate security for the shipping services they had in mind.

Then came the selection of suitable ships (and Commanders) which for any trade always required a fairly fine judgement as there were so many factors involved as explained in a later chapter). But for the Partners in 1858 trying to enter the New Zealand trade without the necessary funds, they were forced to turn to shipowners who were willing to have a stake in the financial outcome of the outward voyage in return for the employment of their ship. Therefore in most cases, initially, the charter was for the outward voyage only, leaving the owner, or his Commander, responsible for picking up profitable freights in Australia, South America or even India and China for the homeward voyage, in which the Partners had no or little interest.

The New Zealand export trade was minimal then and consisted mostly of a little wheat, wool, flax and tallow. However, to demonstrate their stake in New Zealand in a somewhat provocative manner, despite the low visibility of its exports, the Partners appointed agents at Auckland, Wellington, Canterbury and Otago as early as 1858. The first despatches from London must have carried the offer letters. Only the *Avalanche* to Auckland made a decent passage. The agents at the other ports did not receive the happy news until confronted by rather distressed passengers at the end of very long voyages. All agents must have wondered what they were letting themselves in for. But the fact remains that David Nathan at Auckland, William Bowler at Wellington, Dalgetys at Christchurch and Russell, Ritchie at Dunedin saw the Partners splendidly through those difficult early years and, besides dealing with inward bound ships, managed to generate some exports when the Partners' services became more reliable and recognizable.

Finally, it was not merely a matter of despatching just one ship. The Partners had to be committed for at least a year, until the first voyage profits were known and ships then loading had completed their voyages. In short, they had to start with a bang and then keep the berths covered with regular sailings – with an anxious eye on reports of sightings and arrivals in Lloyd's List.

One of the most appalling drawbacks to their kind of operation in 1858 was the almost total lack of worldwide communications (until the *Great Eastern* obliged with an undersea cable in the Far East and Australia in 1880). When ships were despatched for New Zealand, there was no means of knowing whether they had arrived safely for at least six or seven months, probably longer, as it depended on the reporting ship making a direct and fast passage home. During the course of the voyage outwards they might be sighted by other vessels and a report brought back, but the safe arrival at the terminal port could not be reported in London for months. Even so, these means were so unreliable that reports were usually duplicated in the hope that at least one of the ships entrusted with copies of the report would reach home.

Meanwhile, as a blind act of faith, the Partners had to continue to put new ships on the berth to stay in the trade. The enormity of this undertaking by two young men with very limited resources has probably never been fully appreciated. The risks both to life and investment were horrific by present-day standards – but were remarkably consistent with the style of Victorian enterprise and practice when trade was following the flag, to the other side of the world if need be. The goldfields were probably a piece of luck at the time for the Partners or wind of them, and the usual surge of interest in sea passages that followed, could have been partly instrumental in the timing of their break with Willis, Gann.

There were, however, some circumstances in their favour. 1858 was a year of promise in the New Zealand trade as gold had been found in Nelson Province in the South Island and people couldn't travel there quickly enough, after the gold fever generated by the successful diggings in California and Australia. The Nelson finds proved to be rather minor (compared with those in Otago in 1861 and on the west coast a year later) but fortunately for the two entrepreneurs this was not known in the City in the spring of 1858. Their very existence was enough for exploitation by the Partners as 'New Zealand Gold Fields' when advertising their first ship in *The Times* of 15 March 1858: 'the beautiful full poop river-built clipper *Chieftain*', 382 registered tons, sailing direct to Nelson and the

Passenger's contract ticket for the *Chieftain*, 12 May 1858

goldfields, then on to New Plymouth (subsequently changed to Nelson and Canterbury) on about 15 April. The notice was sandwiched between five others advertising packet services to New Zealand. ('River-built' meant built on the Thames. It must have carried some cachet to the discerning.)

In the event, the *Chieftain* sailed five weeks later than advertised, reduced from ship to more humble barque rig to give savings on crew numbers and wages, and she took a tedious 149 days to reach Nelson. The gold-seeking passengers must have been desperate to disembark, despite the alleged 'accommodation of a most superior type', 'unlimited table' for cabin passengers, and second-class passengers being promised meals 'on a scale of the utmost liberality'.

Another early inducement to travel by Shaw Savill was the offer of free grants of farmland in Auckland Province. (Together with Lidgetts, Shaw Savill immediately introduced a service to Auckland more frequent than any other packet line.) The offer of land was generous – forty acres and 'upwards' to passengers over eighteen years of age 'proceeding by this Line and being eligible parties', i.e. who could afford to pay their own fare. Passengers between five and eighteen years of age qualified for twenty acres. Therefore a family of four was entitled to 120 acres – but the Partners advertised the maximum acreage on offer in 1858 as being as much as 500. Other packet lines advertised more modest offers. Perhaps they had had reports on the poor quality of land available, as most of it was still bush to be cleared.

The offer of this land was made by the New Zealand Government's agent in London as part of the rather piecemeal policy to encourage selective settlement in New Zealand. In practice, each Province was responsible for devising its own land policy. In this case Auckland hoped to encourage people of means to emigrate and thus help stabilize the various settlements by creating new jobs for people whose services they had required at home and would therefore probably require in New Zealand to support their life-style: carpenters, blacksmiths, wheelwrights, domestic help, shepherds, tradesmen and stockmen. Even when the *Royal Charlie* sailed from London in 1862, forty of her ninety passengers were female servants. 1858 also saw the provincial government of Canterbury offering assisted passages to 'agricultural labourers, shepherds, carpenters and other country mechanics and domestic servants' – but no offers of free land.

In 1858 ship-owners were somewhat off-balance, with a radical development in ship-design and construction taking place before their very eyes. A few miles down the Thames at Millwall, amid

great excitement, Brunel had at last managed to launch his monster
iron steamship, the *Great Eastern*, 700 feet long and displacing
23,000 tons. She was six times larger than any ship then built. As
the emigrants in the *Chieftain* floated down the Thames on the tide
from St Katherine's Dock in their small wooden sailing-ship, they
must have seen this huge iron ship being fitted out at Deptford and
wondered if they had taken leave of their senses in entrusting their
lives to such a frail shell by comparison to get them safely across
13,000 miles of ocean.

Robert Shaw and Walter Savill, and countless other shipping
men in the City, must have had similar doubts as they watched the
*Great Eastern* being fitted out, sometimes by the light of gas
torches, from January 1858 to September 1859. Shipowners were
apprehensive not only of the enormity of her construction but also
of the repercussions on the thousands of sailing-ships in which they
had invested. The Partners, with no such investments at that time,
probably felt fortunately free to respond to the changes that would
come, especially if it meant picking up a few sailing-ships on the
cheap.

The question the men of the shipping industry were then asking
themselves was: was Brunel merely trying to prove another
engineering point or was there really a sound commercial reason
for the huge ship? At one time India, Australia and the North
Atlantic were all thought possible trades for her. In the event,
however, it was the North Atlantic for a few years, followed by a
web of telegraph-cable laying worldwide. So instead of being a
threat to the livelihood of shipowners, she proved a blessing, as by
1880 she had provided an absolutely vital facility, a rapid and
reliable means of communicating with their fleets in ports all over
the world. Until then shipowners had to continue to rely on the
message held in the maritime equivalent of the cleft stick – a casual
sighting at sea and reports sent home by agents using the same slow
method.

The Partners' ideas for marketing their services for cargo and
passengers were quite well constructed, having overcome an initial
shyness and awkwardness. What emerged was a happy
compromise between the quiet self-confidence of the canny Scot
and the brash enthusiasm of his young English partner.

First, they thought better of trading under their own name for
the prospective passenger side of the business and within a month
had adopted the somewhat pedestrian name 'The Passengers' Line
of Packets' to distinguish it from the other packet services to New
Zealand. A strong reason for the change was that they heard that
the New Zealand Government was not inclined to award contracts

to individuals. Private partnerships with a proposed line of packet ships were not much better but they were better than sole traders. The new name may have sounded impressive but, on the face of it, it was an odd choice, as it indicated no connection with New Zealand or with anywhere else for that matter. It showed a singular lack of imagination if it was meant to capture the thoughts of potential passengers for far-off New Zealand. (Later they had second thoughts and added 'for New Zealand'.)

Their early marketing policy was not, however, entirely devoid of appeal. They had decided they needed a house flag to be worn at the London Docks by all the ships they had chartered and were loading, or were merely loading. They had wanted to establish their own identity amidst that forest of masts and spars and the noisy bedlam of the dockside.

They had a flash of inspiration in choosing as their house flag a design closely resembling the first so-called national flag of New Zealand – that is, the one chosen by certain Paramount North Island Maori chiefs at the British Residency at Waitangi on 20 March 1834 as a standard under which all interests in New Zealand could unite. To the casual observer it *is* the same flag, but there are important differences of detail: Shaw Savill's stars in the flag are six-pointed instead of eight-pointed, and the smaller red cross is not edged with a white border as in the national flag finally approved in London. The national flag had flown stiffly in the breeze on the lawn of the Residency at Waitangi as the approved colonial ensign for six years, February 1840, when the Treaty of Waitangi saw the hoisting of the Union Jack on the assumption of British sovereignty. It had served a very useful purpose at sea as it had offered the protection of the Royal Navy to any colonial vessel flying it.

The national flag has an interesting if not confused history which needs to be understood, if possible, to grasp the significance of the Partners' extraordinarily effective move to purloin it.

The outline design of the national flag closely resembled the White Ensign of the Royal Navy, which is not too surprising considering it is reported to have been designed by an ex-lieutenant of the Royal Navy, the Reverend Henry Williams, who had since become a missionary in the Bay of Islands. It was one of the three designs submitted to the Maori chiefs for their approval in 1834. The interesting question is why did they choose it? No doubt its association with the Royal Navy, their potential maritime protector, left a heavy impression on the minds of those assembled on the lawn at Waitangi.

The New Zealand Company, as the prime sponsor in the United

Kingdom of emigrants to New Zealand, was seemingly the first to purloin the national flag design when its Colonel Wakefield formally hoisted a close copy of it at its first settlement at Port Nicholson on 20 September 1839 as its Company's flag. It is strange that he did not fly the approved flag. As a soldier, he would have been rather particular about correct form. At any rate the Colonel needed a flag when his party landed on a strange shore. What he hoisted was sufficiently close to the real thing to fool the Maoris into thinking friends had arrived and to satisfy the authorities that the Company's representative was not flying the true national flag without permission.

It is equally strange that the Company's surveyor, Charles Heaphy, in his famous drawing in 1841 of part of Port Nicholson shows, even after Thomas Allom had made it into a lithograph of domesticity in 1842 to encourage emigration, neither the national flag nor the Company's version of it, nor the Union Jack, but the White Ensign in two places. It is not inconceivable that true White Ensigns were what potential emigrants most wanted to see at that juncture, rather than home-grown versions, despite their pedigree.

The Company itself was all spent in 1850, well before the Shaw Savill partners appeared on the scene in 1858. Nevertheless, as a new firm they could not have risked failing to seek permission from someone, probably the Company in its final throes of being wound up in the same year, to fly the old Company's flag because it was this flag and not yet another (i.e. their own) adaptation of the national flag that they flew – unless of course all versions were meant to be the same flag, which is quite possible.

At any rate the young firm had linked themselves simultaneously with the Colony and sentiment, and thereby a probable source of much-needed revenue. It was a popular and adroit move. The flag is indeed striking and smart and remains one of the most distinguishable in the British Merchant Navy after 125 years use.

The second adroit move by the Partners before their first ship was placed on the berth was to befriend William Stones, who was on the point of completing his essay on New Zealand for the Society of Arts. The essay was so well received that he was awarded the Society's Medal for it, but there his scholarship would have ended had not the Partners seen some commercial advantage in it. They decided to sponsor its publication as an up-to-date and reliable guide to New Zealand for potential emigrants – but subject to a suffix by them on the services they were offering in response to the requirements of a safe voyage. (They were ingenuously frank about their motives for supporting the essay: 'Every man naturally prefers his own particular interest and therefore if we are asked to recommend any particular Line of Packets we naturally recommend our own.') The Victorian English is stilted and correct, and compatible with the frock coat in the office, mutton chop whiskers, top hat and black walking cane.

From its first appearance, the guide was accepted as a great source of information about New Zealand, not only its physiological and governmental data but also what you could buy there, what you should take out, Customs Duties payable, frequency of mails and basic skills needed – in fact, how to survive in fairly hostile conditions. It was a great point of reference for all concerned and probably indispensable for many. A *vade mecum*. It was even a comfort in time of trouble at sea, with a few deft phrases from the Partners: 'little grumbles' on board could become 'cordial sympathies,' and 'hearty co-operation' with the ship's officers was recommended. The Colonials were reported to detest above all else, lazy people.

Substantial extracts of the Partners' contribution to the seventh edition (1864) of the book are in Appendix A. Much of it reads today like a homily but one mustn't forget the style and culture of Victorian Britain when such efforts were expected to be expressed in rather unyielding prose and in support of firmness of character at all times.

Sailing cards for shippers of cargo needed careful drafting to squeeze out the virtues of each ship, the name of its Commander and any sponsors, so that shippers could see at a glance the answer to the sort of questions they might have. On the back of the cards were scribbled freight deals with shippers who retained them as evidence of the rate agreed for their shipment. The use of the term 'Commander', instead of Master or Captain, followed the practice of the East India Company where he was more than the captain of a ship: in command of the voyage, he was responsible for dealing with all eventualities affecting the ship, its passengers and cargo. In the New Zealand trade it is more than likely that he was equally responsible in the 1850s and 60s for finding profitable cargoes for the homeward voyage. If he was fortunate, there may have been a local agent to help him and the opportunity of making some profits from private trade. At any rate, it was important to publish the name of the Commander of each ship because many established a high reputation with shippers, insurers and passengers. In the end, all had to put their trust in one form or another in his good sense and seamanship.

The sailing cards of the *England* and *Gainsborough* (see p.42) are sufficiently subtly different to cause one to speculate about the difference between 'a regular trader' and 'a magnificent clipper'?

# NEW ZEALAND.

To Follow the "MATOAKA."

Under Special Engagement to the Provincial Government of Canterbury.

## RECEIVING GOODS TILL 10th JANUARY.

DIRECT FOR

# CANTERBURY,

The magnificent Clipper

# GAINSBOROUGH, A1.

997 Tons.

C. CHARLTON, Commander.

## LOADING IN THE EAST INDIA DOCKS.

This beautiful Clipper, built last year, may safely be relied on for Quick Dispatch, and sound delivery of Cargo.

APPLY TO

# SHAW, SAVILL & CO.,

THE NEW ZEALAND PACKET OFFICE, 34, LEADENHALL STREET LONDON, E.C

---

# NEW ZEALAND.

To Follow the "LOCHIEL."

## RECEIVING GOODS TILL 25th NOVEMBER.

DIRECT FOR

# OTAGO,

The Regular Trader

# ENGLAND, A 1, 10 YEARS.

1000 Tons.

JAMES FOX, Commander.

## LOADING IN THE EAST INDIA DOCKS.

This beautiful Clipper, built in 1863, is noted for Speed and sound delivery of Cargo.

APPLY TO

# SHAW, SAVILL & CO.,

THE NEW ZEALAND PACKET OFFICE, 34, LEADENHALL STREET, LONDON, E.C.

Sailing cards for the *Gainsborough* (1867) and *England* (1868)

LETTERS OF CREDIT GRANTED TO PASSENGERS FREE OF CHARGE

# NEW ZEALAND.

## THE PASSENGERS' LINE OF PACKETS

### For OTAGO, GOLD FIELDS, Direct,

The famous fast-sailing full poop Passenger Ship, "GEELONG," A 1, 1,000 Tons Burthen,
W. WALLACE, Commander.

**NOW LOADING IN THE ST. KATHARINE DOCKS.**

*Provisions included.*

CHIEF CABIN FARE—For One Person, the whole Cabin ... ... ... ... ... ... 75 Guineas.
For Two Persons in the same Cabin ... ... ... ... ... ... 50 „ each
Stern Cabins by special agreement.
SECOND CABIN FARE—Enclosed Cabins ... ... ... ... ... ... ... £25 „
STEERAGE { Enclosed Berth, separate Cabins for Married Couples ... ... ... ... ... 20 „
{ Open Berths ... ... ... ... ... ... ... ... 16 „
Children under 12 years to pay one-half Passage Money. Infants under 1 year no charge.

**Chief Cabin Passengers supplied with an unlimited table, including Live Stock.**

**SCALE OF DIETARY FOR EACH ADULT PASSENGER PER WEEK.**

| ARTICLES. | Second Cabin. | Steerage. | ARTICLES. | Second Cabin. | Steerage. |
|---|---|---|---|---|---|
| Preserved Meats ... ... ... | 2 lb. | 1 lb. | Tea ... ... ... ... ... ... | 1½ oz. | 1½ oz. |
| Soup and Bouilli... ... ... ... ... | ½ lb. | — | Coffee ... ... ... ... ... ... | 3 oz. | 2 oz. |
| York Ham ... ... ... ... ... | ½ lb. | — | Butter ... ... ... ... ... | ½ lb. | 6 oz. |
| Fish ... ... ... ... ... ... | ¼ lb. | — | Cheese ... ... ... ... ... ... | ¼ lb. | — |
| Prime India Beef ... ... ... ... | 1 lb. | 1¼ lb. | Currants, or ... ... ... ... ... | ¼ lb. | — |
| Irish Mess Pork ... ... ... ... ... | 1½ lb. | 1 lb. | Raisins, Valentia... ... ... ... ... | ½ lb. | ½ lb. |
| Biscuit ... ... ... ... ... | 4½ lb. | 3½ lb. | Suet ... ... ... ... ... ... | 6 oz. | 6 oz. |
| Flour ... ... ... ... ... ... | 4½ lb. | 3 lb. | Pickles ... ... ... ... ... ... | ¼ pint | ¼ pint |
| Rice ... ... ... ... ... ... | 1 lb. | ½ lb. | Mustard ... ... ... ... ... | ½ oz. | ½ oz. |
| Barley ... ... ... ... ... ... | ½ lb. | — | Pepper ... ... ... ... ... ... | ¼ oz. | ¼ oz. |
| Peas ... ... ... ... ... ... | ½ pint | ½ pint | Salt ... ... ... ... ... ... | 2 oz. | 2 oz. |
| Oatmeal ... ... ... ... ... ... | ½ pint | 1 pint | Potatoes, fresh, or ... ... ... ... | 3½ lb. | 2 lb. |
| Sugar, raw ... ... ... ... ... | 1 lb. | 1 lb. | Preserved ditto ... ... ... ... | ½ lb. | ½ lb. |
| Lime Juice ... ... ... ... ... | 6 oz. | 6 oz. | Water ... ... ... ... ... ... | 21 quarts | 21 quarts |

For all children and infants an equivalent quantity of sago, flour, rice, raisins, suet, and sugar will be substituted for salt meat if required.
Provisions of the best quality are put on board according to the above scale for 22 weeks, together with an abundant supply of extra stores as medical comforts for Passengers generally.

The arrangements of these vessels are based upon long experience. Every improvement which, from time to time, suggests itself as conducive to the comfort of Passengers (without losing sight of economy in the rates of Passage) will be promptly adopted.

## SHIP'S REGULATIONS.

PASSAGE MONEY.—Each Passenger is required to pay a Deposit of one-half of the Passage Money on securing his berth, which Deposit will be forfeited in case of non-embarkation. The other half to be paid, prior to embarkation, at the Office of SHAW, SAVILL & Co. On remitting Deposit, particulars of *Name, Age, Country, and Occupation* of each Passenger must also be given.

CABINS are appropriated in rotation as the Deposits are paid.

LUGGAGE.—Chief Cabin and Second Cabin Passengers carry half a ton, and other Passengers quarter of a ton measurement of Luggage only, *free of charge;* the remainder, if any, is paid for at the current rate of freight. What linen, &c., is required for the first week or two should be packed in a handy Bag, and should be clearly marked "Cabin."—Luggage forwarded from the country for shipment should be carriage paid. The name of the Passenger and the Port of his destination should be *painted* on each case or package; and then each should have a card tacked on bearing the direction:—"Care of SHAW, SAVILL & Co." To be delivered at the St. Katharine Docks, per the New Zealand Ship "GEELONG," when if a letter of advice be sent to SHAW, SAVILL & Co., at the time the articles are sent off, they will be duly shipped All extra Passengers' Luggage and Goods, however, should be delivered at the Docks seven days before the sailing of the Ship. The Dock charges on Luggage amount to about 2*s*. per box or package, according to size.

*N.B.—The Luggage packages most necessary to have in the Cabin should be marked "Cabin;" and those most likely to be "Wanted on the Voyage" should bear these words, so that they may be stowed in the Hold, where access can be had from time to time.*

EMBARKATION.—Passengers embark at Gravesend the day following the Ship's leaving the Docks, or in the Docks if they prefer it.

LIQUORS.—Wines, Beer, &c., of the best quality, are provided at the following prices:—Port or Sherry Wines, 3*s*. 6*d*. per bottle; Ale or Porter, 1*s* per bottle; Brandy, 4*s*. per bottle; Spirits, for Chief Cabin Passengers only, 3*s*. per bottle; but for the better preservation of order in the Ship, the quantity so supplied will be under the regulation of the Commander. No private supply allowed to be taken into the cabins.

CHIEF CABIN PASSENGERS provide their own furniture, bed places, and whatever else they may think requisite within their private Cabins. The Owners of the Ship supply everything that is required for the table, viz.—plate, linen, glass, attendance, &c.

SECOND CABIN AND INTERMEDIATE PASSENGERS have berths built for them, but find their own bedding, and other fittings they may require. They must also provide themselves with the following utensils, viz.—knives and forks, table and teaspoons, one or two deep metal plates and dishes, a hook teapot, cups and saucers or tin drinking vessels, and a water can. The Provisions are daily prepared by the Cook of the Ship, but Passengers must in other respects attend to their own arrangements for messing. They must be provided with a proper supply of Clothing and other necessaries for the voyage. Second Cabin Passengers receive only partial attendance in cleaning the Cabin.

**Shaw, Savill & Co. effect Insurances on Baggage and Passage Money**

*For Freight, Passage, and further information, apply to*

**SHAW, SAVILL & Co., New Zealand Packet Office,**
34, LEADENHALL STREET, E.C., LONDON.

Read the New Pamphlet "NEW ZEALAND—THE LAND OF PROMISE, AND ITS RESOURCES," by W. STONES, Esq. Price 4d. post free, 5d. The Society of Arts awarded their Silver Medal to the Author for this Pamphlet. The 3rd Edition just published, contains the latest statistics information, &c., from the Colony, and can be had at the above office.

Passenger notice for the *Geelong* (1862)

One ship could be 'relied upon for quick dispatch' (i.e. get-away) and the other was 'noted for speed'. You took your choice and paid your money – or was there really no choice in fact when as a shipper you were primarily interested in identifying the next ship in the berth, and the draftsmen's care in the selection of words to appear as an inducement on the sailing card were wasted on you? However, a shipper could not dismiss entirely the idle thought of who might offer the best odds for the safe arrival of his cargo. In the event, both the *England* and the *Gainsborough* made good passages of under 100 days. The *Gainsborough* even managed to cover 300 miles in 24 hours i.e. $12\frac{1}{2}$ knots.

The sailing notices for passengers needed a different kind of appeal. Besides information on the ship and the name of its Commander, such words as 'gold fields', 'free grants of land', 'direct', 'free of charge' and 'unlimited table' (for some) all started bells ringing. Then there were the fares to be paid, scale of food to be supplied, liquor available on board and ship's regulations – with a reassuring reminder that all arrangements made were based on 'long experience'. You could believe anything you wanted to really.

The sailing-notice for the *Geelong* (see p.43) from Gravesend to Otago on 20 March 1862 sets it all out in a plausible manner which must have appeared less than perfect to the passengers when they disembarked 138 days later on 5 August in the dead of winter after a very long voyage of 'slow starvation and agony' but mercifully, or hopefully, in a good cause – gold.

The Partners had despatched nine ships in 1858 before they knew six months later, that the first one to arrive (the *Avalanche* at Auckland) had arrived safely. That called for iron nerves. She was the fourth despatch and made a fast passage in ninety-five days. The safe arrival of the *Avalanche*, reported in Lloyd's List of 21 December 1858, was, however, the best Christmas present the Partners could have. The first three despatched had still not been reported as arrived, although two of them were steam ships. There was some moral there – but who cared about that when the champagne corks were popping in Leadenhall Street, their new offices?

But as the Partners raised their glasses, did not their eyes meet for a fleeting moment enough to convey to one another the same anxious message they held? – those ships were out of sight but they could never be out of mind.

# 4. 'Take Her Out, Mr Pilot'

By mid-May 1858 the open sea beckoned as the commercial effort gathered way. The Partners' first ship was loaded, ready to slip her lines in London Docks and make her way down river for Gravesend, Milford Haven and Auckland.

Lloyd's List was the main source of shipping intelligence and by convention New Zealand destinations were shown at the top of its sailings list, presumably because they were the best evidence to the readership of the full extent of the worldwide shipping services available from the Port of London. It was therefore easy to spot these sailings. Those by the Partners were first advertised with 'Shaw' as the loading broker. 'Shaw Savill' did not appear until 6 June 1860. For passenger sailings, the Partners used the front page of *The Times*. For the *cognoscenti*, the London Customs Bills List had all the detailed particulars of shipping activities in the port.

The first ships the Partners entered at the Customs in 1858 as ready to receive cargo, and advertised in the Press, were the following – which was a considerable achievement in the few weeks since they had broken with Willis, Gann:

| Date entered | Sailed from Gravesend | Ship | Destination |
|---|---|---|---|
| 13 March | 23 May | *Chieftain* | Nelson and New Plymouth |
| 6 April | 19 May | ss *Lord Ashley* | Auckland |
| 6 April | 2 June | ss *Lord Worsley* | Otago and Wellington |
| 8 April | 24 June | *Avalanche* | Auckland |
| 26 April | 6 September | *Lady Alice* | Nelson |

The sailing-ships were all advertised in *The Times* as being 'unrivalled vessels', to be despatched to New Zealand. They were hardly that, compared with the fine vessels employed in the North Atlantic and India trades, but then the New Zealand trade was Cinderella at that date. An even more preposterous boast was to follow: 'These ships are all A1 at Lloyds. They have full poops, lofty and well ventilated between decks, fitted with every modern improvement for the safety, comfort and convenience of passengers. The utmost care will be taken to provide a dietary of the most liberal character.' 'A1 at Lloyds' meant that a vessel had been surveyed by the qualified surveyors of Lloyd's Register of Shipping, and her condition had been found ideal for her class. You could not do better, in that sense – but it was the remainder of the claim about the vessel's charms that was so suspect to the more discerning. True, the *Lady Alice* was a new ship but she was a slow sailer. Her 131-day voyage to Nelson must have tested even the most generous spirits on board. Perhaps the Partners had covered themselves, because she was described in particular as being constructed to the most modern approved lines and had been specially adapted 'to combine the utmost speed with the most complete accommodation for all classes of passengers'. Clearly the passengers had to note the compromise – travel comfortably rather than speedily.

An extraordinary piece of good fortune for the Partners at this moment was the welcome news that the Inter-Colonial Royal Mail Company had recently acquired in the United Kingdom two small iron-screw steamers, the *Lord Ashley* (287 net registered tons) and the *Lord Worsley* (282 net registered tons) for the inter-colonial service between Australia and New Zealand and for inter-provincial voyages. This seemed a heaven-sent opportunity to the Partners. They contrived to be appointed loading brokers for the two vessels and used their position to bring themselves to the attention of the Government, with the offer to carry despatches and mail speedily and directly to New Zealand. That was a considerable inducement, as delivery of mail could be almost guaranteed within a prescribed period and it would be carried port to port instead of being transhipped at Melbourne (as usual). As a result of this initiative by the Partners, the first ship they ever despatched to New Zealand was a steamship – the *Lord Ashley*, from St Katherine's Dock in the heart of the City of London within a stone's throw of Tower Bridge.

The *Ashley* left Gravesend on 19 May 1858 and finally sailed from Milford Haven, where she filled all available cargo space with coal, on 26 May. She had ninety-seven passengers on board and took 148 days to reach Auckland, arriving on 14 October. The *Worsley* did better. She sailed from Gravesend on 2 June with ninety passengers and took 122 days to reach Otago, on 4 October. Hardly the fast passages promised. All agreed that it was still quicker by sail – indeed the Partners' fourth despatch, the *Avalanche*, reached New Zealand before the two steamships, despite having given them at least three weeks' start. And so it was to remain on and off for another twenty-five years, until 1883, when steamship design and back-up facilities were sufficiently advanced and reliable, and public opinion was demanding enough to support a regular steamer service in the trade. Although steamships were not profitable yet for the long haul to New Zealand, because bunkering stations were too scattered to allow a straight course to the destination, they were looked upon as an inevitable improvement on sailing-ships once their back-up requirements and fuel consumption could be economically matched. Meanwhile they sailed or steamed depending on the weather and the coal supplies on board.

The Partners soon built up the number of ships on their berths in St Katherine's Dock and at the East India Docks in London. By 26 April 1858 they had the above five ships loading. A fortnight later they entered another (*Gloucester*). By February 1859 they were advertising six New Zealand sailings to Willis, Gann's four. They had also agreed a number of joint despatches with John Lidgett & Co to give more substance to their claim of a 'Passengers' Line of Packets, sailing at convenient intervals for all settlements in New Zealand'. They needed Lidgett's help at first (until January 1859) because it was hard going for a new organization to get their ships loaded and away, let alone trying to give some semblance of a service.

Within a year of their formation, however, the Partners were dominating the New Zealand trade as a whole from London – a position Shaw Savill went on to hold for fourteen years, until 1873, when the New Zealand Shipping Company was formed. Paddy Henderson, however, continued to offer fierce competition in the trade to Otago, but from Scotland, leaving the London trade to local enterprises. In September 1859 the Partners opened a West End office at Regent Circus off Piccadilly.

Usually they advertised six ships loading at one time. By 1862 the number of their annual sailings was beginning to look formidable. It averaged almost one sailing per week to New Zealand ports, primarily to Otago and Auckland, with Wellington quite far behind. It usually took up to ten weeks to load each ship. In October 1864 they had as many as eleven ships on the berth to Willis, Gann's two.

They also loaded, if not chartered, several ships for the west coast of North America – Vancouver and San Francisco in 1858. This side-line ceased in 1861 because of the demands of their New Zealand sailings, but they were an interesting diversion and no doubt helped improve the cash flow in support of their main effort with New Zealand. In all, seven ships were loaded for North

America. Some were required to carry Royal Engineers to help maintain law and order in the gold rush in British Columbia.

From the beginning, the Partners gave a direct service to Nelson, which was soon coupled with New Plymouth, even Hawke Bay (Napier) in 1859. All were small ports, thus fulfilling one of their earliest declared objectives to serve direct, when they first set up in business together. By 1861 there were despatches to Nelson and New Plymouth every two to three months, and Southland (Invercargill) received one direct service in 1862. Their second objective, to provide a scheduled service to the main ports, Auckland, Wellington and Otago, was reached from September 1861, when there were regular monthly sailings direct to each port. The same frequency of sailings to Canterbury (Lyttelton) was not reached until a year later.

Things were going well for the Partners. Up to the end of 1862 they had suffered only one maritime disaster in 133 sailings – the burning of the *William Brown* at sea in 1861 with the loss of one life (which is referred to in a later chapter).

Between 1859 and 1862 they benefited from three events which kept them firmly placed in the trade.

First there were the Maori Wars, which flickered on here and there like the lightning of a tropical storm for almost ten years. They began with a dispute over land, particularly the misunderstood Waitara Purchase by the Governor. In a sense the wars were inevitable, as Maori lands were encroached upon by the immigrants, leaving the Maoris with a deep sense of injustice. The main fighting was in the Taranaki and Waikato regions of the North Island, and the Partners became involved in the trooping of imperial forces from the United Kingdom and India. Troop ships included the *Sir George Pollock* and *Nourmahal*, which sailed from Gravesend to Auckland on 7 May and 21 August 1859 respectively. In 1860 the *Sevilla* embarked troops at Queenstown for Auckland. In 1861 the *Sir George Pollock* was again trooping from Queenstown, and in 1863 the *Norwood* from Portsmouth, all bound for Auckland.

The Maori Wars were a disruptive influence on shipping services. New Plymouth was no longer available as a suitable port of disembarkation for passengers (but its open roadstead was always a drawback), and the number of immigrants for the North Island fell away as the extent of unsettled districts grew. However, trooping was not unprofitable to shipowners and was acceptable as a temporary experience in support of the flag.

The South Island remained largely unaffected by the troubles further north, and the flow of emigrants from Britain continued to

*Merope* – lithograph by T.G. Dutton

*Cospatrick* – water colour by J. Spurling

increase, as did wool exports from New Zealand.

The second event beneficial to the Partners was the discovery of gold in Otago in 1861. This was such a bonus to the young firm that they had to double their sailings there immediately from one every four months to one every two. It is reported that at one time there were more than 3,000 passengers a day landing in Otago. It is hardly surprising that, with a total population of 27,000, Otago was the most populated province of New Zealand, equivalent to half the total Maori population in the whole country. However, compared with Colorado, the goldfields in Otago proved very small and equally difficult to mine. Fortunately for the young Partners, this news took a long time to reach London and so stem the rush for passages.

The third beneficial event was in 1862 when, through their contacts in London, the Partners secured a New Zealand Government contract to carry emigrants to Otago at £13.10s per head from London and only £12 per head from Glasgow (including the rail fare to London). Naturally Paddy Henderson were not too pleased at this unexpected and competitive turn of events as they had covered the Glasgow-Otago emigrant traffic since 1848 and had even built ships particularly suitable for the trade – which is more than the Partners had ever done, let alone contemplated at that date. The result was that the numbers of Shaw Savill sailings from London to Otago were jacked up again, from one every two months to one every month – and it is doubtful if Paddy Henderson ever forgave Shaw Savill for this impertinence. They certainly alleged there was skulduggery in London. They were probably right.

From the very beginning of all these activities in 1858, a personal partnership existed between the two men, almost that of an uncle and favourite nephew, to which each warmed, both having lost their own fathers when young and in most need of fatherly love and advice. To Robert Shaw, Walter Savill was his 'dear boy'. He had taken him into his family and helped make a man of him long before they joined forces commercially in 1858. The partnership was to remain on these terms until Shaw died suddenly of a heart attack in November 1864 at the early age of forty-one. It was a shattering blow to young Walter Savill who was then only twenty-eight. He looked for comfort and support from his young wife whom he had married some five months previously, now seen as not a moment too soon – but the unexpected death of his senior partner and protector had deprived him not only of a respected and loved friend but also of a key resource who was to be keenly missed by Walter for the rest of his life and may explain his subsequent single-mindedness and self-sufficiency.

Many young men in his fragile position would have cut and run – but it was not as simple as that. He was faced with an enormous practical problem, not to mention fearful responsibilities if he cared to think about them too much. The partnership then had about fifty ships in its employ – eleven loading in London, twenty-two on passage to New Zealand, eight discharging in New Zealand and up to ten loading there, homeward bound or discharging in London.

In the event, the hand and love of his remarkable mother steadied him – and sent him forth again to discharge his responsibilities and fulfil his destiny in the City. She was to be a tower of strength to him for the next thirty years of her life. He slipped off to her whenever he needed her commercial judgement or comfort. At seventy-eight, she felt compelled to write him a loving poem for his birthday. It was one of the few papers he kept, envelope and all, to the end.

When Robert Shaw died so unexpectedly Walter Savill turned awkwardly to his younger brother, Norman, with the offer of a partnership. The offer was refused as Norman Shaw had begun to get his teeth into his chosen profession where he was to rise to pre-eminence. Walter turned next to James Temple for help and his offer of a partnership was accepted. He was expecting Temple to accept as he was the more obvious choice but he had felt obliged to make the offer first to Robert's brother. Temple was possessed of all the resources Walter needed – experience, contacts, cash and worldly wisdom – but his commitment to the trade had yet to be proved.

Despite Norman Shaw's refusal to become a partner in Shaw Savill, there were pickings from it for him throughout his life. He did work for the firm and its partners, for its bankers (Martin's and Baring's) and for other shipowners, particularly the formidable Thomas Ismay, founder of the White Star Line, for whom in 1882 he designed Dawpool, and he drew on their political friends when necessary. In 1884, when Dawpool was half finished, Thomas Ismay agreed to charter his spare fine Atlantic steamship tonnage to his architect's good friend Walter Savill, to help him start a steamship service to New Zealand. Norman Shaw had brought the men together first as business partners, later as friends, and this proved of great value to Walter Savill as he struggled to put Shaw Savill & Albion on its feet as the new public company it had become.

Whether or not Norman Shaw felt safe to take a few liberties with work for Shaw Savill and the families, each work undertaken has been said to be, in its own way, a new departure in his developing styles.

First, there was a rather charming tile-hung warehouse at Eagle Wharf in 1863 built for James Temple for Shaw Savill's use. It was constructed by Walter Savill's eldest brother, Alfred, who had by now started a building firm in the City, and it was Norman Shaw's first major building. Then came Leyswood at Groombridge, in Sussex, in 1870 for James Temple. This was Shaw's first country house. Its homely Wealden style of half tile-hanging, timbering and strong, tall chimneys was to catch the imagination of house-builders in southern England for nearly one hundred years. Third, there was another warehouse at Lower Thames Street in 1871. Here Shaw showed that even the most functional building could have its dignity and beauty.

Then in 1871-3 came his first office building, New Zealand Chambers at 34 Leadenhall Street in the heart of the City. Shaw Savill wanted offices and as much lettable space as possible. Shaw designed a building which had eighty small offices and a suite for the Company itself. It was a controversial but distinctive design. Its front was elegant yet domestic, being distinguished by large oriel windows and elaborate plasterwork (supported by piers of narrow brickwork. Its appearance was most unusual and pleasing for an office block in the City of London. Inside it was said to be a novelty of structure and style – but probably a rabbit warren by today's standards. Walter Savill and James Temple occupied a semicircular room behind the Company's general office which fronted the street on the ground floor. It was all destroyed in the Blitz on London on a Sunday night – 11 May 1941.

Finally, in 1875 Norman Shaw designed Chigwell Hall for Alfred Savill. Here he is said to have perfected his joinery forms and given 'a lesson in composition'. It had no bathrooms, which was not unusual at that time, but it is strange that Norman Shaw as a far-sighted architect let this pass. It is now a Police College.

In 1864, Walter Savill was impatient to find convincing evidence that James Temple could become a real business colleague with the same personal and financial commitment as his former partner. In the event, the disappointment was enough to make Savill hell-bent on his own self-sufficiency, both in business and at home. Despite the new partnership, the firm became known in the City as 'Young Savill's'. Walter Savill took the helm. The spirit of the old partnership was dead.

The opportunities available in New Zealand for a better life for the victims of the Industrial Revolution at home had given Savill a social conscience. He attended and spoke at public meetings in London, wrote pamphlets and joined the New Zealand political scene in London. He became quietly determined to provide these unfortunate people with the means of travel there – and this bee buzzed in his bonnet for the rest of his life. New Zealand, as a new country, was symbolic to him of the fresh start he knew he had to make in Leadenhall Street – not least for the sake of his old mentor and partner, the perpetuation of whose name in the firm's name was a defiant sign that it was business as usual. The job they had started together with so much enthusiasm, loyalty and expectation would be seen through and finished.

# 5. Sail

The success or failure of the enterprise depended to a large extent on the selection of ships for the trade and on the competence and character of their Commanders. Shippers of cargo and passengers had strong prejudices, and the emigration authorities had views, at least, if not regulations. An unblemished marine reputation counted for much at Lloyd's and elsewhere, in accordance with the Victorian convention of evaluating virtues above all else. It was of little use to offer a ship or a Commander of good repute: they had to be fused into a single, indistinguishable successful unit. This required considerable judgement by ship managers. Any failures of ship or Commander had to be given short shrift, unless the sea had already taken its toll.

There was, however, a strong element of luck about the selection of ships and their subsequent confrontation with the perils of the sea. The selection process by the ship managers was far from perfect. Despite management policies for most situations and ports, sometimes berths had to be covered quickly because inward-bound ships were too late for positioning outward or too slow in discharging their cargo, or failed their survey, or because shipbuilders had made late deliveries.

As for Commanders, they faced unusual hazards at sea, and their ships were not always as seaworthy as their surveys declared. Some leaked like sieves and, like the *Agamemnon* bound for Canterbury in 1872, were condemned on passage. Even a small miscalculation or surprise event at sea could produce disaster very quickly. Commanders died at sea, crews mutinied or were washed overboard, boats were stove in, saloons flooded, wheels and binnacles smashed, ships sank in collision with anything including icebergs or capsized in harbour due to lack of ballast, sails were carried away, masts came down, anchor chains parted, especially on lee shores, and cargo caught fire or shifted. As a last resort, the Commander had a revolver or pistol of some kind to enforce his orders — but someone at some time might be less vigilant or less seamanlike than necessary (it was not unknown for repairs to the ship to be on the Commander's account) and disaster would ensue. It was usually human error, although some allowance must be made for bad luck.

The state of the cargo was always a worry to Commanders, not only on passage, when it could shift or catch fire or be thrown overboard to save the ship, but also on its out-turn. On several occasions, owing to rough weather rather than bad stowage, the cargo arrived in New Zealand as a soggy mess or had to be swept into sacks before it could be discharged. When the *Siam* arrived at Auckland in 1868, her cargo was so saturated with salt water that it had to be auctioned. At other times, cargo had to be sold on passage to defray repair expenses, as happened to the *Doña Anita* in 1867 when she put into Rio de Janeiro leaking badly bound for Nelson. It was just too bad if you were the shipper or consignee.

There was a particularly notorious case when some cargo had to be swept into sacks. The *Blundell* arrived at Auckland in 1862 with such a cargo. The Commander was gaoled but he gave the authorities the slip by escaping from gaol and taking his ship out of harbour at the dead of night. Full marks for initiative, none for care.

The Commander also had to keep an eye on the food and fresh water supplies on board. Whilst these should always have been adequate for a normal voyage, as they were worked out according to a scale of victuals per person on board, things could go drastically wrong on a long voyage. In 1872 on a 216-day voyage to Wellington the *Glenlora*'s food supplies, except for rice, were exhausted, despite a forty-day stay in Mauritius for repairs and replenishment of stores. The passengers of the *Black Swan* bound for Wellington in 1865 were on reduced water allowance on a 130-day voyage.

On the whole, Shaw Savill ships were well found and manned. If they had not been, the firm would not have survived twenty-five years in face of the competition available. Of course some owners, charterers and even Commanders skimped occasionally on food and repairs and were tempted to carry too much sail or to make a fast passage at all costs. Some ships were too deeply laden with railway iron before the Plimsoll mark on the hull checked this malpractice finally in 1890. No one could claim that Shaw Savill ships and Commanders did not have their share of blemishes and, on several occasions, did not live up to the Victorian ethic of moral responsibility above all else – but what men of business could afford such a cultivated ideology? They were out to make money. More often than not, the consequences did not bear thinking about. Never look behind you – press on.

Since the repeal of the Navigation Acts in 1849, British

shipbuilders had been suddenly faced with the full might of American shipbuilding skills. No longer were importers required to have their cargoes carried in British bottoms, which had by design kept foreign ships out of the Empire trade in particular. Importers knew that American ships with their clipper lines could make a faster delivery for fine cargoes, such as tea, when special freights would be payable. The British builders were not slow to improve on the American designs and eventually to beat them at their own game. The result for British shipowners and managers was that there was soon a great fleet of British-built sailing-ships designed to suit various trades offering speed or stowage space or various permutations of both. There was a great choice of ship available – but in some you would not wish even your mother-in-law to take a voyage.

The size and rig of a ship most suitable to the New Zealand trade or to particular ports in the trade were always a bone of contention amongst shipowners and Commanders. Shipowners were concerned mainly with a meld of seaworthiness and profitability, possibly on occasions the minimum of one and the maximum of the other. Commanders on the other hand were concerned equally with seaworthiness and with the rig and manning scale, because when it came to the survival of the ship and its passengers, these were the critical factors.

There were three types of sailing-ship for the Partners to consider for employment in the New Zealand trade. Each type was determined by its rig. This is a complex subject but in simple terms the following descriptions give the main differences.

First there was the full-rigged sailing ship. On all her masts, usually three, were set great square sails, but on the aftermast lower mast she could also set another square type of sail from a spar gaff, called a spanker. Then there was the barque, similar to a full-rigged ship except that the aftermast mast had no yards or square sails at all but just fore and aft sails. She required less crew because she had fewer yards and square sails, and her rig was the most popular of all sailing-ships.

Finally there was the clipper – a much-abused term but one which captures the imagination as epitomizing the majesty of sail. The clipper was a full-rigged ship with lofty masts and spars carrying an immense wardrobe of sails. She had fine lines and was tender, needing careful ballasting and outstanding seamanship skills to bring home safely valuable cargoes or passengers at speed and thus able to demand the highest freight rates. The true clipper ship was not well suited to the New Zealand trade as her cargo capacity was not large and there was no need for great speeds to bring home

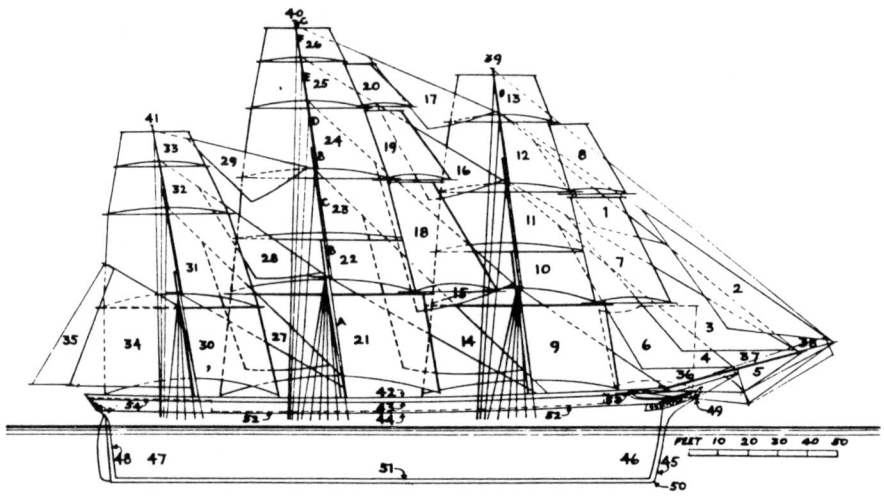

| 1 Jib topsail | 22 Main lower topsail | 43 Main rail |
| 2 Flying jib | 23 Main upper topsail | 44 Planksheer |
| 3 Jib | 24 Main topgallantsail | 45 Stem |
| 4 Fore topmast staysail | 25 Main royal | 46 Entrance |
| 5 Jamie Green | 26 Main skysail | 47 Run |
| 6 Fore lower stunsail | 27 Mizen topmast staysail | 48 Stern post |
| 7 Fore topmast stunsail | 28 Mizen topgallant staysail | 49 Figure head |
| 8 Fore topgallant stunsail | 29 Mizen royal staysail | 50 Fore foot |
| 9 Foresail (or fore course) | 30 Crossjack | 51 Keel |
| 10 Fore lower topsail | 31 Mizen topsail | 52 Deck level |
| 11 Fore upper topsail | 32 Mizen topgallantsail | 53 Monkey foc'sle |
| 12 Fore topgallantsail | 33 Mizen royal | 54 Raised quarterdeck |
| 13 Fore royal | 34 Spanker | A Lower mast |
| 14 Main topmast staysail | 35 Ringtail | B Doubling |
| 15 Main topgallant staysail | 36 Bowsprit | C Topmast |
| 16 Main royal staysail | 37 Jib-boom | D Topgallant mast |
| 17 Main skysail staysail | 38 Flying jib-boom | E Royal mast |
| 18 Main topmast stunsail | 39 Fore mast | F Skysail mast |
| 19 Main topgallant stunsail | 40 Main mast | G Mast head |
| 20 Main royal stunsail | 41 Mizen mast | |
| 21 Mainsail (or main course) | 42 Topgallant rail | |

Diagrammatic sail plan of a clipper of the 1860s

some luxury commodity such as tea. Eventually wool became important for as quick a passage home as possible but the economics of the trade meant that there was need of a careful judgement by shipowners between the needs of speed and capacity. Clippers were, however, employed in the New Zealand trade when the tea trade was over-tonnaged or the ships were past their best. Then their charter rates came down and Shaw Savill could afford to take them up, provided they had not been driven too hard in the China trade, to give a little edge to the competition on outward berths, particularly at the time of gold rushes. They were not, however, comfortable ships for passengers, as their sharp lines made them wet and lively in a seaway. Their chief advantage was that they could glide along in light airs. But to sail at their best they needed a large crew to make frequent sail changes in all weathers, which was an expense the firm preferred to do without on the prosaic New Zealand run. On the other hand, it often suited owners of tea clippers in particular seeking outward cargo to employ them on a triangular round voyage – first to Australia or New Zealand with general cargo and passengers, then to China with coal and finally to London with tea.

In 1858 Shaw Savill thought a vessel of about 500 tons and A1 at Lloyd's was about the right minimum size for the trade, but from the very beginning they chartered full-rigged ships and barques of a variety of sizes and later purchased some quite small ships of under 500 tons (*Anazi* 468 tons, *Chaudière* 470 tons). Several ships of even under 300 tons were chartered and sent out to all the ports, but latterly mainly to Nelson and Southland. None of these made smart passages. The best were the *Racer*, 244 tons, to Southland in 1868 and the *Rapido*, 299 tons, to Nelson in 1871, in 108 days each. Both lived up to their names, compared with the passages by other small ships.

The Partners were inclined to charter from the same shipowners, either because their ships were suitable for the trade or because they had established a friendly link with them. Foremost were Park Brothers of Fraserburgh, Shirres, Leslie of Aberdeen, Somes Brothers of Blackwall, John Lidgett of London, Greens of Blackwall, Devitt & Moore of London and Seymour, Peacock of London.

Robert Shaw's circle of Scottish friends and colleagues in the City, and later Walter Savill's family connections with the Aberdeen area through his wife, produced two particularly useful sources of support and ships.

First there was the firm of Park Brothers, prominent shipowners at Fraserburgh and well known in Aberdeen and Stonehaven. They owned a fleet of small wooden ships employed in the South African and Indian trades when Robert Shaw contacted them early in 1858 for his fourth despatch – the *Avalanche* (692 tons) on 24 June to Auckland. Thereafter Park Brothers, like Shaw Savill, on both a business and a personal level, became inextricably linked in the New Zealand trade for the next thirty-five years. They opened an office at 18 Leadenhall Street, a few steps from Shaw Savill's.

James Park became Walter Savill's closest friend. He was a frequent and popular guest at Finches and was well known to all the family. Later, partly in return for his friendship and support since the early days, Walter invited him to serve as a director of the new Shaw Savill & Albion Company, on its formation in 1882. Although James Temple was Walter Savill's partner, and later co-director, for twenty-nine of those thirty-five years, James Park as a fellow shipowner was the nearest Savill found to being his new mentor, joint schemer and innovator.

Park Brothers supplied not only the fourth despatch of Shaw Savill but also the seventh (*Kinnaird*) and ninth (*Lochnagar*) in the first six months of operations. In fact they were courageous enough to commit half their fleet to the untested enterprise of Robert Shaw and Walter Savill in this initial period. In time, having perceived their trust to be well placed, they offered the young firm some really significant larger ships which served at the heart of the Shaw Savill business – the *Hydaspes*, a new *Lochnagar*, *Celestial Queen*, *Wave Queen* and finally the great *Lady Jocelyn* herself. In all, up to 1882, Park Brothers' ships completed at least sixty voyages to New Zealand (and Australia) under the Shaw Savill flag.

The second useful contact in the Aberdeen area was the firm of Shirres Leslie. They too owned a fleet of small wooden and iron ships which were chartered by Shaw Savill. These included *Queen Bee*, *Calypso*, *May Queen*, *Marlborough* and *Taranaki* up to 1882, by which time they had completed at least forty voyages under the Shaw Savill flag. And there was a bonus in the person of Captain John Leslie, a remarkable owner-captain able to run any ship under his command with efficiency and safety. He was not a passage-breaker, but his attitudes to his responsibilities on board commended themselves both to the charterer and to passengers. Captain Leslie had the knack of getting the best out of a ship and all on board her so that both profited from the experience. In his own way, he set an example to other Commanders flying the firm's flag and was held in high regard for the fifty years he was active in the New Zealand trade. When he came ashore in 1885, he was appointed to co-ordinate in New Zealand the steamship service of Shaw Savill & Albion, and on his return from there he served on the board in London as a director. He too became a close friend and colleague of Walter Savill.

Of the hundreds of different ships chartered by Shaw Savill, thirty-one completed five or more voyages between 1858 and 1882, eight completed ten or more; some, the *Halcione* and *May Queen*, completed as many as fourteen voyages in this period. The *Lady Jocelyn* completed twelve chartered voyages before she was bought in 1882 and included in the fleet transferred to Shaw Savill & Albion, which continued trading with many of the same chartered vessels for several years.

Many were small wooden vessels which would stagger forth or bounce across the oceans and get their passengers to their destinations safely in their own time. Some were famous tea, opium or wool clippers such as the *Miltiades, Blue Jacket, Silver Eagle, Ben Venue, Coulnakyle, Oberon, Challenger* and *John Bunyan*, with lines so perfect that they satisfied the most artistic eye. Some were fine iron vessels specially designed for the passenger trade, such as the 1,447-ton *Rodney* for first-class passengers only. She had a smoking-room (cigars and cheroots), bathrooms with hot and cold water, lavatories in every cabin, and an eighty-foot saloon. Others chartered were handsome bluff-bowed Blackwall frigates used in the trade to India and the East, such as the *La Hogue, Statesman, Coldstream* and *Agamemnon*, and the auxiliary screw ships *Norfolk* and *Durham*.

Some were later special in their own way, like the *Sea King* which completed her maiden voyage in 1863 to Auckland before returning to Britain via China with a cargo of tea. She was an auxiliary screw steamer and had been built to take on the fastest ships in that trade. However, a more colourful career was opening out for her. On her next voyage, to Bombay, she got only as far as Madeira, where she was hi-jacked by the American Confederate States Navy after much deception for several months and became their marine raider *Shenandoah*, over a thirteen-month period successfully destroying thirty-seven ships – most of the Yankee whaling and sealing fleet. When the Yankees had won the American Civil War, she had to seek refuge elsewhere and ended up in Britain before becoming the private yacht of the Sultan of Zanzibar. An interesting end for a vessel of her capacity and reputation.

Other ships employed are best forgotten about, but most were ordinary working vessels, with fancy names to conceal their true performance or with not much touch of class about them, even if some were on their maiden voyage.

The Blackwall frigates, in particular, were rather grand-looking ships though inclined to be short and beamy, which made them more seaworthy, buoyant and dry. They could sail well up to windward, which made up for some of the fast runs by clipper-type ships on a reach. They were built on the Thames in the Blackwall yards of Green & Wigram, in the Sunderland yards of Pile, Laing & Marshall and in Calcutta and Burma. They usually had majestic figureheads and rows of windows in the stern. Their captains, who first enjoyed the title of Commander, entitling them to put Esquire after their name, invoked almost a naval discipline to run their ships. Ship's officers and crews wore a smart uniform, and decorum was important. The Commanders themselves were judged to be superb seamen. It was bad form, let alone bad seamanship, to carry away spars and rigging, which were always of the best, as were the ships, built of lasting oak or teak.

The slow build-up of Shaw Savill's own fleet did not begin until seven years after they had started operations. Initially, shipownership was seen as a mixed blessing, if not beyond the reach of the firm's financial resources. Also, there was probably no necessity for it as suitable chartered tonnage was readily available, profits were more reliable with such tonnage and could be forecast with less difficulty on a voyage-by-voyage basis. Finally, the whole business of ship management was working rather well without the additional responsibilities of ownership, and the firm wanted to see how the trade would develop. But the firm began to dabble in share-ownership (limited by ancient practice and law to sixty-four names) in various ships in the early 1860s because it helped secure the sort of tonnage they had discovered they wanted to cover their berths in the trade.

The first ship bought outright was the *Cossipore* in 1865, a wooden ship of 707 tons, fourteen years old. She made only one round voyage to New Zealand under the firm's flag and that was a disaster. Sailing from Gravesend on 15 October 1865, she had to put into Plymouth for repairs after storm damage and sailed from there nine months later. By the time she reached Auckland, on 22 November 1866, she had been 403 days on passage – an all-time record – and she was still leaking like a sieve despite the repairs at Plymouth. It was a bad first buy by the firm, and with hindsight they must have wished they had questioned the survey on purchase. She was sold on her return to Britain, presumably to another gullible buyer.

Setback or not, the firm bought two ships in the following year, 1866 – the *Monarch* and the *Strathallan*. Both were wooden vessels, of 1,415 gross tons and 548 gross tons respectively. The *Monarch* was twenty-two years old and the *Strathallan* nine. The

*Monarch* was a magnificent ship in the Blackwall tradition, as the following account of her specifications in the *Illustrated London News* of 15 June 1844 shows:

> This splendid mercantile frigate was launched on Saturday from Mr Green's yard at Blackwall. The Monarch is 1400 tons burthen; length of keel 168 feet; length overall 180 feet; depth from upper deck to keelson, 32 feet. The breadth of her beam is 40 feet, and it is only in this particular that she is inferior to the first-class frigates of HM Navy.
>
> She has an entire flush deck fore and aft; is pierced for 50 guns, and capable of carrying a greater number, for besides 16 ports on a side upon the main deck there is also an equal number of large scuttles on the lower deck.
>
> Her timbers and planking are chiefly of teak; the planks next the keel are American elm 5 inches thick, above this is teak to the whales, which are formed of African oak; the topsides are entirely of teak, and her bitts, capstan and most of the interior work are of the same wood.
>
> There are 12 cabins, averaging 11 feet by 10 each, and a dining-room 36 feet by 18 on the main deck, the fore part of which is bulkheaded off for the crew accommodation.
>
> The lower deck has 18 cabins (making 30 in all) of similar dimensions, the two after ones being the largest, 18 by 16 feet each, with stern windows. Before the lower deck cabins is a roomy space for troops.

Despite her impressive specifications in 1844, she was decidedly *passée* by 1866, when the firm bought her. In her first voyage under their flag, she had to put into Rio leaking badly. She was repaired and staggered on to Auckland, where she arrived after a voyage of 152 days from Gravesend. Her second voyage to New Zealand was to Canterbury in 1870, when she turned in a quite decent passage of ninety-eight days. The firm traded her more to Australia than New Zealand before selling her after seven years service. The *Strathallan* was sold two years after her purchase. Probably two more bad buys.

But the firm persevered with their purchasing policy, which was one of principle more than strategy. Also, with the opening of the Suez Canal in 1869, offering potential benefits to steamships and increasing their popularity, there were a number of fine sailing-ships on the market for a bargain price. Second-hand prices were generally low. Some fast American ships were going cheaply because of their shipping slump (following the revival of British ship building skills).

By 1872 there were seventeen ships in the fleet. Then came the big purchases in 1873-4, when the emergence of the New Zealand

Shipping Company created a demand for suitable chartered tonnage which previously the partners could obtain without much difficulty. In those two years Shaw Savill almost doubled their fleet to twenty-nine ships, and it was to remain at between twenty-six and thirty ships until amalgamation with the Albion Line in 1882. In addition, they took up shares in a number of other ships which continued to be managed by other owners (the majority shareholder) or, by arrangement, by friends in the trade. For example, in 1869 the firm owned $\frac{32}{64}$ths of the *Halcione* and *Electra* but both ships were managed by John Parker & Son of London. In 1872 the firm owned $\frac{43}{64}$ *ths of the Hydaspes*, and in 1873 the same share of the *Lady Jocelyn*, but both vessels were managed by James Park who owned merely $\frac{21}{64}$ths of each.

The average age of the forty ships bought between 1865 and 1882 was eleven years. Ten ships were over fifteen years old and three (the *Edwin Fox, Lady Jocelyn* and *Monarch*) over twenty years old when bought. When they were disposed of (some after transfer to Shaw Savill & Albion) or lost, the average age of the same ships was twenty-three years. Others were over thirty-five years old when finally disposed of (the *Euterpe, Soukar, Lutterworth* and *Lady Jocelyn*). One ship, the *Chile*, had completed twenty voyages by 1880 when she was sold. She must have been popular, which, together with the name of her Commander, was an important consideration before deciding to dispose of a ship. Clearly a ship's age was not necessarily a factor in the trade, or in her popularity. In fact, it has been said that the regular old-timers seemed to do rather well in the trade. Perhaps it was because they never had a dull moment at sea and were being constantly worked.

Most were full-rigged ships as opposed to barques, which is surprising considering the fewer crew members required by barques without a square sail on the mizen mast. Some were cut down to barque rig later to make this economy. Wood and iron hulls were evenly balanced as the table below shows:

| Hull | Barques | Ships | Total |
|------|---------|-------|-------|
| Iron | 5 | 13 | 18 |
| Wood | 4 | 12 | 16 |
| Composite | 3 | 3 | 6 |
| (Wood and Iron) | — | — | — |
| | 12 | 28 | 40 |

There seemed to be no particular purchasing policy except to have available appropriately sized owned tonnage to help support a service covering all ports, within resources available – which were obviously very tight to have had to be used for so many old wooden vessels. Some (the *Monarch* and *Edwin Fox*) were almost museum pieces and nothing but trouble, but the firm was still buying them up to 1874. Some of the iron ships bought were, however, splendid vessels, giving long service and smart passages. The size of ship varied from 468 tons (the *Anazi*) to 1,418 tons (the *Golden Sea*) with the average size being about 950 tons, excluding the *Lady Jocelyn* (2,138 tons).

The full list of ships bought and managed is given in Appendix B, but the number of ships at the Partners' disposal was, in fact, larger, due to the firm's part-ownership in a number of others regularly employed by them in the trade but managed by other firms.

The fleetest and sweetest of them all was that little beauty the *Crusader*, an iron ship of 1,058 tons bought in 1869 which completed fourteen voyages for Walter Savill and a further fifteen voyages for Shaw Savill & Albion. She turned in an average passage time to New Zealand of only ninety-one days land to land throughout this very long period. Once, in 1877 autumn in the South Atlantic, she made a record passage from Lyttelton Heads to the Lizard in sixty-five days, a truly remarkable performance by any standards for a quite small ship. She was so phenomenally popular that a Crusader Association was formed in New Zealand. At one time her Commander was only twenty-five years of age. Her overall performance was such that she was said by the experts to be more highly regarded by seafarers of the time than the famous *Cutty Sark*.

Shaw Savill ships were painted with dark green hulls and light brown masts and deckhouses. The figurehead, ship's boats and deck fittings were painted white, and the name and gingerbread carved scrolls on the bow and stern were picked out in gold. This livery was the smartest feature of their mixed bag of a fleet, and several ships on long-term charters also assumed it.

When it came to build a ship, the firm spared no expense – but sadly they built only six ships between 1858 and 1882, in the following sizes, hull construction and rig, based on their forecasts of how the trade would develop, without envisaging the explosion following the successful carriage of refrigerated cargoes (in 1882):

| Year Built | Name | Gross Registered Tons | Hull Construction | Rig | Builder | Fate |
|---|---|---|---|---|---|---|
| 1869 | *Zealandia* | 1165 | Iron | Ship | Connell, Glasgow | Scrapped, 1911 |
| 1870 | *Merope* | 1082 | Composite | Ship | Oswald, Sunderland | Burned at sea off the Azores, 27 June 1890 |
| 1874 | *Avalanche* | 1210 | Iron | Ship | Hall, Aberdeen (Cost £19,973) | Sunk in collision in the English Channel, 11 Sept. 1877 |
| 1876 | *Hermione* | 1176 | Iron | Ship | Hall, Aberdeen | Scrapped, 1913 |
| 1876 | *Pleione* | 1139 | Iron | Ship | Stephen, Glasgow | Wrecked, 1922 |
| 1881 | *Akaroa* | 1334 | Iron | Barque | Osbourne, Sunderland | Sunk by a German submarine, 1917 |

Except for the *Akaroa*, they were all full-rigged ships, larger than the average size of vessel in the fleet and elegant tall clipper-types with distinctive lines. They were built of iron, although steel was beginning to be used for shipbuilding in 1870. (The only steel ships built to order by Walter Savill were the *Lindfield* and *Mayfield*, four-masted barques of 2,280 and 2,285 gross registered tons in 1891-2 for bulk cargoes.) Most survived into old age.

The reason for this modest building programme was to be able to put some new ships specially designed for the top bracket of the passenger trade on the berth when competition from the new Albion Line of Paddy Henderson and New Zealand Shipping Company was strongest. These ships were for emigrants with a bit of money, taking out their family and household to make a permanent investment in New Zealand.

Ships built of iron, as opposed to wood, which was in any case in increasingly short supply in the 1870s except in North America, could meet the demand for more cargo space to carry the greater cargoes on offer, especially the bulk cargoes including wool. They did not need the great wooden beams and pillars of a wooden ship to support the hull structure and the lift from the sails. This strengthening took up valuable cargo space. Without them, cargo was also easier to stow, provided this advantage was not lost by failure to use adequate shifting-boards to hold the cargo in place on passage. Iron ships were also less likely to be burned by a fire in the hold or stores (although the *Merope* became a mass of flames down to the water's edge when her homeward mixed cargo caught fire at sea in 1890). Above all, higher freights could be charged for the carriage of cargoes in strong iron hulls, and they did not leak! No longer would crews be required to do a spell at the pumps or plug deck seams as part of their watch routine. However, some later iron ship designs, drawn in an effort to maximize carrying capacity, had no depth of keel and too much superstructure, with the result that they easily capsized unless carefully loaded and ballasted.

*Outward Bound* – oil painting by R.B. Spencer

*Halcione* – water colour by G.W. White

*Miltiades* – water colour by J. Spurling

In terms of performance at sea, iron had the strength to support a longer hull shape, which meant that such ships need not be slow. The hull itself was strong enough to support iron lower masts and yards held up by wire, as opposed to hemp shrouds needing constant maintenance, and therefore encouraged a great spread of canvas. There was, however, always the temptation to owners and builders to pile on the sail area to match the strength of the hull construction and masting on the drawing-board – and Commanders at sea took some time to adjust to the correct balance. The rigidity of the resulting superstructure caused many dismastings and unseamanlike efforts to drive the ship beyond its maximum performance in the weather conditions prevailing at the time. How many Commanders failed to shorten sail in time? A slight error of judgement or inexperience was enough to bring it all crashing down. And failure to allow for the marked deviation of the compass could prove even more disastrous as the look-out cried, 'Breakers ahead!' Other drawbacks were corroded plates in the hold, unless covered by cement or asphalt, and more frequent docking than a wooden ship, to clean away the marine growth. Effective anti-fouling techniques were still to be learned.

With the use of iron for hulls, or in composite form with the traditional hardwoods of oak and teak on an iron frame, came improvements to deck fittings and rigging which could mean that fewer crew were needed. The main improvements were with steam winches, Donkey engines, windlasses and capstans – all key aids to anchoring, sail-changing and working the yards and traces. Roller-reefing sails, more efficient pumps, boat-lowering gear and davits were other improvements. Where possible, muscle power gave way to steam.

The next area for technical improvement was sail plans. This was the most personal area of all, where owner, builder and Commander of the ship had strong views. The owner related the sail plan to the numbers of crew required to be on the payroll, the builders to the correct design balance between hull and superstructure, and the Commander to his natural needs based on experience.

To the casual bystander on the dockside, a glance aloft to a sailing ship's superstructure would have suggested lack of planning, lack of any order and a hopeless mess – and yet nothing was haphazard. It had all evolved gradually over the years. Everything was in its place for handling up to thirty-six sails. Seamen knew by instinct and training where to lay their hands on the sheets, the braces, the lifts, the halliards and the warps. Besides the square sails on each mast, there were the triangular staysails between the masts, and the jibs on the bowsprit. If further sail area was required, there were the square stunsails hoisted as an extension on each side of the square sails, a Jamie Green hanging from the bowsprit just above the water, and a moonsail or skysail at the very top of the main mast. The square sails provided the main drive for the ship. They were the topsails, top gallants (which possibly were divided into shallow upper and lower sails for ease of handling) and royals. They were all sheeted up the masts one above the other. The triangular sails, especially the jibs, edged the ship more up into the wind and improved steering. Particularly heavy canvas was required for use in strong winds or dirty weather.

The matching of this canvas to the ship's characteristics, her cargo, her crew and the weather was the Commander's responsibility. Regardless of the number of her sails, there was still a limit to her speed through the water – but time and time again Commanders proved that fast passages (under ninety days) could be done. What was particularly maddening for them was to run past or be prevented from entering their final port through a final quirk in the weather, such as fog or a sudden gale. The *Himalaya* had to wait ten days outside Wellington in 1878 before she could slip into port.

Passage times were important to shipowners, charterers, Commanders and passengers. Shipowners were acutely aware that days on passage and turn-round time at the end of a long voyage were critical to profit and loss. The faster the ship, the smaller the outlay on food and pay – but probably less freight because of the fine hull shape. Passengers wanted to minimize their period of discomfort and danger, but not at the expense of a Commander prepared to put padlocks on sails to prevent a frightened crew shortening canvas in dirty weather. Commanders wanted to obtain a fast passage so that they could expect further employment. There were many boasts of, and much confusion as to, fast passage times and fast speeds, even up to seventeen knots for several hours. All were due to some extent to good fortune with the weather, rather than to navigational skill or seamanship, although it required the latter to make the most of the former. Some ships, however, such as the *Crusader* and the *Ida Ziegler* made such consistently good passages that credit must be given to their designers and Commanders.

At the end of the voyage Commanders knew that they would have to account personally to Walter Savill, sitting four-square behind his big desk in Leadenhall Street and subjecting all to the direct gaze of those piercing blue eyes.

Of the 1,310 sailings under the Shaw Savill flag between 1858 and 1882, a third made passages in under one hundred days. The firm's ships and Commanders could not, however, compete with the fast, sleek clippers built by the Albion Line in 1874 for their Otago trade, which regularly made passages in under one hundred days. But not everyone wanted to travel to Otago: Shaw Savill served about ten other New Zealand ports requiring differing tonnage. However, no doubt more spectacular passage times would have been appreciated by their weary passengers.

The fastest sailing-ship passages recorded under the firm's flag between 1858 and 1882 to each port were the following:

*Hudson*   Gravesend to Napier 20 Nov. 1874 to 12 Feb. 1874 – 84 days

*Blue Jacket*   Gravesend to Canterbury 15 June 1867 to 30 Aug. 1867 – 76 days

*Sam Mendel*   Gravesend to Otago 9 May 1874 to 23 July 1874 – 75 days

*Merwanjee Framjee*   Gravesend to Auckland 4 Jan. 1876 to 21 March 1876 – 77 days

*Jessie Readman/Schiehallion*   Gravesend to Wellington (22 Sept. 1872 to 15 Dec. 1872-21 April 1873 to 14 July 1873) – 84 days

*Camperdown*   Gravesend to Nelson 14 April 1876 to 3 July 1876 – 80 days

Except for the *Hudson*, all were chartered tonnage at the time. The fastest outward passage by an owned ship was by the *Merope*, which sailed from Gravesend on 9 June 1871 and arrived in Canterbury on 25 August 1871 in seventy-seven days – only a day longer than that celebrated flyer *Blue Jacket*.

From 1870, when larger ships were employed, there was a notable improvement in passage times as Commanders could afford to bend on more sails knowing that the improved and larger hull shapes and the stronger masts, sails and running gear could take a greater strain, even if it meant a rather wet voyage for those passengers who ventured on deck when a moderate or worse sea was running. With stauncher ships, Commanders could also sail closer to the wind and shorten normal sailing tracks.

About five per cent of all voyages took over 140 days. The longest voyages were the 403 days by the *Cossipore* bound for Auckland in 1865 and 300 days by the gallant *Dallam Tower* in 1873, after being dismasted and repaired in Melbourne when bound for Otago.

The track from Britain to New Zealand was governed by the direction and strength of the winds at various seasons of the year and by the power of the vessel – and by Mathew Maury's remarkable *Physical Geography of the Sea*. Basically the track was south-south-west from the English Channel to make a landfall at St Paul Rock, (half way on the Equator between West Africa and South America) or, if you missed that, with the South American coast at Cape San Roque north of Pernambuco. Then the Commander had to pick up the South-East Trades to fight the vessel due south before bearing up to the south-east for the Cape of Good Hope for another landfall – except for the intrepid who sailed further down the South American coast before turning to make their easting – a direct run for South Australia through the Roaring Forties, and through ice if the navigational calculations had gone wrong. All Commanders had their own favourite tracks – and had to gamble considerably without weather forecasts to guide them. They relied a great deal on their notes and observations taken during previous voyages, on Maury and on the management skills (seen then as big fists and a stony heart) of the mate. They were not suicidal maniacs, as some claimed, just rather gifted men doing their job as best they could in difficult circumstances.

Despite the competition between Commanders and the vagaries of the weather, it did happen that ships sailed and arrived within a few hours of each other after the long voyage. Both the *British Merchant* and the *Maori* sailed from Gravesend on 3 September 1864 and reached Nelson and Auckland respectively on 24 January 1867 after voyages of 143 days each.

Also, there is confusion over who can claim what feat of passage-making. For example, the *Spray of the Ocean*'s claim to fame in 1859 in her record passage to Auckland of eighty-seven days has been attributed to the Shaw Savill flag. In fact, she was a Willis, Gann despatch. Nor can the enterprise of the first commercial steamship passage to New Zealand by the *Mongol* to Otago in 1873 continue to be attributed to Shaw Savill: she was a New Zealand Shipping Company despatch. Shaw Savill challenged with the *Atrato* two months later.

As a mark of respect to builders and Commanders alike, it is fitting to conclude this chapter by recording that the following owned ships each completed over twenty-five years service under the Shaw Savill (and Shaw Savill & Albion) flag:

| Ship | Service Years | Age on Disposal or lost | Age Finally |
|---|---|---|---|
| Crusader | 29 | 33 | 45 |
| Euterpe | 28 | 36 | 123 (still afloat) |
| Glenlora | 25 | 34 | 53 |
| Hermione | 30 | 30 | 37 |
| Hudson | 25 | 29 | 48 |
| Lutterworth | 27* | 38 | 38 |
| Pleiades | 27 | 30 | 30 |
| Soukar | 25 | 35 | 47 |
| Zealandia | 34 | 34 | 42 |

* 34 including years on charter prior to purchase.

It took a German U-boat to sink the *Glenlora* and *Hudson*. The others were scrapped, presumably reluctantly, with the exception of the *Euterpe*, or came to grief (the *Pleiades*).

The *Euterpe*, as the *Star of India*, has been restored and is the showpiece of the Maritime Museum at San Diego. She now has a full set of working sails. Indeed, she is more than a sight for admiring eyes whenever she takes to the open sea again, virtually as staunch, game and functional as she was well over a hundred years ago when she lumbered and screwed her weary way round the world twenty-seven times, mostly for Walter Savill and his colleagues. She was always desperately slow, but a comfortable and happy ship not given to sensational escapades or nasty habits. The Maritime Museum have done wonders for her and deserve universal acclaim from all who care about old ladies of the sea.

It is an extraordinary phenomenon that of all the many thousands of sailing-ships under the British flag one hundred years ago, only seven have been identifiable from the wreckage to be chosen to represent for ever that vast fleet, carefully restored as museums, of which three are in the USA: the *Euterpe* (built 1863), the *Balclutha* (built 1886) at Los Angeles, the *Southgate* (built 1885 and renamed *Wavertree*) at New York, the *Falls of Clyde* (built 1878) in Hawaii, the *Polly Woodside* (built 1885) at Melbourne, and the *Cape Finisterre* (built 1874 and re-named *El-Faroukieh*) at Alexandria. Whilst the seventh one – the *Cutty Sark* (built 1869) in London – is in a class of her own in terms of grace, beauty and speed, the others are more typical and symbolic of the fleet of workhorses plying their trade year after year in an unspectacular manner across the oceans. John Willis' *Cutty Sark* and Walter Savill's *Euterpe* are probably the two whose performances were most in contrast, but both served equally usefully and arrived at the extremes of the laws of survival, with the result that they now share the honour of preservation as fitting representatives of their kind. But the greatest survivor of them all must be the *Euterpe* – the oldest – in her new glory under all plain sail again at sea as the *Star of India*.

Possibly another old Shaw Savill ship could have been preserved, in New Zealand, if spirit and cash had been as forthcoming as in San Diego. A unique opportunity to re-create an indivisible part of that country's history has probably been missed. The ship is the *Edwin Fox*, now a hulk at Picton. She was built of teak in India for the East India Company ten years before the iron hull of the *Euterpe* went down the slipway in the Isle of Man. In a way she is of even greater interest – not only because of the survival of her wooden hull but because of her historical past. She was involved in trooping for the Anglo-Russian War in the Baltic and Crimea, and for the Indian Mutiny. After her voyage to Australia with convicts, Walter Savill bought her in 1873 and ran her in the emigrant trade until 1884, when he fitted her up with refrigerating machinery to be used as a meat-storage ship at Dunedin, such was the demand for cold storage in New Zealand following the successful shipment of frozen meat in the *Dunedin* in 1882.

As an emigrant-carrier she had had her moments. She grounded on the Goodwin Sands off Kent and was refloated, suffered a crew too drunk to man the pumps in a gale and had to hoist aloft ladies' red petticoats to indicate her distress at sea. Emigrants usually had more than the usual discomforts to put up with on board her, yet, on her arriving in Wellington it was once reported that there was not a cleaner or more comfortable ship entering New Zealand waters, her 'tween decks in the pink of order and cleanliness and in a manner to indicate the superior character of her passengers. Perhaps the reporter had broached the cargo of spirits.

Nineteen of the twenty-six ships in the Shaw Savill fleet were transferred to the new Shaw Savill & Albion Company in 1882. Only two of these were less than twelve years old. The venerable age of the rest caused a stir in the City when the new Company was floated but the fact remains that they were off-loaded onto the public without any difficulty, seemingly on the basis that the older the ship the greater the privilege of possessing her!

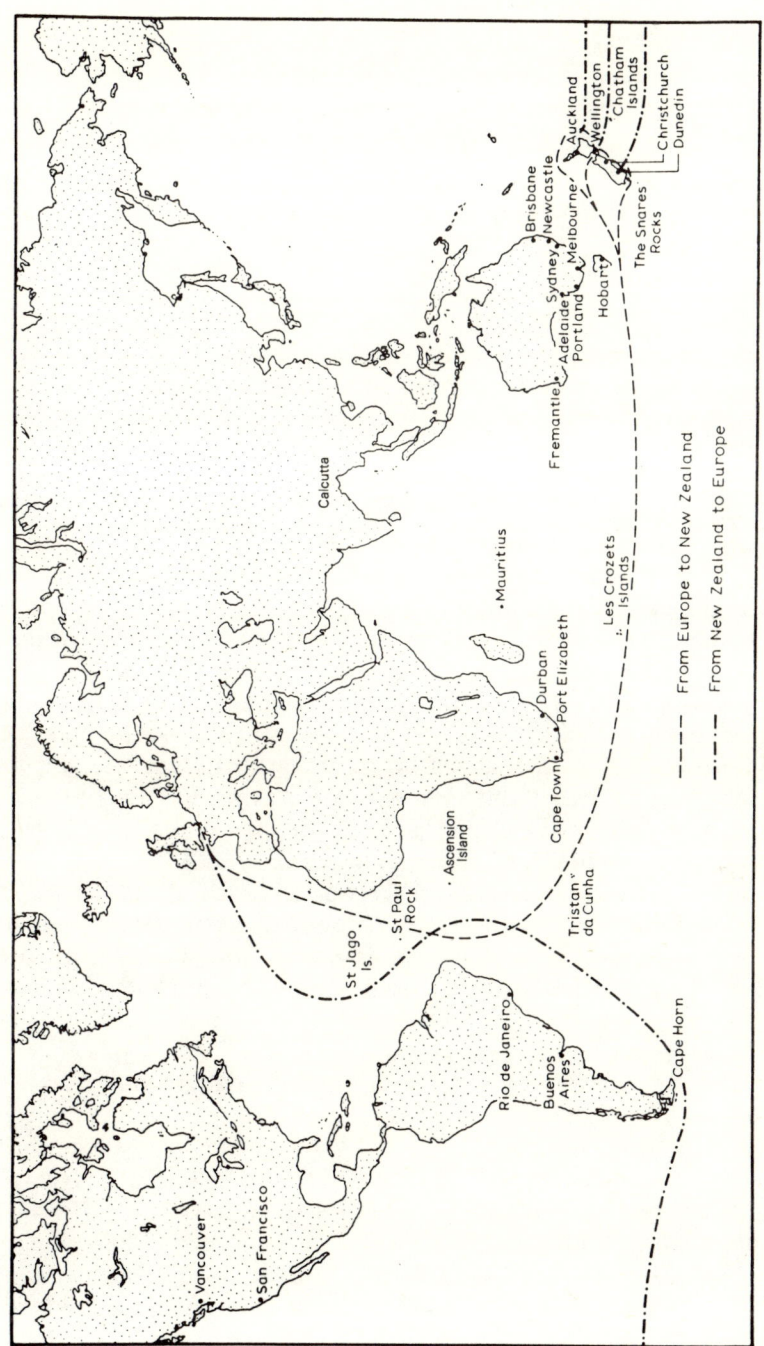

Sailing-ship routes

Labels on map:
- Vancouver
- San Francisco
- Rio de Janeiro
- Buenos Aires
- Cape Horn
- St Jago Is.
- St Paul Rock
- Ascension Island
- Tristan da Cunha
- Cape Town
- Port Elizabeth
- Durban
- Mauritius
- Calcutta
- Les Crozets Islands
- Fremantle
- Adelaide
- Portland
- Sydney
- Melbourne
- Hobart
- Newcastle
- Brisbane
- The Snares Rocks
- Auckland
- Wellington
- Chatham Islands
- Christchurch
- Dunedin

Legend:
- – – – – From Europe to New Zealand
- – · – · – From New Zealand to Europe

# 6. *The Voyage Out*

Passengers, whether emigrants or fare-paying, faced a long and often hazardous experience of up to six months from the time the decision was taken to travel to New Zealand until they first set foot ashore there.

The reasons for travel were many – the search for a better life, adventure, improved health from the sea voyage, the prospect of making a future, evangelism, escape, boredom and curiosity. Regardless of the reason, the reality was that most passengers converged either at the foot of a gangway in London Docks or at the windy pierhead at Gravesend, to be taken off in boats to join the ship lying at anchor in the river – with a severe attack of second thoughts or absolutely petrified at the inevitability of a fearsome chain of events in which they were trapped. How many had packed and followed some passing whim, command from the head of the household or the call of duty? At any rate, pamphlets 'descriptive of all the New Zealand Settlements' could be obtained free of charge at the Colonists' Room, 61 Cornhill in the City.

For fare-paying passengers, there was a choice of rates, type of accommodation on board, scale of food, departure date and, of course, ships, as well as of home comforts from which a private supply of liquor had sadly to be excluded. No such facility was allowed in cabins.

At the top of the fares' table were chief cabin passengers, followed by second cabin passengers in small, simple cabins, possibly a converted sail locker or at the after end of the 'tween decks and roughly bulkheaded off from steerage passengers in enclosed or open berths in the 'tween decks. The steerage passengers were not emigrants but fare-paying passengers. It was a divide, albeit a slender one.

The scale of outward fares in 1862 in the *Geelong* was as follows (equivalent 1986 values in brackets as per Bank of England sources.):

Chief Cabin Fare  £52.10s  (£1309)  –  £78.15s  (£1955)
    depending on whether a cabin was shared.

Second Cabin Fare £25 (£624).

Steerage Berth Fare £16 (£399) – £20 (£500) depending on whether the berth was open or enclosed.

Contrary to popular belief, fares by sailing ship were far from cheap, and passengers still had to provide a number of items for their own comfort but the shipowner would have said it was a long time to feed passengers and pay for the overheads.

Some of the best cabin type of accommodation was to be found, from 1874, in the trim clippers of the Albion Line, many of which, particularly the *Auckland, Invercargill* and *Westland*, were chartered from time to time by Shaw Savill prior to the later amalgamation with the firm. This accommodation was probably unsurpassed by most of the other Shaw Savill charters, although by 1877 all shipowners were making special efforts to attract passengers by higher standards all round. A plan of the accommodation in the Albion ships is given on pages 74-5 – but prior to 1874 most accommodation could be measured only in terms of varying degrees of discomfort.

By and large in the 1860s and 70s even the top-rate chief cabin passengers had to furnish their own cabins and provide bedding and any other comforts they might require. The ship supplied them only with tableware. These passengers were offered 'an unlimited table' including livestock (allowed for at the rate of one pig, one sheep and a dozen ducks and hens per passenger). It sounds marvellous compared with the fare for the other passengers who merely had a scale of simple food per week. It was also a selling-point for Shaw Savill as the normal practice in other firms was a limited scale of rations for all passengers relating to the fare paid. Second-class and steerage passengers had to provide their own bedding and tableware, including teapot and metal pots. Their provisions were daily prepared by the ship's cook, but they had in other respects to attend to their own arrangements for messing. According to the passenger tickets, there was a substantial difference in the type and scale of victuals to be provided by the ship even for these passengers and emigrants. For the latter, soup, York ham, fish, barley and cheese were all off the menu but they were entitled to more generous rations of peas, oatmeal, suet, flour, rice and potatoes, and of carrots and molasses, which were entirely their own perks.

The ship's victualling scale held good for twenty-two weeks (154 days). No doubt the prudent passenger also planned for an even longer voyage, of which there were a few notorious and frightening experiences, with several hard and wet slogs to windward.

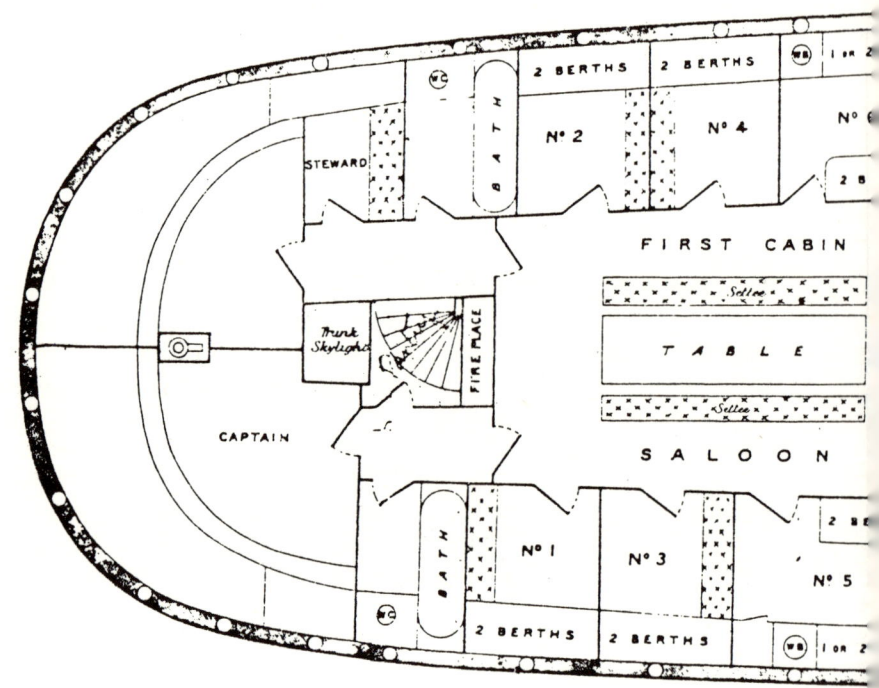

STEWARD

BATH N° 2 2 BERTHS N° 4 2 BERTHS N° 6 1 OR 2
2 B

Trunk Skylight

CAPTAIN

FIRE PLACE

FIRST CABIN

Settee

T A B L E

Settee

S A L O O N

BATH N° 1 2 BERTHS N° 3 2 BERTHS N° 5 2 BE

1 OR 2

PLAN OF ACCOMMODATION OF THE MA

"AUCKLAND" "NELSON" "WELLIN
"CANTERBURY" & "INVERCARGI

"OAMARU" & "TIMARU"

Accommodation plan of *Auckland*-class sailing-ship

COMPANY LIMITED.

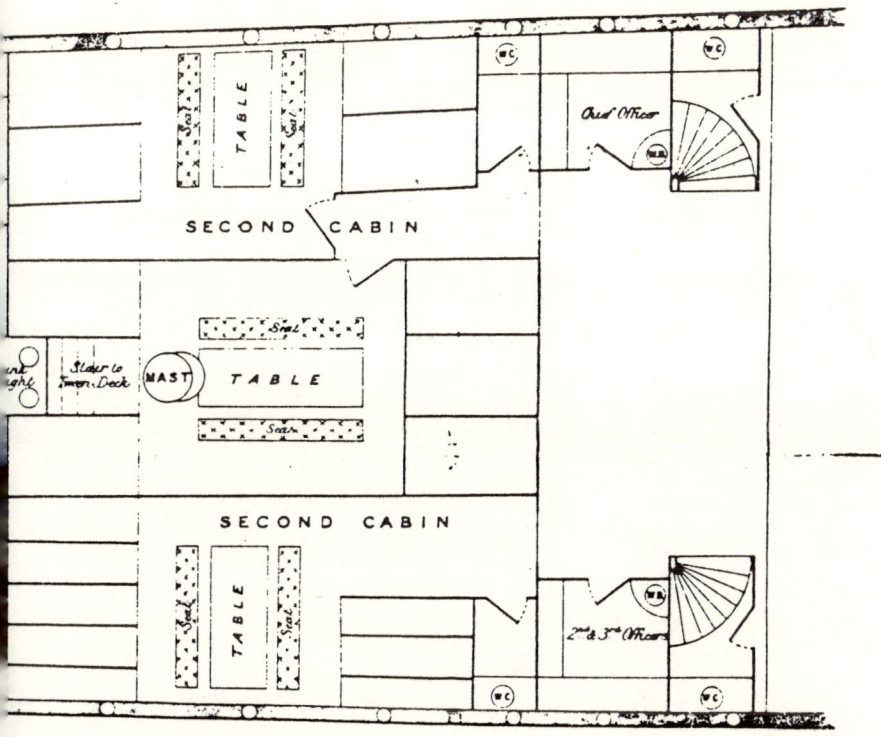

ENT CLYDE-BUILT CLIPPER SHIPS

1250 Tons Register.
} A.I. at Lloyd's.
1306 Tons Register.

For full particulars apply to
SHAW SAVILL & ALBION COMPANY. LIMITED.
34. Leadenhall St. LONDON.E.C.

# SHAW, SAVILL & Co., 34, LEADENHALL STREET.

**No. 1131**    **PASSENGERS' CONTRACT TICKET.**

1.—A Contract Ticket in this form must be given to every Passenger engaging a passage from the United Kingdom to any place out of Europe, and not being within the Mediterranean Sea.

2.—The Victualling Scale for the voyage must be printed in the body of the Ticket.

3.—All the Blanks must be correctly filled in, and the Ticket must be legibly signed with the Christian names and surname and address in full of the party issuing the same.

4.—The day of the month on which the Passengers are to embark must be inserted in words and not in figures.

5.—When once issued, this Ticket must not be withdrawn from the Passenger, nor any alteration, addition, or erasure made in it.

Ship *Merope* of *1082* Tons Register, to take Passengers at *London* for *Canterbury* on the *Twentyfourth* day of *June* 1876

I engage that the person named in the margin hereof shall be provided with a { Second Cabin } Passage to, and shall be Landed at, the Port of *Canterbury* in *N.Z.* in the Ship *Merope* with not less than { Twenty } Cubic Feet for Luggage for each Statute Adult, and shall be victualled during the voyage and the time of detention at any place before its termination according to the subjoined Scale, for the sum of £ *26-5-0* including Government Dues before embarkation, and head money, if any, at the place of landing, and every other charge except Freight for excess of Luggage beyond the quantity above specified, and I hereby acknowledge to have received the sum of £ *26-5-0* in { full } payment.

The following quantities, at least, of Water and Provisions (to be issued daily) will be supplied by the Master of the Ship, as required by Law, viz., to each Statute Adult Three Quarts of Water daily, exclusive of what is necessary for cooking the articles required by the Passengers Act to be issued in a cooked state, and a Weekly Allowance of Provisions according to the following Scale :

| NAMES. | AGES. | Equal to Statute Adults. |
|---|---|---|
| Mr H. Todd | 26 | 1 |

**Scale of Dietary for each Adult Passenger per Week.**

| ARTICLES. | Second Cabin. | Steerage. | ARTICLES. | Second Cabin. | Steerage. |
|---|---|---|---|---|---|
| Preserved Meats | 2 lb. | 1 | Coffee | 3 oz. | 2 |
| Soup and Bouilli | ½ lb. | — | Butter | ¼ lb. | 6 |
| York Ham | ¼ lb. | — | Cheese | ¼ lb. | |
| Fish | ¼ lb. | — | Currants, or | ¼ lb. | |
| Prime Indian Beef | 1 lb. | 1 lb. | Raisins, Valentia | ¼ lb. | |
| Irish Mess Pork | 1¼ lb. | 1 lb. | Suet | 6 oz. | 6 |
| Biscuit | 4½ lb. | 1 lb. | Pickles | ½ pint | |
| Flour | 4½ lb. | 3 lb. | Mustard | ¼ oz. | |
| Rice | 1 lb. | ½ lb. | Pepper | ½ oz. | |
| Barley | ½ lb. | — | Salt | 3 oz. | 2 |
| Peas | ½ pint | ½ pint | Potatoes, (fresh) or | 3½ lb. | 2 |
| Oatmeal | 1½ pint | 1 pint | Preserved ditto | ½ lb. | |
| Sugar, raw | 1 lb. | 1 lb. | Water | 21 quarts | 21 |
| Tea | 2 oz. | 1½ oz. | Lime Juice | 6 oz. | 6 |

Substitutions, at the following rates, may at the option of the Master, be made in the above Dietary Scale :—

| 1 lb. of Preserved Meat | for | 1 lb. of Salt Pork or Beef |
|---|---|---|
| 1 lb. of Flour, or Bread or Biscuit or | " | {1} lb. of Oatmeal or |
| 1 lb. of Beef or Pork | " | {1} lb. of Rice or Peas, |
| ½ lb. of Rice | " | 1½ lb. of Oatmeal, or rice versa |
| ½ lb. of Preserved Potatoes | " | 1 lb. of Potatoes, |
| 10 oz. of Currants | " | 8 oz. of Raisins, |
| 3½ oz. of Cocoa or Coffee, Roasted and Ground | " | 2 oz. of Tea, |
| 1 lb. of Treacle | " | ½ lb. of Sugar, |
| ½ gill of Mixed Pickles | " | 1 gill of Vinegar. |

Signature in full *For Walter Savill W.R. Sutherland*

34, LEADENHALL STREET,

LONDON, *19th June* 1876.

‡ Deposit...... £ *26-5-0*

Balance...... £ to be paid at 34, Leadenhall Street, London, prior to embarkation.

Total ...... £ *26-5-0*

## NOTICES TO PASSENGERS.

1.—If Passengers, through no default of their own, are not received on board on the day named in their Contract Tickets, or fail to obtain a passage in the Ship, they should apply to the Government Emigration Officer at the Port, who will assist them in obtaining redress under the Passengers' Act.

2.—Passengers should carefully keep this part of their Contract Ticket till after the end of the voyage.

N.B.—If Passengers are not maintained on Board after the above-named date, they will be paid Subsistence Money after the rate of 1s. 6d. per day for each Statute Adult. N.B.—This Contract Ticket is exempt from Stamp Duty.

\* SHAW, SAVILL & Co. will not undertake to land more than the above quantity of Luggage.

✝ All charges on board the vessel between embarkation and disembarkation.

‡ It is understood that this Deposit will be absolutely forfeited in case the parties named herein fail to embark in a fit state of health for the voyage at the above-mentioned place and date.

Passenger ticket for the *Merope*, 1876

Having chosen his style of accommodation on board, as either fare-paying passenger or emigrant, the traveller then had to consider the question of suitable clothing for the voyage. There was plenty of good advice available about that – in London, according to Shaw Savill's contribution to William Stones' booklet on New Zealand. It is probably tempting to dismiss the consideration of clothing for the sea voyage as a luxury many passengers could ill afford to do much about. It was important, however, because they would suffer extremes of heat and cold, and because there were no drying facilities on board (except the fresh air), so laundry was done in salt water in a bucket on the upper deck in fine weather. They also washed in salt water.

*The Times* carried an advertisement from Messrs Hanning & Co of 93 Gracechurch Street in the City offering 'outfits for all classes of passengers' for use on the voyage and in New Zealand. They claimed to be the cheapest outfitting establishment in London and were also prepared to fit up cabins 'with every requisite'. Lists of the absolute necessities for the voyage were available gratis either on application or by post. (Besides clothing for the voyage, there was clothing needed in New Zealand. The main requirement was several pairs of strong boots to stand up to the outdoor work in a 'rainy country'.) How was the passenger to pass the time on the voyage? The firm recommended reading and 'learning useful matters connected with the sea, such as lending a hand with the sails'. Women passengers were advised to take some calico or printed cotton, needle and thread 'to amuse and occupy their time'.

Although most passengers were probably prepared to build their new homes on arrival, it must have been somewhat disconcerting to be advised by Shaw Savill to dispose of all furniture before sailing as the freight for it was high and it would be 'an encumbrance' on landing. Possession of cash on arrival was a better asset in every way, and it could be used to purchase 'the requisites' of furniture. The free baggage allowance for cabin passengers was only twenty cubic feet, and many better-off passengers disregarded this advice, paid the freight rate and took out with them their favourite china, silver, paintings and furniture to help make a home as soon as possible.

Finally, thought had to be given as to how to overcome the break in schooling of children and keep them occupied at sea, which cases were 'wanted on voyage' and what special provisions to take to relieve the monotony of the ship's fare. Fancy biscuits, jellies, jams, sago, milk powder and condensed milk were all recommended.

Arrangements for carrying emigrants were negotiated separately with the New Zealand Government's Agent in London and were enforced as strictly as possible. The accommodation and victualling arrangements were inspected prior to departure, and the Commander of the ship and shipowner had to give various undertakings they would observe. This was no perfunctory occasion. However, once the ship was on passage, there was no inspector available to safeguard the emigrants' conditions of travel, and inevitably these became the responsibility of the Commander, like everything else on board. For a Commander used to the disciplined passengers in the Indian trade, the prospect of a long voyage with a shipload of New Zealand emigrants could be daunting.

Emigrants were carefully accommodated in different parts of the ship according to their circumstances – single men forward, married couples amidships and single girls aft. There was only one partition between the married couples, which was hardly the kind of privacy they needed. As for the single girls, though their virtues were planned to be unassailable, some male passengers managed to slide down the ventilators to their quarters and declare their admiration.

The emigrants were divided into messes on board and drew their provisions weekly from the ship. These they prepared for cooking by the ship's cooks in the galley. Even if the scale of provisions appeared plentiful, the food would become monotonous by the end of the voyage.

A 'Surgeon-Superintendent' had to be carried to care for the emigrants. He was technically an employee of the shipping company even if working his passage. When the New Zealand Company was shipping out emigrants in the 1840s, the Surgeon was their employee, and this was probably a better arrangement for all concerned as, always subject to the safety of the ship, standards could be enforced. On the whole, however, Commanders, shipowners and the Surgeon-Superintendents did the best they could for the comfort and welfare of emigrant passengers. It was hardly in their interest to do otherwise if they wanted their contracts to be renewed for another voyage – but the elements, the health of the passengers on boarding the ship and the reaction of many to a long sea voyage were often more than they could cope with, despite strict supervision of alcohol (other than beer) in the 'tween decks and crew's quarters, spotting the troublemakers early, and efforts to provide a fairly organized social life on board.

The Surgeon-Superintendent was to the Commander a godsend,

The Emigrant Ship

Thou semblance of the Angel Death,
    With thy dark dismal shrouding wings,
Whose fluttering seems to catch the breath,
    The very latest breath that wrings
The soul from body, thou art there
Like Hope half soothing wild Despair!

In thee is promise that thou'lt bring
    A change of season to the mind
Of those who chance a distant spring
    For the dull wintry waste behind!
Yet – what's the wintry waste they leave?
Alas! all hearts with theirs must grieve!

They quit their Native Land for life,
    A land they'll weep for when away,
Sister and Brother – Husband – Wife
    May never meet another day!
The living Death of absence, quite
    Obscures the gloom of endless night!

Perchance to some hope will be true
    And lead them on to riches – fame –
But all they lov'd, and all they knew
    In early days, just like a name
Upon a tombstone will appear,
And mem'ry vainly, wish them near.

Some may return with pow'r to bless
    The weeping wretches left behind –
And see that home all loneliness
    Where they expected them to find!
The son for mother look in vain,
Then seek the wide – wide world again!

The signal's given – away to shore –
    Break ties of every dearest kind! –
One parting kiss – one look – one more
    Farewell to those now left behind!
Divorcer Ocean! thou dost make
Many a gentle heart to ache!

Oh! Emigration! thou'rt the curse
    Of our once happy nation's race!
Cannot our Fatherland still nurse
    Its offspring without taking place
Of dislocated men to make
More cause for thy disturbing sake?

Thou art an enemy to peace,
    Thy restless hope but ends in grief –
When comforts in the mother cease
    How can we hope step-dame's relief?
'Better to bear the ills we have'
Than seek in foreign climes a grave!
                    W.                          (From the *Illustrated London News*.)

to the emigrants a godfather – guide, philosopher and friend to many, even after landing in New Zealand. But to safeguard himself from charges of complete omnipotence on board he appointed assistants from the emigrants who were known as ship's constables. There was also a matron for the single women, who at sea had to be below by 8 p.m.; other passengers could stay on deck with their lingering thoughts until 9 p.m.

Despite all these elaborate distinctions and arrangements, what difference in misery did they really make once things started to go wrong? Certainly the rats on board were no respecters of these divisions and were a common sight for all.

Ports of embarkation for Shaw Savill passengers were London, Gravesend, Portsmouth and Plymouth, where the last mails were often picked up, and occasionally Middlesbrough, Sunderland, Belfast and Cork. At some ports there were special emigration barracks; elsewhere marquees were put up, if necessary. The traveller usually had quite a journey across country by train or coach-and-four before reaching the ship. It could be a nightmare counting each piece of baggage and child at every transfer. It was compounded for the emigrants if they did not join the ship at some point on the Thames and she was delayed by contrary winds in the Channel. They were then faced with a rather unpleasant stay in the barracks, which could be a shocking and unnerving experience for those used to privacy and consideration in their former homes.

Most passengers joined the ship in London Docks, especially if they wanted to see their loads and luggage safely hoisted on board and stowed, or wanted to fit up their basic cabin accommodation with their own furniture and bedding or were marshalled to do so.

On arrival at the East India Docks in London, the traveller was faced with a scene of pandemonium and filth. There was a forest of masts and bowsprits of ships berthed bow-to on the quay, providing an elegant and lofty arch for the human traffic passing up and down on the quayside below. There were shouts of 'Mind your backs' as porters trundled their barrows of baggage and cargo through the milling crowds of passengers, dock-workers and crews. Fretful children tripped and fell on the uneven cobbles, and horses stood patiently whilst their carts were unloaded. Everywhere there was a smell of horses and tarred rope, and small steam-engines. Baedeker's guide-book may well have been correct in its comment that, 'Nothing will convey to the stranger a better idea of the vast activity and stupendous wealth of London than a visit to the docks.'

The scale of the chaos was determined by the numbers of passengers arriving to board the ships in dock. Their carrying-capacity varied enormously. On the whole there were

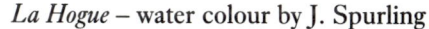

*Rodney* – water colour by J. Spurling

*La Hogue* – water colour by J. Spurling

*Taranaki* – water colour by J. Spurling

Towing out

never fewer than twenty passengers for each Shaw Savill ship, but the average was about eighty passengers per ship. Some ships, however, lifted as many as 600 passengers (the *Stad Haarlem* in 1879); *La Hogue* and *Rodney* each lifted over 500 in 1874 and 1875.

As the passengers stood in frightened groups on the dockside, there was still time, and no doubt some took it, to turn back before ascending the ship's gangway. But for many it was too late by then. The ship offered them their only home for the next few months.

The day of departure for the open sea came in a comparatively leisurely manner. The ship battened down her hatches, the carpenters finished their last-minute work in the confined spaces of the emigrants' accommodation, putting up the temporary wooden bunks and long mess tables, all of which had to be ripped out for the voyage home when space had to be found for cargo. The emigrants themselves and other passengers completed their unpacking and safe stowing of their home comforts (little realizing that the lurch of the ship in the first big sea would send them all flying onto the deck).

With a final splash the lines were cast off and the ship edged out from the noise and confusion of the docks. She was taken by tug down river to Gravesend, where the last passengers would board from the Town Pier and the ship would be prepared for sea.

On passage down the Thames representatives of the New Zealand Government or its Provinces may have been on board for a formal send-off of large numbers of emigrants. This was quite an occasion, with everyone in their best clothes, a band playing, the ship bedecked with flags, and speeches from important people. A good meal with beer was served. With their mutton-chop whiskers, high collars and frock coats, the departure party were representative of the stiff upper lip of Victorian England and believed in doing things properly. Sometimes there were farewell peals from churches, and a gun salute at Tilbury.

It all helped give the emigrants Dutch courage for the long voyage ahead of them, and a special day to remember a very moving experience. They never expected to see their families, friends and homeland again. They hardly sailed without a care in the world. (For an account of the departure from London of 800 Non-Conformists in three Shaw Savill ships was given in the *Illustrated London News* of 7 June 1862, see Appendix C).

On arrival at Gravesend, the ship anchored and jollyboats came out with fresh food and provisions, sails, stowage nets and eating-utensils. Boat- and fire-drills were carried out. Sometimes a River Missionary came on board to conduct a service or even hold a baptism if the ship was long delayed waiting for a favourable wind. If the wind was fair, the pause at Gravesend was short. The hatches were finally battened down, all loose gear was stowed, and the anchor was hoisted and catted. Woe betide the Commander who forgot to unship the headboards with the ship's name painted on them. If they were lost overboard at sea and recovered by another, the ship could be feared to have gone missing.

There could be delays even at Gravesend if the ship was 'waiting for despatches', or if the carpentry work on the tiered bunks in the 'tween decks was not complete. On these occasions, if passengers had to stay on shore, Shaw Savill paid 1s. 6d. per day subsistence per adult.

From Gravesend the ship with the Channel pilot on board made her way to Deal, where he would normally be dropped. However, if the south-westerlies were blowing hard, the ship was delayed near there in the great anchorage of the Downs as she could not

At dinner on an emigrant ship

make any headway down the Channel. Two to three hundred vessels could be waiting there for an easterly wind, the first sign of which would be signalled by the clanking of anchor chains in the anchorage as ships made ready for departure. Ships were known to need the paddler tugs as far as Beachy Head and pilots to Portland, Torbay and Dartmouth. Sometimes ships took three weeks to clear the Channel and were damaged enough to put into Portsmouth, Plymouth and Falmouth for repairs or shelter, at which point the voyage could even be abandoned, if the ship was badly damaged.

For many, the voyage even down Channel was a terrifying experience if they had never been to sea before. The movement of the ship as she met the waves, the roar of the down-draught from the towering sails piled tier upon tier, the creaking noises in the 'tween decks' and from the swinging blocks aloft, the shouted orders to the crew to alter the sails, the slatting of wires and rigging, the slight heel of the deck, the darkness below except for a solitary lantern, and the strange smell of tarred cordage, induced a nervous terror, particularly amongst the women and children. The blue-water experience was too much for some. They jumped overboard in desperation.

Occasionally there were collisions in the Channel and a marine disaster ensued. At least fifteen Shaw Savill ships were involved in collisions when outward bound: three sank – the *Leichardt* bound for Wellington in 1868, the *Avalanche* bound for Wellington in 1877 (when almost all lives were lost) and the *Hydaspes* bound for Melbourne in 1880; the rest put into south-coast ports for repair and sailed later. The passengers were then usually put ashore on subsistence rates. In view of the hazards of the Channel, crew and passengers were probably heartily relieved to get clear of the land and away. If there was a long spell of headwinds, passengers would find a number of ships in company. (On one occasion in 1897 the *Pleione* had fifty-one sail in sight in the North Atlantic.) Many ships were compelled by bad weather in the Channel to turn back.

After that they may not see land again the whole voyage. At most, the passengers might catch glimpses of Madeira, Brazil, Tristan da Cunha, the Cape of Good Hope, St Paul Isle and Tasmania. In fact, a landfall such as Cape Town, Mauritius or the Australian coast was possibly a bad sign, meaning help was required – but sometimes a ship called at Rio de Janeiro and re-stocked with fresh provisions, if the Commander wanted to be sure of a good slant for running his easting down to New Zealand without trouble from the south-east tradewinds further north.

Once on passage, the ship and its passengers settled into a routine closely monitored by the Surgeon-Superintendent. Initially there were the usual problems of sea-sickness, which aggravated the conditions in the steerage accommodation. Passages had to be kept clear and as well aired as possible, which was where the Surgeon-Superintendent first made his presence felt. He saw that the emigrants washed daily, did their laundry, scrubbed out their bunks and floors and aired their bedding. It also kept them all occupied and happy – hopefully.

His main concern was of course the health of all on board, regardless of individual disposition. Many of the emigrants lacked education and hygiene habits. Lice were often found on them. An infectious disease such as scarlet fever could cause havoc, even death, to the very young, who did not in any case take well to a diet of ship's stores. Daily doses of lime juice, the boiling of all drinking-water and strict control of alcohol and personal cleanliness helped to keep passengers reasonably well. The Surgeon-Superintendent's other concern was to devise ways of relieving the monotony of the long voyage by entertainment, school, hobbies and, if any passengers cared for it, helping the crew with the sail changes. He also kept a sharp look-out for any action amongst the passengers likely to lead to the greatest peril of all at sea – fire.

Inevitably there were births and deaths on passage. Infectious diseases were particularly alarming, and the relatively primitive conditions on board coupled with the savagery of the sea soon found out the weaker brethren and the elderly. On the other hand, some passages were remarkably trouble-free in fair weather; in fact, downright boring. Many passengers, who had never seen a ship, let alone the sea, had no idea of what they were undertaking. For them, it had been a desperate step into the unknown. For others it was no more than an adventure, at worst. For some, they were better fed and cared for on board than they ever had been in the Old Country.

As the ship sailed south, the seas became calmer and the sun hotter, much hotter. The passengers began to enjoy the voyage and sat on deck. The women sewed and made cakes and toffee, the men talked in groups as they leaned over the rail, and the children played. As the evenings grew warmer, a mandolin could be heard playing some haunting air in the soft darkness, and hidden singers hummed a melody or sea shanty as the moon flickered across the deck and the sea swished by the ship leaving a phosphorescent wake. There might be dancing on deck to tunes hammered out on the saloon piano brought up from below. On the *Mermaid* bound for Canterbury in 1863 there was scarcely an evening when they did not dance on deck during the voyage. On the *Famenoth*'s voyage to Auckland in 1877, the topsails never had to be reefed, such was her fine-weather passage. And then of course Crossing the Line was never allowed to pass without some tomfoolery.

Probably passage through the Tropics was the most difficult part of the voyage, especially when the winds were light or non-existent. It was so hot below that passengers preferred to sleep on deck. Awnings were rigged to provide shade during the day. Passengers fished or caught birds, wrote letters and diaries or slept in a shady corner. Deck games were organized. Sometimes fights broke out and passengers had to be restrained, if necessary locked up. Children went missing exploring the ship.

Fresh water supplies were carefully noted, as was the coal required to run the condensers that supplied the water. Fresh water for drinking was not usually a problem once condensers had been installed in the 1870s. There was always livestock carried on board – rabbits, chickens, geese, pigs, sheep, goats and calves. All were destined for the cabin table. The farmyard noises were probably re-assuring to the passengers, although some would have deplored the animals' suffering.

Occasionally a passing ship was sighted, signals exchanged by flag hoists and the event duly reported to London when each ship next reached port. Passengers were allowed to bathe over the side and to indulge in various entertainments, including shuffleboard and charades. Passengers on the *May Queen*'s voyage to Otago in 1874 published a weekly newsletter (see p.86 – many ships did this.) Church services were held most Sundays.

The trials of the voyage were not over until the passengers had

# THE MAY QUEEN WEEKLY NEWS.

PUBLISHED ON BOARD THE "MAY QUEEN," DURING HER VOYAGE FROM LONDON TO OTAGO, NEW ZEALAND.

## ADDRESS TO OUR READERS.

As under the most favourable circumstances, a long sea voyage must necessarily be more or less monotonous, the Editors of "The May Queen Weekly News," in issuing their First No., trust that their journal will tend in some degree to afford a little diversion to their fellow passengers and the good ship's company. Generally during the voyage, it will be the aim of the Editors to make it "The May Queen Weekly News," an entertaining as possible, they hope to receive weekly contributions from correspondents in all parts of the ship. The Editors embrace this opportunity of wishing success in the future to the Commander, officers, and all officially connected with the "May Queen"; to their fellow passengers they wish hearty success in the land of their adoption.

### LOG OF THE "MAY QUEEN"
TO MONDAY, AUGUST 31, 1874.

Latitude, (noon), 35° 58' N.; longitude, 14° 2' W., Distance from Lizard, 1100 miles.

The wind since leaving has been mostly N.E. and fine, the ship, during the last few days, it has been light and variable, with calms.

We may reasonably expect to reach the N.E. Trades soon.

Barometer, 30°00; Thermometer, 75 in the shade.

NAUTICUS.

"*Lucea non uri.*"

Our good ship the "May Queen," under the command of Captain Tatchell, finally took her departure from Gravesend at about 4 p.m. on Wednesday, the 19th August, bound for Otago, New Zealand, having on board 100 souls, distributed as follows:—

| | |
|---|---|
| Saloon Passengers | 20 |
| 2nd Cabin Passengers | 16 |
| 1st Cabin Passengers | 34 |
| Ship's Company | 30 |
| **TOTAL** | **110** |

## SUNDAY SERVICES, 23rd AUGUST.

Divine Service was held on the Main Deck. The texts of Captain Tatchell's discourses were:—

MORNING.

6th Chapter of Hebrews, 18th verse.

EVENING.

46th Psalm, 1st to 3rd verses.

Evening Prayers were read by Fathers Mathews and Higgins in the 3rd Cabin.

30TH AUGUST.

Texts of Captain Tatchell's discourses:—

MORNING.

6th chapter Mark, verses 45 to 52.

EVENING.

49th Psalm, 8th verse.

Fathers Mathews and Higgins held Morning and Evening Services.

Father Higgins preached in the morning of her. Text from 6th chapter of St. Matthew, verses 24 to 33.

### NO. 2. WEDNESDAY, SEPTEMBER 9, 1874.

#### TO OUR READERS.

As it is our wish that "The May Queen Weekly News," should it be deemed of sufficient merit, be printed on our arrival at Dunedin, we inform our readers that previous to its being placed in printer's hands, "The May Queen Weekly News" will be thoroughly revised, and items we have inserted for the amusement of our readers during the voyage, but which it might be undesirable not to insert in the printed issue, will be excluded. We hasten to correct an error which inadvertently appeared in our column last week. In noticing the "May Queen" as passing the Lizard, on Friday, 21st ultimo, it should have been stated Saturday, the 22nd August.

### LOG OF THE "MAY QUEEN,"
7TH SEPTEMBER, 1874.

## ADVERTISEMENTS.

### MISLAID.

A volume of Robert Browning's Poems. Anyone finding the same will oblige by leaving it with the Chief Steward.

### THE
### May Queen Weekly News.
7th SEPTEMBER, 1874.

"*Lucea non uri.*"

We have had cause for great thankfulness and congratulation, for our voyage so far advanced in having been most prosperous. Our good ship having proved herself to be a vessel of no ordinary sailing qualities, and no doubt ere long she may be more severely tested, and we doubt not but she will maintain the good opinion now generally formed of her. True, one or two uncomfortable days have been experienced in consequence of the rolling of "The May Queen," but we must bear in mind, that ships sailing before the wind are all more or less subject to a rolling motion.

We must prepare our readers to anticipate shortly an interval which we trust will be of short duration of somewhat calm weather on the water, subject only to the Atlantic swell, though the sails should hang like boards about the stately masts, and though a tropical sun pour down its heat upon the deck, yet we trust one and all will preserve their equanimity and do all in their power to condition to make this part of our voyage as pleasant as possible.

We should feel ourselves wanting in gallantry did we omit in our "Leading Article," on the events of the past week to congratulate three of our lady passengers who have suffered from sea-sickness on their return to consciousness. We have noticed during the last two or three days that the bloom of health is gradually rising, and we trust may not again fail in that thermometer influenced by ill health.

### NO. 3. WEDNESDAY, SEPTEMBER 16, 1874.

#### LOG OF "THE MAY QUEEN."
14th SEPTEMBER, 1874.

Latitude, (noon), 7° 27' N.; Longitude, 24° W.

Distance run during week, 900 miles.

The weather, for the "Variables," has been rather rough, but the wind favourable, on the whole, rather less than I expected at this season. I am in hopes of reaching the S.E. Trades in a few days.

NAUTICUS.

### VESSELS SPOKEN.

On Sunday last, at about 1.30 p.m. quite a German ship, name unknown, from Africa bound for Bremen, she evidently had experienced heavy weather.

To the Editors of "The May Queen Weekly News."

Dear Sirs,—The military state of the ship in all that could be desired, and the spirit displayed by the passengers more than commendable. I am glad to notice that the cabins and berths are kept in perfect order, and neat and clean.

Believe me,

Faithfully yours,

M.D.

### SUNDAY SERVICES, 1874.

MORNING.

15th September, 1874.

Captain Tatchell's discourses had for its text St. Luke, chap. 15, verse 25.

Father Higgins preached from St. Luke, chap. 1, verse 46.

### THE
### May Queen Weekly News.
16th SEPTEMBER, 1874.

"*Lucea non uri.*"

For "life on the ocean wave," the events of the past week on board our good ship,

*Extract from the May Queen Weekly News*

faced another severe change of climate, but at least by then they should have become toughened to ship-board life and able to cope with most things. To make their eastings, ships sailed within the Roaring Forties; some went even further south to pick up the westerlies, but hopefully not the icebergs. In these latitudes it was cold, wet and rough for passengers and crew alike. Hatches were firmly closed. No passengers were allowed on deck for a breath of fresh air except under strict supervision. Below, the atmosphere was dank if not wet. No fires could be lit. Candles and lamps were often in short supply. If the ship was built of wood, there would be leaks through the seams of the wooden decks as the ship corkscrewed her way eastward. The winds whistled and screamed in the rigging for days, and spirits were low. If the voyage was stretching out, there might be a scramble for food put on the table. Then there were the constant smells, enough to make many passengers reek. Above all, there was misery and great loneliness as the ship ploughed on for weeks without a single sighting of another living soul on the heaving sea stretching from horizon to horizon under the big sky, with little comfort anywhere on board and the sea giving the ship a good going-over in its own remorseless way.

Then there were the emergencies when passengers had to turn to to help the crew save the ship. Quite frequently they were asked to man the pumps, occasionally to work the sails. On the *Hydaspes* bound for Auckland in 1873, three were knocked overboard when on such work and were lucky to be rescued by the quick reaction of the Commander. Passengers could also cause an emergency, as they did on the *Dauntless* in 1865, when some joined in a mutiny by the crew – probably with good reason, as the conditions on board were reported to be poor and it was a long voyage to Auckland.

As the voyage drew to its close, the passengers watched eagerly for a sight of their new homeland. The Commander usually took the ship south of Tasmania before making for the destination port in New Zealand. Here he was faced with a choice of options but, unless bound for Wellington or Nelson, most Commanders went northabout or southabout of New Zealand to reach the east coast ports rather than chance a passage through the hazardous and frustrating Cook Strait between the islands, where it could take a ship a week to enter port battling against contrary winds.

Even at this late stage of the voyage, there was still a strong element of danger for the passengers – indeed, after the English Channel it was the most dangerous period of any voyage, and still is, as any seafarer will confirm. Shaw Savill had two particularly disastrous landfalls so near journey's end. In 1877 the *Queen Bee* bound for Nelson was wrecked approaching port just far enough

away for it to go unwitnessed. After three days the passengers were
rescued, having been castaways. They were starving and cold, had
lost everything and were lucky to be alive. A year later the
*Schiehallion* when homeward bound fróm Auckland ran aground at
St Catherine's Point in the Isle of Wight. The heavy swell and
foggy morning made rescue difficult but somehow the survivors
were hauled ashore through the surf, more dead than alive.

Now, as the new land closed in on the emigrants, the pilot came
out to take the ship in – usually to a sheltered anchorage where
boats took off passengers and their baggage. There were no
deep-water wharves until the 1870s. Although there was relief that
the voyage was over safely (remember, the average length of
voyage in a Shaw Savill ship was about a hundred days), it was a
moment of sadness for many as friends made on the voyage took
their departure and all measured up in their own often bizarre way
to the enormity of their decision to leave their families in Britain in
favour of the unknown and strange but beautiful land immediately
before them. For some it was all too much. They were almost
hysterical as they clung hold of crew members, embraced them and
whispered their prayers and thanksgiving before joining the others
standing at the top of the gangway ready to disembark.

# 7. Tradewinds

A summary of the 1,310 ships Shaw Savill despatched to New Zealand between 1858 to 1882 is given in Appendix D. Sailings in a few typical years are given in Appendix E. They served a wide range of ports and harbours. In addition, there were ninety-five joint despatches from Glasgow in tandem with the Albion Line.

But it did not end there. In 1869 the firm began loading for Australia in either their own or chartered vessels conveying passengers and cargo. There were also occasional sailings to New Zealand from Middlesbrough, Newport and Liverpool and occasional despatches continued to San Francisco and the Far East. The fact that the Suez Canal had been opened in the same year increased the threat of potential competition from steamships should they be able to remove the remaining obstacles to entering the New Zealand by this quicker route for them. These were coaling stations at convenient intervals, more reliable engines and a fuel consumption to match an economic speed. This threat spurred the firm on to greater efforts by sailing-ship via the Cape of Good Hope. Although meanwhile this meant for passengers a good blow round the southern seas before the prevailing winds, it was at least an experience which saved them from the oppressive Red Sea heat and the prevarications of the Middle East. To the shipowner, the wind was free and reliable – but Government contracts for mail forced on Shaw Savill a more regular service to New Zealand from which their passengers benefited.

However, as a result of their declared policy to provide a liner-type service to New Zealand from the beginning, the firm must have often found themselves obliged to despatch ships with empty space – short on fare-paying passengers, emigrants or cargo, and this was quite a heavy price for their public commitment to the trade. The following examples show how the human load carrying factor could vary enormously from voyage to voyage in the same ship:

| Ship | Year | No. of Passengers |
|------|------|-------------------|
| Norwood | 1863 | 177 |
|  | 1866 | 65 |
| Silver Eagle | 1863 | 346 |
|  | 1865 | 73 |
| Winterthur | 1865 | 126 |
|  | 1866 | 59 |

The number of sailings (almost entirely from London) built up steadily, as the following table shows; it also reflects the ups and downs of Government policy for settlement in New Zealand:

| | | | |
|------|----|------|-----|
| 1858 | 9 | 1866 | 68 |
| 1859 | 25 | 1867 | 50 |
| 1860 | 21 | 1868 | 50 |
| 1861 | 33 | 1869 | 57 |
| 1862 | 45 | 1870 | 44 |
| 1863 | 70 | 1871 | 42 |
| 1864 | 62 | 1872 | 64 |
| 1865 | 56 | | — |
| | | | 696 |

It was almost a ferry service. One has only to look at the London *Times* from 1863 to see that the New Zealand trade from London was totally dominated by Walter Savill. Ten ships at a time were advertised for various ports. No one else had a look in. It was his exclusive domain.

Standing on the windy shore of a coastline on the other side of the world, you could hardly set your calendar by the welcome sight of the fluttering sails of a rust-stained Shaw Savill packet as she gently nosed her way into the anchorage, but you could stand there and cry and pray.

The arrival of a ship was much more than just that. It was a very special public, and private, event. Relief would be coupled with anxiety about the casualties on the voyage, the condition of the cargo and the health of the survivors. The whole event was drowned in a flood of emotional satisfaction and wellbeing, for it was the re-assuring evidence of the small, fragile but regular link with the Old Country. Despite the thousands of miles of sea and constant dangers, the link still held firm. News, letters, parcels and friends had arrived safely from home. Home and the family were still there. So were Britain and the Empire. God save the Queen and New Zealand. And thank you to that fearless young man in the City, making it all possible. Something like that.

| Name | Tons | Destination | Cleared | Sailing | | Spoken | | Arrived | | Days | Remarks |
|------|------|-------------|---------|---------|---------|--------|-------|---------|------|------|---------|
| | | | | From | Date | Date | Place | | | | |
| 1866 | | | | | | | | | | | |
| Queen Bee | 726 | Otago | June 22 | Gravesend | June | | | October | 11 | 109 | |
| Star of Tasmania | 632 | do | July 11 | Gravesend | July | | | do | 13 | 91 | |
| Blue Jacket | 1442 | Canterbury | do 12 | Deal | | | | do | 14 | 91 | |
| Ega Ziegler | 860 | Auckland | — 16 | Deal | | | | do | 22 | 96 | 87 pass |
| Electric | 661 | Wellington | — 18 | Gravesend | | | | do | 15 | 89 | |
| Empress of Indies | 737 | Nelson | — | Gravesend | | | 13 N. 26 W | do | 14 | 87 | |
| Lancing | 883 | Otago | — | Gravesend | August | 12 | 3 N. 24 W | Novr | 24 | 115 | |
| Leichhardt | 621 | Canterbury | — 30 | Gravesend July | 2 | 8 N 11 27 W | do | 23 | 106 | |
| Chile | 768 | Auckland | — 30 | Gravesend Augt | | | Decr | 4 | 115 | |
| Wild Duck | 737 | Wellington | August 10 | Deal | | 6 22 S. 30 W | do | 8 | 104 | |
| Strathallan | 551 | Napier | — 14 | Deal August | 16 10 N 26 W | do | 2 | 106 | |
| Maulin | 621 | Otago | — 24 | Deal | | 19 N Gr Jany | 12 | 126 | |
| Stormark | 953 | Canterbury | — 24 | Gravesend Plymouth | | Decr | 20 | 98 | |
| Maori | 499 | Auckland | Septr 1 | Deal October | 2 12 N. 26 W | Jany | 24 | 137 | |
| British Merchant | 374 | Nelson | August 21 | Deal | | | do | 24 | 137 | |
| Glamo | 402 | Otago | Septr 2 | Gravesend | | | do | 8 | 111 | |
| Water Nymph | 585 | Invercargill | — 4 | Gravesend October | 30 7 30 N 21 W | do | 28 | 90 | |
| Southern Cross | 562 | Wellington | — | Gravesend October | 3 34 N 14 W December | 16 | 120 | |
| Mermaid | 1283 | Canterbury | — 10 | Deal | | | January | 5 | 104 | |
| Electric | 1106 | Auckland | — 18 | Gravesend | | | do | 22 | 114 | |
| Warrior Queen | 988 | Otago | — 18 | Gravesend | Oct | | do | 8 | 99 | |
| Commodore | 518 | Wellington | Octr | Deal | | | do | 22 | 100 | |
| Mataka | 1224 | Canterbury | — 6 | Deal | | | do | 9 | 94 | |
| Glostat | 804 | Nelson | — | Deal | | | Febr | 7 | 110 | |
| England | 353 | Auckland | — 19 | Gravesend | | | do | 8 | 105 | |
| Countess Russell | 965 | Otago | — | Gravesend | | | do | 22 | 121 | |
| Joseph Phillips | 510 | Canterbury | — 24 | Gravesend | | | March | 11 | 130 | |
| Barualaya | 1005 | do | Novr | Gravesend Novr | | | do | 10 | 103 | |

Extract from the Sailings Book for 1866

The organization and planning necessary to despatch those ships so frequently for so many years, and probably involving over 100,000 passengers, between 1858 and 1882, staggers the imagination, considering the simple facilities available for most of the time. In the office, it was stuffily and murkily Dickensian, depending on the season of the year. There was paraffin or gas lighting, heavy ledgers, scratchy metallic pen nibs, laborious copying of letters, high stools to perch on, juniors busy running messages and constant noise from the streets as the iron rims of the carts and buses rumbled past on the cobbles and as their drivers, the newsboys and the street traders shouted their cries of warning and of wares for sale. There was no central heating but some offices had coal or gas fires. The clerks hunched over bills of lading and cargo manifests for the Customs, making the essential special copies to be sent by separate ship to New Zealand in case the originals were lost on passage. Arrangements had to be made for agents to collect some freight in New Zealand on arrival of cargo and for the money to be remitted. The scope of insurance cover to support the risks taken by the infrastructure of shipowning in Victorian England was enormous.

Outside the office there was horse-drawn transport everywhere, horses slipping about on wet and muddy cobbles, street-sweepers with pans and brushes, and messenger boys darting in and out of the traffic with shipping papers. The yellow London fogs added to the confusion. It was quite possible to become lost, even to the railway station, so dense were the fogs, and the Underground was always smoky and dirty. In cold weather, straw was laid on the floor of the buses. Down at the docks there were congested wharves, limited basic ship's lifting gear and narrow hatches to contend with before getting a ship away.

Even in 1870 the methods of communication were still very limited. There were no telephones, typewriters or overseas cables to New Zealand. Within the UK there was the postal service, and telegrams could be sent by wire in morse code.

The homeward voyages from New Zealand could lay no claim to being a service for several years. Indeed, the firm were hardly involved initially, as the ship's owners or the Commander were responsible for her further profitable employment once the outward charter had expired. Gradually, however, as they grew more confident, they became prepared to take up round-voyage charters or charters for several voyages or even just homeward charters as New Zealand export cargoes found more overseas markets and the firm's agents saw profitable opportunities. Many ships were taken up for two round voyages, especially when good tonnage was going cheap. However, special care had to be taken before chartering particularly old ships, which were liable to suffer more damage from storms, and some of the fast American wooden hull ships, which could be waterlogged.

It was not necessary to send ships out from London in ballast (i.e. without any cargo), in order to provide the extra tonnage required for seasonal cargoes homewards, as there were plenty of opportunities for trade with the Empire under the Red Ensign, particularly with India. A cargo of sorts could always be found which took a ship in the direction of the East and New Zealand.

Initially homeward voyages for ships whose outward voyage had ended in New Zealand were often via Australia, where export cargoes were available, mainly wool and coal, but some chartered ships were sailing home direct in 1860. Coal (a dangerous, self-igniting cargo) was discharged in the Dutch East Indies, Hong Kong or India. The voyage then continued via New Caledonia (for nickel ore), North America (for grain) or the nitrate and guano ports of Guam and South America, picking up whatever profitable cargoes were available before sailing to Falmouth for orders. Most ships went tramping – but a few were sailing homeward direct to London in 1860 with the wool clip. Practically all, however, ended up rounding Cape Horn, that being the direction dictated by the prevailing winds.

Even when New Zealand exports could fill a ship homeward bound, it might take three or four months to load her before she finally sailed. One of the earliest round-voyage charters was when the *Bosworth* sailed for Otago in October 1859 but did not return to Gravesend until August 1860, a round voyage of about ten months. In 1866-7 the speedy *Blue Jacket* completed a round voyage to Canterbury in seven months, but she was exceptional, and probably her homeward cargo was already offering to be loaded on her arrival at Lyttelton. Most ships were away about a year, even if sailing under the scheduled service of the Passengers' Line of Packets.

Scheduling ships homeward was more an imprecise art than outward programming but as long as there was a ship on the berth ready to load when homeward cargo and passengers were offering, that satisfied most people. The only real urgency was to have your best tonnage available to bring the wool clip home in time for the wool sales in London in May, with holds jammed tight and decks almost bursting at the seams under the pressure of the screwed-in bales. Several New Zealand ports were still exposed open roadsteads – Napier, New Plymouth and Timaru.

Without gold strikes, Maori Wars and special contracts, Shaw

Savill could have been in difficulties in the 1860s as emigration did not really expand until 1871, under the Vogel Scheme for free passages. But first the Wars had to end. It took extensive military action and constitutional reform before Sir George Grey, New Zealand's masterly and long-remembered Governor, could unite the country, during his second long term as Governor. (In all he served nineteen years as Governor and later as Prime Minister. If ever a man left his stamp on a country, Grey did in New Zealand; many would say he was its architect.) The end of the wars came in 1868, and with it more emigrants saw opportunities for land purchases following the confiscation and later scale of substantial tracts of Maori lands. It was a messy end to over twenty-five years scrapping and fighting, often of an unusually heroic and compassionate kind, and it led to an understandable latent bitterness by the Maoris.

In 1870 Sir Julius Vogel, the New Zealand Treasurer, obtained support for a massive and imaginative scheme to finance, through London bank loans, public works and free passages for selected immigrants, who in turn were expected to create sufficient wealth for New Zealand to be able to repay the loans. For ten years there was a boom in New Zealand with better wool from a new breed of sheep, the Corriedale, and more wheat. More settlers moved inland.

At the start of this period, in 1872, there was some evidence to indicate either that Shaw Savill's standards of service and care were slipping or that emigrants and New Zealand exporters and importers were seeking higher standards and lower freight rates respectively. It was probably a little of both. Certainly the firm completed two outward voyages best forgotten.

The *Helenslee*, 798 net registered tons, had taken 142 days from Gravesend to Auckland, where she had arrived on 5 June 1872 with her cargo in a bad condition. Then there was the *Bulwark*, 1332 net registered tons, which had taken 215 days for the same voyage and had arrived a little later. Her cargo was so badly damaged that it had to be dug out. She had had the worst of the seas. Her fresh-water tanks had leaked and there was five feet of water in the hold. The huge seas she had encountered had made a clean sweep of her upper deck.

The first sign of dissatisfaction with the service in New Zealand was the formation of local freight associations. Then came a meeting of 'Gentlemen' in Christchurch in November 1872. The prime exporters at the time of wool and wheat, they wanted a regular homeward service of ships as well as a clean-up of the outward service. They probably also wanted a share of the British shipowners' profits, if they were honest with themselves – and the introduction of the Vogel schemes of expansion saw the right moment to seek them.

At any rate, at the close of 1872 a new spirit was abroad in New Zealand. Several immigrants had been settled for more than a generation and were influential, wealthy and self-confident. It was fully opportune for them to start dictating terms to those who traded with the new country it was fast becoming under the quiet leadership of Sir George Bowen, the Governor. There was countrywide support for the efforts being made in Christchurch.

In January 1873 a new company was registered there as the New Zealand Shipping Company Ltd, and by 2 June its first ship (on charter), the *Punjaub*, 883 net registered tons, sailed from Gravesend to Canterbury. The occasion was recorded in Walter Savill's Sailings Book, without comment.

The new company started strongly and sweepingly. Its London sailings alone almost matched Shaw Savill's – in 1876-7 they actually exceeded them. The table below shows their total number of sailings to New Zealand from London and the dramatic change in Shaw Savill's hitherto exclusive possession of its New Zealand trade.

|  | London | |
|---|---|---|
| *Year* | SS | NZSCo |
| 1873 | 67 | 26 |
| 1874 | 71 | 63 |
| 1875 | 63 | 54 |
| 1876 | 51 | 53 |
| 1877 | 51 | 56 |
| 1878 | 71 | 60 |
| 1879 | 60 | 56 |
| 1880 | 54 | 48 |
| 1881 | 57 | 53 |
| 1882 | 65 | 55 |
|  | 610 | 524 |

The formation of the new company was closely followed by the Immigrants Land Act 1873 of the New Zealand Government, a great spur to immigration. The Government contracted a passage fare with the shipping companies, and the emigrants travelled free of charge.

In the previous year the Albion Line had again been worsted by Shaw Savill in a New Zealand Government emigration contract, which had resulted in the withdrawal of approved passages in Albion ships from Glasgow in favour of Shaw Savill ships from

London. This was a very serious matter for them and was another cause of dissatisfaction in New Zealand, where they had many friends and Shaw Savill a few long-suffering customers. Walter Savill thought he had the emigrant trade sewn up for a while. How wrong he was.

With the new contract in 1873, however, both Shaw Savill and the Albion Line knew they had to expand their fleets fast to cope with the new traffic and the fine tonnage being introduced by the New Zealand Shipping Company. So they went out to build, buy and charter the best tonnage they could afford.

The Albion Line's Otago emigrant trade from Glasgow was again secured, and they even began berthing the occasional ship in London for Auckland. Their agent in London, the courteous Edward Pembroke, and Walter Savill began to bury the differences between their organizations. Together they forced the new company into a freight war with the result that it showed a loss of £14,360 in its first year of operation. Having thereby bought a little time to re-organize themselves, the old companies were ready in 1874 to agree with the new company to carry cargo at uniform rates – with the result that the New Zealand importer and exporter had by their actions created a shipping monopoly (within whose reasonably friendly hands they were to remain captive for a very long time, until the New Zealand Government formed a state deep-sea shipping company in 1982). The New Zealand traders were probably little better off in 1874 than they were before the new company was formed, except that they perceived that they had, at a price and in return for mutual obligations, probably a more regular service of homeward sailings (subject to cargo availability), freight rebates for loyalty to the Lines and improved ships in the trade.

Competition in terms of the quality of service between all three shipping companies became fierce. There were now double the number of ships in the trade to carry the thousands of emigrants, particularly in 1874-5. The vagaries of the periodic awards of emigration contracts could not, however, be relied upon for the profitable employment of tonnage. Indeed, by the end of 1873, whilst the New Zealand Shipping Company were advertising their contractual obligations for emigrants, Shaw Savill were advertising only first-rate passenger packets not carrying emigrants. They were after the top end of the market. In 1875 they advertised some first-rate ships with 'new' after their name. A further declared benefit to passengers was that some ships would not carry railway iron, a dangerous cargo if it shifted.

In 1876 the assisted immigration policy was seen to be

Maria Savill – oil painting by
Samuel Bellin

Walter Savill – as a young man

Walter Savill taking a morning ride

Walter Savill in later life

*Star of India* (ex *Euterpe*) restored at San Diego, 1965 – photograph by M.W. Guest

overheating the economy and social structure of New Zealand, and numbers were substantially reduced. So were fares in the Government contracts – and, of course, shipping company profit margins.

Shaw Savill's interest in steam was like a flickering candle or a virgin's dalliance in the rose garden. The two Partners were not keen about it, for a number of good reasons: scattered bunkering ports, loss of valuable cargo space, its unpopularity with passengers, who preferred a clean ship to a few days saved on the voyage, risk of fire (and damage to the sails if set), general expense and liability to break down or run out of coal. It was difficult to estimate fuel consumption which depended so much on the seaway. Shipowners had to curb the enthusiasm of marine engineers, and they compromised initially by insisting that steamships were acceptable only if they could be rigged with sails.

There is no evidence to suggest that Shaw Savill were anxious to introduce steam vessels into their service. In fact, the evidence points the other way. First, there was Walter Savill's known aversion to steam. He was a sailing-ship man through and through. Secondly, the firm despatched only six steamships to New Zealand in twenty-five years, apart from the early two inter-provincial mail steamers (which were of no real consequence) in 1858: 1863 *Sea King* to Auckland, 1874 *Atrato* to Otago and Canterbury, 1879 *Stad Haarlem* to Otago, Canterbury and Wellington, 1880 *Norfolk* to Canterbury and Wellington, *Durham* to Canterbury, 1881 *Norfolk* to Canterbury and Wellington. They were in fact auxiliary screw or auxiliary sail ships as no-one was quite ready to put all their eggs in one basket.

Thirdly, one of the six sailings (the *Stad Haarlem*) was in conjunction with the New Zealand Shipping Company to show willing to the New Zealand Government, which was a generous gesture considering the results of the voyage proved to be the financial disaster forecast by the old sailing-ship hands in the shipping trade. And the three steamship sailings in 1880-1 were part of Walter Savill's obligations as a member of their owner's board, Money Wigram, to help find employment for their surplus tonnage. Money Wigram were the proud owners of a magnificent fleet of frigates built at their Blackwall Yard in Deptford, primarily for the Indian trade but later for first-class passengers bound for Australia under the quiet discipline of their distinctive and distinguished commanders. Contamination with steam by Shaw Savill was very rare indeed.

In January 1877, in face of increasing competition from the New Zealand Shipping Company, the two old rivals, Shaw Savill and the

Albion Line, decided that, despite their earlier differences, they must pool their tonnage and start joint sailings from the Clyde to Otago, which would then be served fortnightly from the United Kingdom, and to other New Zealand ports – Wellington and Canterbury. The Albion Line had a fine fleet of graceful sailing-ships and Shaw Savill were not averse to sharing in their glory until both firms amalgamated in 1882. The new arrangement would enable a number of emigrants to be embarked at Greenock, who might otherwise have had to travel to London or Liverpool to join a New Zealand Shipping Company ship in preference to what Shaw Savill had on the berth. In return for allowing Shaw Savill to participate in the Glasgow trade, the Albion Line were invited to help load Shaw Savill ships in London. With some pride they advertised particulars of their combined fleets of fifty-two ships in *The Times* on 1st January 1877 as being at the service of the New Zealand trade in the following terms under the names of three ships already loading: 'To be succeeded at regular intervals during the year by the following magnificent fleet of high-classed iron and composite ships. These vessels, so favourably known, have been specially constructed for this trade, and are fitted with all recent improvements for the comfort of passengers.' Both firms hoped it was an unbeatable fleet and would scare the living daylights out of the New Zealand Shipping Company.

The scale of New Zealand's immigration effort between 1858 and 1882 was impressive and can only be attributed to the concentrated determination of the New Zealand Government and various agencies in the UK to colonize the country as quickly as possible lest any other European nations in the area, such as the Dutch and the French, began to doubt the British commitment. Also it was necessary, in accordance with conventional wisdom in London, that the colony should be no exception to the rule that it should be self-supporting (apart from the supply of imperial troops for its defence).

In 1858 New Zealand's European population was 61,224. Twenty-five years later it was 517,707, of whom about 226,000 had arrived as immigrants from the United Kingdom. This had been the result of a major effort by the shipping companies and a major step into the unknown by thousands of families showing extraordinary courage and fortitude. Obviously some thought they had no choice but to take this opportunity to escape from slums, poverty and misfortunes in Victorian England, but the great majority must have set sail because of the spirit of the times. The Empire beckoned; there were new frontiers to conquer, new starts to be made. The British people were on the move all over the world, many just for the hell of it.

The mass movement of people meant inevitably more ships in the trade, more imported goods and, as the new arrivals generated more wealth, more exports, as the following figures from the New Zealand Government statistics show dramatically:

|  | 1858 | 1882 |
|---|---|---|
| Nos. and size of British vessels cleared inwards | 266 (62,616 tons) (av. 235 tons) | 723 (393,614 tons) (av. 544 tons) |
| Value of imports ex UK | £532,596 | £5,553,324 |
| Value of exports to UK | £242,523 | £4,709,393 |
| Wool exported worldwide | 3.8 m. lbs. | 65 m. lbs. |

During this period Shaw Savill had built up a quiet reputation for an efficient service (on the whole). They had not sought the headlines, although their disasters had not spared them a few. Their top priority remained to have a ship on the berth on schedule for a New Zealand port, sailing on the tide as advertised.

# 8. *The Price Paid*

Inevitably, Shaw Savill did not escape their share of marine disasters and accidents. Sailing-ships were always dangerous to crew and passengers alike once voyaging with the wind. Many sailed on crippled, but game. The most notorious tragedies concerned the *Cospatrick*, the *Strathmore* and the *Avalanche*. The following accounts of their individual ends are not meant to dwell on them in terms of Shaw Savill's overall performance of transporting tens of thousands of passengers safely to New Zealand – rather to recount the awful circumstances with which emigrants were faced, the hazards chanced by sea-travellers when they set off into the unknown, to the other side of the world to build a new nation, and what extraordinary courage it needed to face them as they did. No wonder many dropped to their knees and prayed on their safe arrival there.

The *Cospatrick* disaster was the grimmest tale of all and ranks amongst the great accidents at sea. Four hundred and seventy people perished as a result of a holocaust which sent the ship to the bottom one calm night when making her easting south of Cape Town. She had taken two days to die, only eighty-five escaped in boats, and only three survived this ordeal. All 429 emigrants, mostly young farm labourers and Irish country girls indentured to help develop the new pastures, perished.

   The *Cospatrick* was a wooden Blackwall frigate-type ship built in teak at Moulmein in 1856 for Duncan Dunbar for his London-Cape Town-India liner service. She was a first-class passenger ship of 1,200 tons, no passage-maker but safe, comfortable, dry and thoroughly reliable, a typical East Indiaman. Seamen would give their eye-teeth to command her, especially in the Duncan Dunbar fleet, where they reached the height of their profession. She made several round voyages to India, trooping during the Mutiny and carrying the ebb and flow of brides, families and leave reliefs of the British in India, before being sold to Shaw Savill in 1873 as an emigrant-carrier. The *Edwin Fox* was bought from the same fleet at the same time.

The *Cospatrick* was seventeen years old when bought but her timbers were still sound, and her Commander, Captain A. Elmslie, came over with the ship. Walter Savill had liked the cut of his jib and his ship when he had chartered her for a voyage to Otago the previous year. Before he bought, he often insisted on a trial voyage or two to make sure the ship and Commander were a good team and likely to reach New Zealand safely without too many fractious passengers or anxious mishaps.

Her second voyage to New Zealand was on 11 September from Gravesend to Auckland in 1874. She had cleared Start Point on 14 September, made a landfall at Bahía, Brazil and was spoken by another ship on 18 and 28 October when fate intervened with a fire in the bosun's store in the fore peak of the ship. The store was full of inflammable material – oakum, oil, tarred rope, paint and cotton waste. The cause of the fire was never established. The three survivors could only conjecture: either the bosun's oil lamp fell off a shelf as the ship rolled (he was said to be a little careless) or a passenger threw a lighted match through the grating over the store. A passenger could have been surprised by the fire patrol on board responsible for enforcing the 'no smoking below decks' rule and in charge of the locked lamps on the stairways leading down to the emigrants' accommodation.

At any rate, at about two o'clock in the middle watch on 18 November, when most passengers and crew were in a dead sleep, fire broke out in the store. The ship was rolling gently along in light airs on a sea surprisingly calm for these latitudes, barely answering her helm (these frigates could be heavy steerers) – this was the cause of major trouble later on. At first the fire pumps were manned but every time the ship rolled, valuable suction was lost. A chain of fire buckets was then formed by crew and passengers, who had emerged on deck in their night attire to try to quench the fire, but the cramped headroom made working difficult, and the thick black smoke and heat of the fire eventually drove people back.

The next setback was when the ship's head came round up into the wind, so that the fire was offered a feast of nearly 200 feet of woodwork and canvas from stem to stern. It went to work with a vengeance: within an hour and a half the ship was ablaze fore and aft and aloft. There has been a good deal of argument about this development. It has been claimed that she would not have gone up into the wind and stayed there if the Commander had granted the mate's request to take out a boat to pull the ship round, as the wind was too light to make her pay off under her own sails, or if the large forecourse had not been brailed up so soon to save it catching fire, or if, instead, all her sails had been brailed up immediately and thus kept the ship in balance.

It was probably at this stage that panic ensued on board as the flames and smoke swept aft, causing confusion. The Commander cocked his pistol but hesitated fatally, with the result that he lost control of emigrants and crew and indeed of the situation as a whole. Previous fire-drills at Gravesend and the voyage had no relevance to the set of circumstances facing all on board.

The chain of events seemed irreversible and swift. There were seven life-saving boats on board – two cutters, two quarterboats, one longboat and two small lifeboats – enough to take only about half the passengers and crew. The first two boats were stowed amidships, bottom up on chocks. There was no hoisting tackle to get them over the side quickly. They would have had to be manhandled. One was rotten; the other had been holed by falling masts and spars and was therefore also unseaworthy. The fire quickly enveloped both boats. One quarterboat was then lowered from its chocks but was quickly overloaded by eighty frightened passengers and soon capsized. All were drowned. The other quarterboat and the longboat were burned in their chocks. The remaining two small lifeboats were housed on their own davits further aft, one on each side. They were already hoisted outboard for emergencies, such as passengers falling overboard. These were eventually got away, one with forty-two passengers and three seamen under the command of the second mate, Macdonald, the other with thirty-nine passengers and crew under the command of the chief mate.

Neither boat had food, water, masts or sails, and one boat had only one sound oar and one broken one. Their occupants wore only the flimsiest of clothes. For two days the overcrowded boats stood off, watching the hopeless situation on board the *Cospatrick* and the screaming passengers jumping into the sea as the masts crashed down and the fire got closer to them. The sharks were waiting. No effort was made to construct rafts. All on board were too exhausted.

Near midnight the ship's stern, where 400 tons of explosives were stowed, blew out and she became a tunnel of fire from stem to stern. A little later the Commander and his wife jumped overboard and the ship went down in a great hiss of steam.

The two lifeboats drifted together all night and the next day as the wind and sea got up. By morning on the following day only one lifeboat was left. The other was never seen again. For the next thirty hours the survivors lay in a stupor – fifteen were tipped over the side, dead. The one good oar slipped overboard and was lost, and there was no shelter from the sun. The seas were now rough. A ship hove in sight but failed to see the lifeboat. The survivors were now half demented and began eating the livers of the dead bodies and drinking their blood.

They had drifted for 540 miles when three days later, on the 27th, the *British Sceptre* saw the lifeboat and took on board the survivors – Macdonald and just four men out of 473 souls – and landed three of them at St Helena, two having died.

When the news was telegraphed to London, it was not believed at first. It was too overwhelming, too utterly ghastly and horrific. For a passing moment the public caught its breath, men paused in their work, and the churches filled – then, somewhat raggedly, life resumed. Life was held cheaper in Victorian Britain than it is today, and standards of care and safety other than in the factory were seldom generally acknowledged or given priority, but on this occasion the Lord Mayor of London opened a fund for dependant relatives.

As for Shaw Savill, the only record that exists of this disaster is a laconic note in the Sailings Book for 1874: 'Burnt lat. 37 S long 12 E'.

The *Strathmore*, 1,472 tons, sailed from Gravesend for Otago on 19 April 1875 with fifty passengers and thirty-eight crew. The following account of her shipwreck on the Crozet Islands in the southern Indian Ocean appeared in the *Scotsman*, based on the experience of Thomas Peters, the second mate (who was later to command the Shaw Savill ship *Helen Denny*):

Mr Peters states that on 30th June the weather was so thick that the lookout could not see further than a ship's length ahead and the speed of the *Strathmore* at the time was only about six knots an hour. It was understood that the course which was being steered would take the ship well to the south of the Crozet Islands: but a close look-out was kept for them. At midnight, the second mate while in his berth, was awakened by the cry 'Breakers ahead' and immediately the ship struck.

Mr Peters ran on deck when he saw the first mate and some of the crew clearing away the port quarterboat. The captain seemed to have lost his head altogether so Mr Peters mustered together a few hands to clear away the starboard quarterboat; but no sooner were the gripes cut and the boat lifted a few inches with the tackle than the sea came rolling over the poop, washing away the two men that were knocking away the chocks. A second attempt was made but by this time the seas came over in quick succession carrying several others of the crew overboard and making it impossible to get the boat out. The port quarterboat also had to be abandoned as she had been stoved by a sea and rendered useless. As the ship was now fast, most of those who had been working at the quarterboats got into one of the lifeboats which floated clear of the wreck by nothing less than a miracle. Eighteen of the crew and passengers, a lady among the number, were in this boat. The captain and first mate were washed overboard by the sea which floated off the lifeboat and neither of them was seen afterwards.

But before the boat got off, Mr Peters saw a saloon passenger standing holding on to the poop rail with a little boy in his arms. Mr Peters took the child and carried him up the mizzen rigging where the second steward took charge of him. The mate then went down again to see if he could help any other unfortunates. But no sooner had he struck on the deck than a heavy sea swept the poop and came rolling over him and but for some of the rigging of the jury mast getting entangled about him he would have shared the fate of so many of his shipmates.

Getting hold of the mizzen topsail sheet Mr Peters reached the mizzen top where he found a number of the crew and passengers being assembled. The after part of the ship was by this time completely underwater. Some of the men managed to get on the top of the forward house where the gig and dinghy were lashed. The gig was got ready for launching at daybreak as it had then become too dark for lowering it in safety. Mr Peters then found that the ship had jammed herself between two rocks forward which accounted for her not going down.

At daybreak the shipwrecked men found themselves within thirty yards of perpendicular cliffs some hundreds of feet high, with rocks all about them. The gig was got out without accident but the dinghy got badly stoved. She was able however to carry three of our group to safety and eight of the party got into the gig. Mr Peters told those left behind that he would come back for them as soon as he could find a landing. After a good deal of trouble they found a place where they could scramble up although with great danger. As they were pulling in they came upon the lifeboat stoved and full of water but her eighteen people so far safe still. The gig took her in tow and brought her to land. All but three men and Mr Peters then got on shore. These four returned to the wreck – faithful to their promise, and took off some of those still clinging to the rigging, the little boy being among them. A number were still left in the forecastle and Mr Peters told them he would be back in the morning for them. A miserable night was spent on the rocks without any shelter. On the way to the shore they picked up a case of spirits which were allowanced out during the night.

Mr Peters goes on to say 'I was glad when daylight began to make its appearance so that I could go back to the ship which I found as we had left her the night before. I made the men that were in the forecastle head get all the clothes they could out of the forecastle and pass them into the boat, most of those on shore being only half clad. We also got a few boxes of matches: and about a dozen biscuits that being all that could be found in the shape of provisions. On landing we gave these to Mrs Wordsworth as the bird's flesh was so wrang that she could not eat it. After making a poor meal of half-cooked birds we returned to the ship for the purpose of getting a sail to make a tent with but we were quite unable to board her on account of the surf. A few cases of spirits, a cask of wine and a box of confectionery were however picked up, the tins of the latter having afterwards come in use for cooking purposes. Coming back to the landing we found the lifeboat had also been pretty successful having come across a passenger's chest out of which we got a few articles such as blankets, table cloths, knives, forks and spoons. Firewood was also picked up whenever that could conveniently be done there being no wood on the island.

'During the time we had been away those that were ashore had built a wall before an overhanging ledge of rock so that with the boats' covers for a roof we had a little better shelter than we had the night before, although the place was so small we could only sit huddled together as close as we could possibly pack. We had wished the lady to use this shelter but she would not listen to our making such a sacrifice and insisted upon all sharing with her the slightest comforts of the situation. Even the biscuits which we desired to keep for her use she'd divide between some of the ailing ones of the party. Owing to our cramped condition and the bitter cold weather we were unable to sleep that first night and during it we had the misfortune to lose our boats. These were moored in smooth waters and a watch set over them; but the wind dropping suddenly broke them adrift and we had the pleasure of seeing them floating about bottom up completely out of our reach. If there had been a beach anywhere on the island we might have saved them by hauling them up; but the rocks were so steep and rugged that we could scarcely scramble ashore. During the next day some of us walked to a part of the island where we could have a look at the vessel: but nothing was to be seen of her save a few small spars entangled by some of the gear and so kept floating over the side of the wreck.

'During all the time we were on the island we were miraculously provided with food. Although sometimes it seemed as if there was not another bird on the island we always managed to catch a few to keep us alive until they got more plentiful. We also ate a sort of herb the top of which resembles carrot tops. Our fire would last a month and after that we found a substitute for wood in the shape of bird skins which do burn pretty well. Five of our number died on the island: the last of these was the little child who was taken on Christmas day. We had then been six months on the island and though four ships had passed pretty close none of them seemed to see our signals. But on 21st January we had the extreme satisfaction of seeing a ship heading in towards the island which afterwards lowered two boats. This was a whaler and her captain agreed to take us off. There were forty-four of us in all and were treated with great kindness on board the *Young Phoenix*. Crosses were placed over the graves of those who had been buried on the island.'

A few more particulars were received from one of the passengers who escaped. He describes the Crozet Islands as 'twenty-six in number and the one we were on was one of the twelve rocks called the Twelve Apostles. Rocks upon rocks everywhere, seabirds' home. Very few level places, some grass and weeds growing about. Plenty of young albatross about which we could at first easily knock down with a stick. They had then no fear of us nor had any other of the seabirds. We found a spring of water which was our great good fortune in all our trouble. We had no doctor amongst us. The ship didn't carry one, else some who died might have been saved. We kept blankets flying on the masts of the lifeboat as a signal but none of all the vessels which passed seemed to see it. One vessel came so near that we cannot doubt that we were seen but she sheared off from us. Our lady passenger survived and with her son was the first to leave the island. The whaler hoisted the Stars and Stripes and sent boats to us. Her captain gave each of us a suit of clothes and a pair of boots and was short on his provisions so that he had to put into Galle to make up his sufficiencies. Half our number had been transferred to the *Sierra Morena* which fortunately met the *Young Phoenix* and cheerfully relieved her of that portion of her unexpected task.'

The absence of a doctor on board is surprising. Although the survivors spent as long as seven months on the island, nothing was heard in London of their plight until some ten months after the ship had sailed outward bound.

The *Avalanche* was a smart-looking iron ship of 1,210 gross tons built for Walter Savill by Alexander Hall of Aberdeen in 1874. Her fine lines and neatness aloft bore the impeccable stamp of that famous clipper-ship builder who had turned out some of the fastest and most beautiful ships afloat, such as *Cairngorm, Black Prince, Flying Spur, Chrysolite* and *Yangtze*. She was the third ship specifically built to the order of the young shipowner and was a fast sailer, having consistently turned in ninety-one, ninety and ninety days for each of her first three Wellington voyages, all of which had been September or October departures from Gravesend. In the spring of 1877 she returned from Wellington on her fourth, after a thrilling race homeward with the *Crusader, Rangitiki* and *Ocean Mail*, arriving second in eighty days to Gravesend, against the *Crusader*'s sixty-seven and *Rangitiki*'s eighty-two days. (The *Ocean Mail* never saw Britain again for she slammed into the Chatham Islands at dawn three days after leaving Wellington, having been caught in the islands' notorious tide race as a result of faulty navigation.)

Working her way down Channel on the port tack at about 9.15

p.m. on 11 September 1877 into a stiff sou'westerly wind on a hazy night, fifteen or so miles south by west of Portland, with her flickering oil side-lights burning, the *Avalanche* collided with the Canadian wooden ship *Forest* of 1,422 tons in ballast on the starboard tack. The force of the collision amidships was so great that the wooden ship pierced the iron hull of the *Avalanche* and she sank in less than five minutes, taking down with her all sixty-three passengers and all but three members of her crew of thirty-four, who with a few others had managed to leap onto the forecastle of the *Forest*, which also was abandoned within fifteen minutes (although she did not sink until several days later). Three ship's boats were launched from the *Forest* but only one was afloat next morning off Chesil Beach, in which were the Commander of the *Forest*, Captain Lockhart, eight of his crew and the third officer and two seamen from the *Avalanche*. Showing immense skill and courage, the crews of two local fishing-boats put out from the shore, transferred the shipwrecked seamen and brought them in through the surf breaking on the beach.

In memory of those who died in the disaster, a church consecrated to St Andrew was built at Portland by public subscription in 1879. Contributions were received from New Zealand and Britain, and they are still being received, as the church enters its second century in Avalanche Road. The wreck of the ship has recently been found, and certain items of Victoriana have been recovered, including bottles of champagne and pottery.

The loss was reported tersely and prosaically in Lloyd's List, as the extracts in Appendix F show. Particularly poignant and not devoid of humour are the reports of how the hull of the *Forest* refused to sink and became a danger to shipping until twelve days later the Royal Navy managed to sink it. The *Avalanche* was in charge of a pilot, and her Commander was therefore in the clear.

No one has reported the thoughts of Walter Savill as the dreadful news came to him by telegraph as he sat in his office the following morning shortly after the rescues on Chesil Beach had been completed. He was stunned at the loss not only of life but of one of his best ships as he wrote simply in his Sailings Book 'Foundered off Portland Sept. 11'. Over one hundred drowned in the Channel was a disaster too close for comfort in London, where credibility had always to be sustained by good performance. He resolved that henceforth more passengers would join their ships at Plymouth rather than risk collisions in the Channel, of which Shaw Savill had already had a number but without loss of life.

Other disasters took the form of collisions in the Straits of Dover (even at Gravesend), parted cables or dragged anchors on lee shores in New Zealand resulting in wrecks on the beaches, destruction from fire when in New Zealand ports, collisions with icebergs in the South Atlantic when homeward bound, and dismasting, shifting cargo and flooding. Not all caused loss of life, but most did.

There were several narrow escapes. For example, the *William Brown*, a small wooden barque of 403 tons, caught fire at sea as the passengers were finishing their tea on 2 October 1861 when outward bound for Nelson. Fortunately she was on a main trade route off Madeira, and twenty-two of the twenty-three passengers and crew were picked up by a Swedish brig (the *Hedwig Charlotta*) after about twelve hours in an open boat, having abandoned the burning ship in rain and darkness and with a heavy sea running.

Although this may seem to have been a straightforward quick rescue of a small party of people, it was a shocking experience for them as there was no guarantee of rescue. They had suddenly lost all their possessions and, wrapped in wet blankets, had tossed about all night in the Atlantic in two waterlogged boats, sustained only by prayer, a bag of biscuits and a cask of water. They owed their rescue to the fact that they had had the good sense to stay all night by the burning ship, which had been sighted by the brig, and also to the superb presence of mind and seamanship of their Commander, Captain Barclay, in conducting an orderly evacuation of their ship, especially of the women and children, in shepherding the two boats in rough seas throughout an anxious night and finally in having the courage to send off one boat with crew members to intercept the brig whilst he remained with his passengers.

The survivors were landed at Madeira and returned to Britain, whereupon some passengers again set off for New Zealand within a period of three weeks, despite their ordeal. What extraordinary stoicism!

The sad record of other losses (and near-losses) is set out opposite:

It is amazing there were so few disasters which ended in the loss of a ship, considering the number of near-misses which only superb seamanship overcame and loadlines not being compulsory until 1876. Sudden squalls dismasted the ships, threw them on their beam ends and ripped out their sails. Great waves broke on board and swept the decks from end to end until the ship was almost awash before she staggered up again and pushed on into the next deep trough of the sea. Each time she plunged down and disappeared, or was pooped by a big wave astern, there was the fearful delay and doubt whether she would ever come up again. If you were aloft on these occasions, all you might see on looking

## Collisions in the English Channel

| Year | Ship | Bound for | Result |
|------|------|-----------|--------|
| 1862 | *Silver Eagle* | Auckland | Not sunk |
| 1863 | *Coldstream* | Otago | Not sunk |
| 1863 | *Rangoon* | Hawke Bay | Not sunk |
| 1864 | *Strathallan* | Napier | Not sunk |
| 1864 | *Victory* | Auckland | Not sunk |
| 1868 | *Leichardt* | Wellington | Sunk |
| 1872 | *Edinburgh Castle* | Auckland | Not sunk |
| 1874 | *Alice* | Canterbury | Not sunk |
| 1874 | *Edwin Fox* | Wellington | Not sunk |
| 1876 | *Bebington* | Auckland | Not sunk |
| 1877 | *Zealandia* | Wellington | Not sunk |
| 1877 | *Western Monarch* | Otago | Not sunk |
| 1879 | *Schiehallion* | London | Wrecked |
| 1880 | *Calypso* | London | Sunk |
| 1880 | *Hydaspes* | Melbourne | Sunk |
| 1882 | *Famenoth* | Otago | Not sunk |

*Dragged anchors, or parted cables, driven ashore in New Zealand and wrecked*

| Year | Ship | Place |
|------|------|-------|
| 1863 | *Royal Bride* | Napier |
| 1865 | *Gazehound* | Oamaru |
| 1868 | *Star of Tasmania* | Oamaru |
| 1868 | *Water Nymph* | Oamaru |
| 1868 | *Echunga* | Napier |
| 1869 | *Ida Ziegler* | Napier |
| 1882 | *City of Perth* | Timaru (salvaged) |

## Destroyed (or damaged) by fire in New Zealand

| Year | Ship | Place |
|------|------|-------|
| 1867 | *Montmorency* | Napier |
| 1870 | *Hera* | Port Underwood |
| 1871 | *City of Auckland* | Auckland (scuttled and re-floated) |

*Missing – Lost without trace homeward bound*

| Year | Ship | Sailed from |
|------|------|-------------|
| 1869 | Matoaka | Canterbury |
| 1872 | Glenmark | Canterbury |
| 1883 | Kilmeny | Wellington |

*Wrecked or sunk on passage*

| Year | Ship | Sailed from | Place |
|------|------|-------------|-------|
| 1863 | Great Britain | Gravesend | St Jago, Cape Verde Islands |
| 1866 | Lizzie Scott | Wellington | Chatham Islands, off New Zealand |
| 1869 | Blue Jacket | Canterbury* | Falkland Islands (fire at sea) |
| 1877 | Queen Bee | Gravesend | Nelson |
| 1881 | England's Glory | Gravesend | Bluff |

* with £63,390 in gold and 20 passengers

*Condemned on passage*

| Year | Ship | Bound for | Place |
|------|------|-----------|-------|
| 1872 | Agamemnon | Canterbury | Cape Town |

down would be three sticks standing in the sea which stretched unbroken from horizon to horizon. It could seem years before there was a horrible shudder from the depths and the poop or forecastle broke the surface, with the seas cascading off her wallowing topsides. There would then be an anxious glance to see whether the hatches had been stove in and what was left on the deck. Usually everything that could go had gone. She was up, but what destruction!

Whole watches could be swept overboard, and men could be washed even from the yardarm as the ship rolled in a sudden broach-to. Wheels were often smashed by a sixty-foot comber crashing onto the poop and carrying away the helmsman and everything before it, as so much matchwood. Great seas poured into the accommodation, and passengers were swimming for their lives in their own cabins. Hatches burst open and flooded holds. Ballast and cargo shifted so that the ship stayed down on her beam ends whilst courageous men went below in the maelstrom and started shovelling cargo and ballast until she righted herself. Hours of back-breaking labour were spent in darkness in a lurching hold wondering when the ship would take her final plunge. The bulwarks were always being carried away, which meant that it was all too easy to fall over the side with a sudden lurch of the ship or by a slip on the wet deck.

The *Dallam Tower*, the *Bombay* and the *Zealandia* suffered such voyages, but practically every voyage of every ship had its moment of tragedy and terror. Some were more protracted than others or plumbed greater depths, but all were met by the extraordinary fatalism and quiet courage of the passengers from Victorian Britain. In adversity they committed themselves to God and stood ready to make whatever sacrifice He demanded, including dying at sea as the icy waters closed over the heads of their loved ones and themselves in one cataclysmic rush.

Then there were the dangerous cargoes. Coal could smoulder away until it became red hot. There was very little you could do about it. An iron hull would become a floating oven; a wooden hull would go to the bottom. Nitrate was also sensitive. A spark could lead to an almighty explosion, spelling doom to the ship.

Perhaps one of the greatest losses at sea was when the ship's boats were smashed or washed overboard – quite a common occurrence. For passengers and crew there was then a fearful anxiety as they realized that the ship's safe arrival was their only lifeline. Also it was not unknown for the boats to tow a ship out of danger, as happened to the *Queen of the Deep* on passage to Auckland in 1864 when she was in danger of being wrecked on Tenerife.

Ice was another menace at sea and is believed to have been, with shipwrecks known only to God, the main reason for ships going missing in the South Atlantic. There were reports of 400 miles of ice with bergs a thousand feet high. It was not unusual to sight 200 bergs at once. At night collision was almost inevitable unless ships hove to. Even by day, collisions occurred if a ship missed her stays when tacking and was caught aback.

Some ships were the devil to steer – for example, the *Soukar* – even in the best conditions. Loss of steerage way was always a tricky, if not nervous, business. A ship could even be blown backwards for several miles if she lost her way ahead. This was particularly alarming, as the masts were braced only for way ahead.

The most remarkable voyage of any Shaw Savill ship on charter was that of the *Dallam Tower*, on passage to Port Chalmers in 1873 when she was totally dismasted by hurricane-force winds (and dubious seamanship) some 2,000 miles from Melbourne, whither she managed to sail under the sweetest of a jury rig. She was repaired and completed her voyage without having lost a single passenger or crew member despite her seven-week ordeal. Thereafter she continued to make good voyages to New Zealand in under a hundred days, which demonstrated her fine lines, sea-keeping qualities and strong construction.

It is difficult to imagine a ship wallowing in great troughs of waves, appearing at times to be almost no more than a floating log. Great holes had been made in the *Dallam Tower*'s hatches and deck by the falling top hamper, and her iron sides were being hammered by floating spars and masts. She could have been in trouble if she had had a wooden hull. There was no cover on deck, as the seas had swept it clean several times. The saloon was flooded and timber floated around there. Water was passing into the holds – and yet on board this hulk were people alive, pumping out the water, stopping the holes, re-stowing cargo and even thinking of rigging new masts and sails with anything that could serve. Shortly after the seas abated, the crew began to clear the decks with axes for stepping a jury rig. All boats had gone the same way as the charts, compasses and some prize bulls – smashed to pieces or washed over the side. Fourteen days after the hurricane struck, they were ready to go, as the *Dallam Tower* slowly answered her helm and was pointed in the direction of Melbourne, thanks to reference to an almanac found undamaged in a passenger's baggage. On a good day she made seven knots as the following wind blew her all the way into port, and despite her ordeal she was only one hundred days out from the Channel, a fine example of British shipbuilding pedigree and of the *Dallam Tower*'s reputation as a flier.

The mate became a local hero, if not someone more celestial. He had spent thirty consecutive hours at the wheel at the height of the gale and had led the salvage effort. The Commander on the other hand suffered the ignominy of dismissal. Like so many others believing in the dubious practice of full speed ahead regardless, he had carried too much sail for too long. Many believed this same sort of maritime arrogance or madness was alive even in the best of commanders when exhausted in mind and body their judgement deserted them and they sought an unnecessary contest with the sea.

In contrast, some ships had extraordinary good luck. For example, the *Famenoth* hardly had a strong blow in five passages to Auckland and, as if to compound this good fortune, was able to be refloated and repaired after going aground on the Kent coast when outward bound in the teeth of a Channel sou'westerly. The *Famenoth* could slip along. On one occasion she logged $15\frac{1}{2}$ knots under a main topgallant sail only.

*Westland* – water colour by J. Spurling

The *Bombay*, a wooden ship of 937 tons, had an experience similar to that of the *Dallam Tower*, terrifying for the passengers but again dealt with in a seamanlike manner by the crew. Ten days out from Auckland on an outward voyage in 1865, she was hit by squalls which partially dismasted her. For two days she lay helpless, wallowing in the stormy sea but dry below. Her plight was noticed by a passing ship which gave her a tow and allowed her time to set a jury rig. The Royal Navy then took over the tow into Auckland. It was four months before the *Bombay* was ready for sea again. Once more, no lives had been lost but the passengers had had a frightening experience.

The *Zealandia* had at least two alarming experiences. She collided at midnight with the *Ellen Lamb* in mid Atlantic on 7 July 1877, when outward bound for Wellington. The sea was calm and she collided with such force that the *Ellen Lamb* sank in three minutes. The *Zealandia* rigged a sail over a hole in her iron plating and sailed safely on to Rio, where repairs were effected. Although the ships were in company before darkness fell, it is extraordinary that neither allowed the other sufficient sea room at night. Probably neither ship was burning sidelights, a common practice in calm conditions to economize on lamp-oil. Like the poor *Avalanche*, the *Ellen Lamb* was hit amidships.

Then in September 1882, outward bound for Otago, the *Zealandia* ran into a hurricane and ran under bare poles whilst the mountainous seas did their best to send her under. The seas swept her deck clean, washed out the accommodation and pooped her time and time again. The bridge was washed away and the forecastle smashed in. Meanwhile the terrified passengers clung to each other as the water sloshed about below them. But she arrived safely, thanks again to remarkable seamanship supported by the fortitude of the passengers.

The safety of the ship depended of course on the Commander's seamanship skills and the mate's management's skills, subject to the abilities and attitudes of the crew. A sailing ship of, say, 1,100 registered tons usually carried a crew of about thirty made up as follows:

| | | | |
|---|---|---|---|
| 1 | Commander | 1 | sailmaker |
| 1 | mate | 12 | able seamen |
| 1 | second mate | 3 | ordinary seamen |
| 1 | third mate | 3 | apprentices |
| 1 | boatswain | 2 | cooks |
| 1 | carpenter | 2 | stewards |

*Invercargill* – water colour by J. Spurling

Their diet on board was even plainer than the emigrants'. It consisted of salt beef, salt pork, tinned boiled Australian mutton, biscuits, bread three times a week, brown sugar, lime juice and little else. In port, the fare was mainly strong liquor, and life was more dangerous amid the vice and crimes found the waterfronts and in the sailor towns. Nevertheless, the temptation to desert was strong, if not enforced by the brothel-keepers and press gangs always on the look-out for a likely victim of their sordid activities. Even if their efforts had been frustrated, there was always the lingering thought of a girl left behind, when a concertina among the crowd standing on the dock wall picked out a haunting tune as the ship was towed out.

A special supplement to the dietary scale was the crew's tobacco ration. All hell could be let loose if Commanders tried to short-change on this entitlement.

The crews were as mixed a bag as the ships. Most were British, with some other Europeans. Some were first-rate able seamen but many signed on in desperation to find employment and were totally unprepared for the hardships of life on board ship and the exhaustion of keeping watches during a long passage. Some jumped ship in Australia or New Zealand and broke their articles for a round voyage. The lure of gold ashore was too strong for them, or the conditions on board were intolerable. Some ships had endless crew trouble, and the loggings for offences were a stain on the ship's life.

The crew of a sailing-ship were individuals, each of whom knew the limit of his own skills and strengths which had pulled him through so far during his time at sea. Each had experienced those private lonely moments when life stood in the balance. When a seaman joined a new ship, those moments were not spoken about but were not forgotten. His priority was to learn to trust his fellow crew members, to work with them as a team and above all to 'learn the ropes' and sails of the ship so that he could seize the right gear by feel in pitch darkness on a heaving deck on a wet, cold night, with water up to his waist each time the ship rolled her lee rail under. He might have to recognize between thirty and forty sails and over 400 ropes of one kind or another, each having its own name. A hand on the wrong rope at the wrong time could mean a friend pitched overboard or a mast brought down.

It was the mate's responsibility to find a crew, and the Commander's to lead them. No doubt, as in other walks of life, each officer got what he deserved. A sneaking regard for each other between crew and officers soon built up if the ship seemed well found, food was adequate, the crew were trying and the officers were fair in their treatment of crew members. The Commander had to show above all else that he was a seaman and navigator and would not put the ship at risk. He could be forgiven a few foibles, even old age and bad temper, if in his own way he completed the voyage safely. The crew wanted to give him their respect because they needed to put themselves in his care but they sometimes found a devilish pleasure in playing for high stakes before the proper relationship was established. So too did Commanders and pilots. On the *India*, the Commander was fined for wilful interference with the pilot in the discharge of his duties as he brought her into Auckland in 1875.

But it was with the crew that the Commander was fair game. For example, during the *John Bunyan*'s passage to Wellington in 1860, the crew mutinied, having first broached a cargo of spirits. The Commander had to hold the poop with a pistol until the mutineers were placed in irons. The magistrate's court for the culprits was their first destination on arrival in New Zealand, followed by a six-month gaol sentence.

The crew of the *Flying Foam* on passage to Auckland in 1864 also mutinied, and sixteen were placed in irons or in stocks. Mutinies occurred on the *Dauntless* (supported by passengers!), *Chapman*, *Blue Jacket*, *Mallard* and *Mary Low* – but all were chartered vessels. There is no record of a mutiny by the crew of a Shaw Savill owned vessel between 1865 (the date of their first purchase) and 1882.

The Commander was not always safe from the aggressive attentions of his officers. The first officer of the *Chieftain* was locked up after assaulting his Commander.

Sometimes cargoes of spirits were broached, fights ensued and fire-arms were issued – not exactly a picnic on the high seas, but understandable. There was one case, the *Anazi* arriving off Auckland in 1874 after a long voyage, when the Commander was so drunk, with relief or joy, that he ran the ship aground at midnight. She was a Shaw Savill owned ship so this was a bad lapse.

Besides mutinies, refusals and desertions by crews, they suffered casualties. Falling from aloft or being washed overboard and drowning were the main hazards. On the *Zealandia*, homeward bound in 1872, the Commander was washed overboard and drowned. Several Commanders, in fact, died at sea. Apprentices were accident-prone from working up to 200 feet aloft stopping buntlines on skysails or standing precariously on the sagging footropes at the end of a swinging mainyard helping to furl a great mass of frozen canvas in a westerly gale. Eight hours aloft without relief were not uncommon when the ship was fighting for her life. It was training of a kind for command but seen mostly as cheap and willing labour. One apprentice was exceptionally lucky on the *Langstone*: he fell from aloft onto his Commander. Neither was any the worse the wear. But far too many fell to their deaths, exhausted and unnoticed. Perhaps they were expendable.

Even able-bodied seamen stood no chance when handling sail near sea-level on the jib boom in moderate weather. Five seamen were washed away there from the *Ben Ledi* in 1877 when bound for Wellington. A freak wave could be a killer. So could be a squall. The first officer of the *Edward Thornhill* was lost overboard in one despite his experience at sea. Then there were the victims of fever, scurvy and the rudimentary medical treatment for accidents. Some loss of life on each voyage was taken for granted.

Napier and Oamaru could be graveyards for sailing-ships owing to their exposed beaches when a nor'easterly was blowing. On one night, 3 February 1868, Shaw Savill lost three ships anchored on a lee shore and loading homeward cargoes – one at Napier (the *Echunga*) and two at Oamaru (the *Star of Tasmania* and *Water Nymph*). Wrecked ships in New Zealand fetched very little salvage money – *Royal Bride* £77, *Star of Tasmania* £40, *Water Nymph* £172, *Montmorency* £110.

In the end the survival of a ship came down to the seamanship and shipmastership of the Commander. Most were dignified, courageous and courteous men, not without the odd idiosyncracy, like Captain Roberts of the *Mayfield* and *Lindfield*: at sea he smoked a long clay churchwarden pipe and after a few days' use he would give it to the seaman at the wheel, until as the voyage progressed all the crew were smoking churchwardens. (The same man had the strength to cling to the top of a mast for thirty-six hours until rescued when the *Mayfield* was wrecked in the Bass Straits in 1904 winter.)

Right up until the Great War (1914-18), the only way to command at sea in the principal liner companies such as Shaw Savill was through an apprenticeship in sail – not for the special knowledge gained but for the lessons learned in safe seamanship and in how to cope calmly with emergencies.

· Walter Savill also paid a price for his success. Towards his children, he showed not too much of a commitment. He was not always able to understand their needs and often took the view that having fed, clothed and educated them he had discharged his duty. He was inclined to distance himself from them, so much that he was known to cross the street in the City whenever he saw one of his sons coming towards him. He feared they would be asking for money, which had been in short supply at home as long as they could remember. They were given no pocket money when young and had to search his trouser pockets for change and stamps which they encashed at the nearest kiosk. One way of finding favour with father was to pull off his boots when he returned home from the City in the evening.

Walter Savill actively discouraged his sons' interest by them in his business, although later he relented sufficiently to allow his eldest son, Walter H. Savill, to join him. However, once encouraged by his mother, W.H. stood up against his father in the boardroom on some issue, which sealed his fate: he was placed under closer supervision than ever and confirmed his father's view that his other sons should not be allowed near his business. Instead they were placed on the Stock Exchange and Baltic Exchange and even further afield – in Ceylon as a tea-planter and in New Zealand, whither one went before the mast to learn the skills of sheep-farming in the South Island. Although he prospered there to become one of the country's biggest wool-growers, at St Helens sheep station near Hanmer Springs, his father never lived to see his success, which would have probably surprised rather than pleased him.

Four of Walter's five daughters never married in his lifetime. Perhaps their legitimate aspirations to a dowry were not encouraged. At any rate it was made very difficult for them to slip out to the stables unnoticed and take a carriage to make a call or visit a friend – but despite that, he was always their 'Poppa'.

As Walter grew older, he developed a hard and unforgiving manner both in the office and at home. He became more emotionally remote from his family and given to moralizing. Religion was always a serious matter for him. Compared with later, more liberal parental standards, he became a bit of a tartar. No doubt this was due partly to the Victorian work ethic which was obsessed with high moral tones and fervent piety, giving the possessor of these virtues the impression that he was endowed with a monopoly of wisdom and propriety.

There is a story of the office boy at Shaw Savill who carried Walter's case over London Bridge to the station ahead of his master, who invariably took a cab. One day in dirty weather the boy also took a cab but he was refused a refund of his expense in no uncertain terms.

His more human side in the office is, however, probably best found in his practice of spending quite a lot of time in a nearby eating-house where there were high-backed little nooks. Here he used to meet his cronies and drink champagne out of harmless-looking beer tankards. When anyone called or telephoned the office, they were told he was not available, as he was in 'the outer office'.

Walter Savill had no particular interest in the arts, other than the theatre. Perhaps he could see no quick profit in a great painting or sculpture. He liked to turn his money over quickly, to keep it in constant use and to make it work for him. One of his favourite expressions was 'SPQR' – not the lofty political philosophy displayed at the masthead of the standards of the Roman Legions as they led the armies into action ('The Senate and People of Rome') but more simply and poignantly, 'Small profit quick return'. Was this impish disrespect for an imperial catchphrase something he had seen and remembered from a desk at school where some boy had busied himself with a penknife during the Latin lesson? Or had he concluded that the Roman Empire would have been better advised to follow this economic truth rather than over-extend itself as it did with the inevitable disastrous result?

If he had had a greater interest in the arts or had been less responsive to the burdens of his business, he would have been able to unbend a little more both at home and in the office – but the truth seems to be that his work came first. He was totally dedicated to it. Perhaps in his upbringing, with his widowed mother having to provide for a large family and run a business, there was no room for the frivolities and pleasures of life. Work was all-important for a man, and success at it the only proof of his worth in the scheme of things.

# 9. *Straws in the Wind*

In 1880 a long depression settled in with a vengeance in New Zealand as the expansion of its economy under the Vogel Scheme coincided with similar expansion in America and Australia. This forced down export prices and caused unemployment in New Zealand. Also, many people had lost money on false prospectuses of conditions there. By 1881 the flow of emigrants was almost greater than those coming the other way from Britain.

It was at this moment that the paternalistic, self-supporting settlements implanted by the New Zealand Company in 1840-50, still recognizable as the basis of the social structure in 1880, began to be found wanting in offering the new immigrant population the leadership it required, and a new breed of vigorous and radical liberal politicians pushed their way through the social structure to take over the reins of government. One of their first efforts was to examine the viability of the New Zealand economy on a national as opposed to settlement basis and devise some pattern of trade which, within whatever inescapable restraints there were, would bring some outlet for the head of steam in the economy built up by the Vogel Scheme. Unless a major export trade could be found, there would be no foreign exchange to purchase the plant and machinery needed to develop the virgin soil and exploit the farming skills of its citizens.

Private enterprise was equally determined to break the mould. This William Davidson and colleagues did in a most dramatic fashion on Wednesday 15 February 1882, when Captain John Whitson took the Albion Line's little *Dunedin*, on charter to the New Zealand and Australian Land Company, from her berth at Port Chalmers, with her holds stuffed full of frozen meat and headed her east for the open sea, Cape Horn and Smithfield Market in the City of London. If ever a ship's cargo can be said to have held a nation's hopes and destiny, this was it – until the famous Malta convoy of August 1942, when strangely enough the same shipping company, as Shaw Savill & Albion, was again heavily involved in another island's fight for survival.

The loading of the meat cargo did not go smoothly at first, as the refrigerating machinery failed and the 500 carcasses already loaded had to be discharged and sold locally. This setback had been enough to discourage all but two of the sixty passengers from sailing on the *Dunedin*, as they feared that if the machinery again failed at sea it could drive a hole through the bottom of the ship. The *Dunedin* finally sailed from Otago with a cargo of 4,909 carcases of frozen meat at a freight of $2\frac{3}{4}$d per pound. This was the first occasion a major shipment of frozen meat had been made from Australasia in a sailing ship (the SS *Strathleven* had sailed from Melbourne in December 1879 with only a small shipment of frozen meat). The *Dunedin* arrived in London on 26 May. Three days later the cargo began to be sold there at an average of nearly $6\frac{1}{2}$d per pound after a voyage of a hundred days port to port, with only one carcase condemned. The credit is due entirely to the Albion Line of Paddy Henderson, whose vessel and enterprise it was, spurred on by the New Zealand & Australian Land Company. This sailing took place very shortly before the Line's amalgamation with Shaw Savill, but in many ways the amalgamation was its cause and effect. The epic and heroic voyage proved such a success that it was beyond the resources of the Albion Line to exploit and beyond doubt could be neglected by Shaw Savill only at their peril if they wished to stay in the trade.

It was not just that the Albion Line had proved the technical feasibility of shipping a frozen cargo 12,000 miles which had arrived in London as if it had come up from a Kent farm. The consequences of this achievement were devastating and far-reaching. In Britain growing demand from the new industrial workforce for meat at a modest price could not be met from home farms, and the New Zealand economy, with agricultural products of meat, fruit, butter and cheese, was bursting for overseas markets. The finest sheep country in the world need no longer breed sheep merely for their tallow and wool – or, in desperation without a market, to drive them over cliffs into the sea.

In a leader *The Times* said: 'Today we have to record such a triumph over physical difficulties as would have seemed incredible and even unimaginable a very few years ago. Had any protectionist told Parliament in the heat of the Free Trade controversy that New Zealand would send to our London market five thousand dead sheep at a time, and in as good condition as if they have been slaughtered in some suburban abattoir, he would have brought upon himself a storm of derision – but this has actually come to pass.'

The economic and social effects of this shipping triumph put

New Zealand on the map more than anything else. At last New Zealand was able to trade at will, to offset the vicissitudes of the wool market, to build up sterling balances, to earn foreign exchange and to provide greater employment for its people. (Following the success of the *Dunedin* there was an immediate call for more farmers and farm labourers.) Substantial exports to New Zealand would soon be needed to match the consumer demand of the local economy. More shipping would be pursuing the spoils and more demands made for faster and more reliable ships. Indeed, the New Zealand Government was already offering a substantial subsidy for a direct service of refrigerated steamers to the United Kingdom.

The refrigerated carriage of meat by sea at 12° to 15° Fahrenheit was not, however, a perfected science. The *Dunedin* had had some serious problems, particularly on voyage, when the Commander risked his life to clear a ventilation shaft. There had been some disastrous frozen cargoes from Australia even in steamships. Installation of the machinery was expensive, and its operation from the main boiler system reduced the ship's speed and increased coal consumption considerably, especially when the vessel was in warm waters. The whole operation was cheaper by sail, but for how long would the trade be prepared to suffer the longer voyages and uncertain arrival dates?

Walter Savill had a lot to think about as he went home in the train to Sussex that evening of the safe arrival in London of the *Dunedin*. He knew he had not much time to secure his future, but he was in a strong bargaining position because of the scope and pre-eminence of his involvement in the New Zealand trade, the fine quality of his New Zealand agents and the volume of tonnage for which he had found profitable employment. Above all his credit in the City was good. He was recognized as a thoroughly professional shipowner, with even a wayward touch of genius. He had had to develop a strong sense of public accountability and he had a track record for surviving. But was that enough? When he arrived at Brighton he probably slipped off either to the Theatre Royal or to the Hippodrome, as was his habit when anxious, before going home to face the family. The sight of a pretty ankle and the melody of a catchy song helped his perspective and sense of well-being. But it was nine months before he could put his name to a cargo of frozen meat from New Zealand, in the *Lady Jocelyn*, lifting the first such cargo from Wellington in February 1883. He had been caught off-balance, as he never expected the *Dunedin* shipment to succeed. He thought sailing-ships too temperamental for such a perishable cargo to be carried safely for a hundred days at sea over 12,000 miles of belligerent ocean.

Although the *Dunedin*'s epic voyage was an overwhelming triumph, there were a number of other factors which caused Shaw Savill in London and Patrick Henderson's Albion Line in Glasgow eventually to join forces.

In general in the early 1880s, there was a mood of optimism and benevolence towards the Empire. It stirred men's thoughts and hearts. Whatever view one took – political, economic, commercial, religious, philanthropic or military – there was available a captive market of over 300 million people and 9 million square miles. And there was no major war in Europe. The situation was ideal for the entrepreneurs in whose hands the imperialist initiative often lay, though governments, however reluctant, had also found themselves increasingly committed. Certainly whenever they were obstructed in their overseas commercial policy of free trade and the open door, they used force to fulfil it and force to consolidate their commitment.

Government support and sometimes rescue were also needed by traders, explorers, missionaries, officials and indeed the huge emigrant population who had opted for a new life overseas. All were making their own new frontiers and responding to the call of duty as each saw it. They were encouraged by the Press and popular songs to push on and on until inevitably and haphazardly Britain came to obtain an imperial pre-eminence and a whole heap of responsibilities in distant places. Sir John Seely, Professor of Modern History at Cambridge University, publicly claimed that the British had 'conquered and peopled half the world in a fit of absence of mind'. This celebrated remark had wide support and set people thinking. It encouraged the Government to adopt a more co-ordinated and virile policy towards the Empire.

Businesses reviewed their practices. A large amount of capital had been invested in industrial equipment in Britain, and there was a large reservoir of skilled labour. Even if the technology was a little outdated compared with that in Europe and America, it was adequate to supply the basic needs of the Empire at a reasonable profit for the foreseeable future until further investment was absolutely essential. Meanwhile the most worthwhile area for further investment was the United States and South America where there was more British investment even than in India. But this did not compare with the sheer satisfaction of improving on God's creation, whether it was transporting flora and fauna as well as emigrants around the Empire where they had never been or being a popular uncle to millions of 'half devils, half children' (as Kipling later wrote) or just plain ruling almost a quarter of the world. The sentiment of empire was, according to Gladstone, innate in every

Briton. Walter Savill would have concurred.

The Government's approach had become more formalized both internationally and nationally. In North America, Canada had already been given permanent identity as a British Dominion. In the West Indies, Crown Colony Government had been imposed in an effort to pull their chaotic economies together following the debilitating effects of the abolition of the Slave Trade in 1833. The scramble for Africa was due to be regulated, as it was by the Berlin Treaty of 1885. In South Africa British annexations of territory were complete, the Zulus had been put down and, more important, the long sea route to India had been secured, with the British, as opposed to the Boers, in control of the coastline. Further north, Cecil Rhodes was planning, with Government connivance, to push into the interior to acquire vast tracts of land and in quest of his Cape-to-Cairo 'all-red' route: 'I would annex the planets, if I could,' he said.

It was the same story in India, the Far East and Australia. Following the Indian Mutiny in 1857, India was now tightly governed and garrisoned. The British were digging in for a long stay; the populace could not be trusted. The Queen had become Empress of India. The Russian threat through Afghanistan had at last been neutralized by British control of the Khyber Pass and a military defence treaty. The short sea route was secure as long as the British continued to be masters of Egypt, the Suez Canal and the coaling ports and coastline of Arabia. In the Far East, Singapore and Hong Kong and a whole mass of Pacific islands the Union Jack was flying vigorously, and in Australia a new nation was being formed based on British stock, gold and unlimited frontiers.

New Zealand had long finished with the Maori Wars and had begun to realize the need for economic planning to build up a new nation. It had started to generate overseas demand for its potential resources, which had hardly been tapped, but wool prices were still weak. The planned immigration schemes had produced the necessary skills and labour to create the infrastructure of towns and villages and basic industries – but the depression was holding these forces temporarily at bay. The people's credit was over-extended. It was, however, thought only a matter of a short time before there would be a break-through in trade between Britain and New Zealand in both directions as the demand for each other's goods was already clear, provided they could be shipped and sold at prices each country could afford. Suitable shipping space would soon be at a premium, and demands from governments, shippers and passengers for an improved service would grow. To survive, the shipping companies would have to find substantial sums of money for new steamships, which would require refrigerating equipment not only for meat but also for dairy produce.

For several years Shaw Savill and the Albion Line, on behalf of Paddy Henderson, had covered the New Zealand trade in a friendly and competitive spirit. On the whole, they had not had any serious confrontations with each other, except over the Otago emigrants contracts of 1862 and 1872. The emergence of the New Zealand Shipping Company in 1873 was first seen by them as an inevitable development of a new country flexing its muscles following the establishment of settlements and the growth of trade. From the beginning it always had a nuisance value to the old companies, especially because it was politically inspired and had influential backers in both New Zealand and London.

By 1882 the new Company had become a persistent and vigorous competitor, with loyalties to steamships rather than sailing-ships, and was exploiting its position as New Zealand's own shipping company. Its friends and resources seemed as unlimited as its emotional appeal to New Zealand merchants and shippers was strong.

The two older Companies had drawn alongside of late and had tried to close ranks. It was not easy with their separate head offices in Glasgow and London. Communications between them were slow. Nevertheless, they had established a friendly working relationship for covering berths in the UK-New Zealand trade. Shaw Savill had been chartering Paddy Henderson's tonnage since 1869. From the time each had entered the trade, in 1848 and in 1858 respectively, they had endeavoured to bring more regularity and comfort into travelling conditions, and the measure of their success is that within a short time they had forced the other participants to withdraw. They had introduced a liner service of sailings with the full backing of the emigrant-sponsoring organizations and had made an honest attempt to show care. (Nevertheless, there had been some unmitigated disasters by Shaw Savill.)

Since 1877, both organizations had been working well together on an informal basis, Shaw Savill felt keenly their position as the senior company in the trade (although Paddy Henderson had first sailed a ship to New Zealand ten years before their own had sailed). They were the biggest operators, covered the whole of New Zealand, and thought they had almost a divine right to the loyalty of many thousands of erstwhile passengers now in profitable employment in New Zealand. Shades of Willis, Gann in 1858!

For nearly twenty-five years, Walter Savill had kept the business of 'Young Savills' going, almost by his sole efforts. He was in the mould of many Victorian entrepreneurs. He had drive, courage, flair and method. Within a fairly regular life he was a restless spirit seeking new frontiers to conquer abroad. He kept strict office hours. He was a hard worker and an organizer and had little time for idle gossip. He believed strongly in discipline in the office and of course at home. Everything in its place and a place for everything.

His business self-confidence and convictions had swept all difficulties aside. Who could blame the Victorian leaders of business, commerce and industry if they showed a certain arrogance and self-righteousness? Nearly a quarter of the world's population was at their feet encapsulated in the British Empire which in their lifetime reached heights of splendour, scope and sovereignty. A private world market of seemingly unlimited millions of people and of acres of undeveloped land, forests and resources were strong meat for anyone with even a spark of commercial initiative and interest in making money – always an important priority for Walter Savill. The office could always tell when business was going well: 'Money's very cheap today', he used to say with a sparkle in his eye and rubbing his hands with some glee.

But the trade was now becoming increasingly competitive. At forty-seven years of age, he was ready to share the heavy responsibilities which at the age of twenty-two were not so evident, and with the energy of youth could be brushed off. He had despatched over 1,300 ships to New Zealand from London alone at the average rate of one sailing each week (besides despatching ships also to N. America, Australia, India and the Far East). It had been a prodigious effort. In effect he had given substance to the Treaty of Waitangi and given the Colony its most valuable resource – people with new skills and knowledge, probably over 100,000, which represented about twenty per cent of New Zealand's European population in 1882.

The firm had assumed that with the Albion Line in bed with them since 1877 as associates they could withstand the New Zealand Shipping Company's efforts for a few more years, provided nothing untoward occurred. Also, they knew that there was surplus steam tonnage available for charter if necessary.

What sent cold shivers down the spines of the Shaw Savill partners in 1882 were two related events within a few weeks of one another.

The first was the tentative frozen meat shipment in the *Dunedin* by the Albion Line, which had turned out to be such a roaring success for them. No longer could these friends be trusted to keep in step in future by informal arrangements. They must be formally invited to join in a partnership terms which they could not refuse and which would obviate any further examples of independent enterprise by them likely to put Shaw Savill in jeopardy.

The second bombshell was notice of an extraordinary meeting in Christchurch of the shareholders of the New Zealand Shipping Company for the purpose of agreeing to increase their capital from £250,000 to a million, in response to an appeal from the local government (and the possibility of a subsidy) for the purposes of introducing a direct steam communication to the UK. The frozen meat trade would need this service, as would better-placed emigrants from the UK who were no longer prepared to put up with the discomforts and vagaries of sailing-ship travel for over a hundred days on a voyage south. The meeting was held on 23 May 1882, only three days before the arrival of the *Dunedin*'s meat in London. Of the twenty-five shareholders present, only four voted against the resolution to increase the capital of the Company. One of these, W.H. Lewin, was the Shaw Savill agent in Wellington. He was being loyal to his London principals.

When this news arrived from Wellington, Walter Savill realized that he would have to build steamships to compete with the Shipping Company in future, and he did not have the personal resources to do so alone. Nor did he think the Albion Line were any better placed. Individually they could not face the future with equanimity. Together there was just a chance.

Within five months of these two events, the two old firms had merged, on 10 November 1882, to form the Shaw Savill & Albion Co Ltd.

# 10.  *A Public Offer*

The terms of the merger were at best extraordinary; at worst, they were cobbled together as a rush job. The two partners in Shaw Savill, namely Walter Savill and James Temple, agreed to serve as joint Managing Directors of the new company. The Albion Line, despite their success with the *Dunedin*, virtually opted out as principals in the New Zealand trade to concentrate on their Burma interests. They agreed, however, to become the new company's managing agents in Scotland.

The share prospectus listed thirty-one sailing-ships amounting to 34,672 net tons. The average age of the nineteen Shaw Savill ships was sixteen years, and of the twelve Albion ships only ten years. Although they were all registered as first-class ships, the Shaw Savill contribution was decidedly seedy compared with the trim fast clippers of the Albion Line. Indeed, one Shaw Savill ship, the *Lady Jocelyn*, was thirty years old. The fact that she had been recently fitted with a refrigerating chamber (at a cost of £6,000 – a lot of money in 1882) was probably her saving grace for being included in the deal. She was also dear to the heart of Walter Savill, who had employed her very successfully since 1869 and finally part-owned her in a joint venture with his old friend James Park, who managed her and had agreed to include her in the prospectus under the Shaw Savill flag as a means of obtaining a place on the board of the new company. At any rate the journal *Vanity Fair* referred to her as a 'veritable Noah's Ark', and to the Shaw Savill fleet as a whole as 'antediluvian'.

*Vanity Fair*, 'a weekly show of political, social and literary ware' (its own claim) was despite its style a respected and well-informed journal with the privilege of publishing Spy's cartoons of interesting people. It was read by anyone who was a student of the lighter side of the political, social or business scene. One section of the journal was devoted to business under the provocative title 'Other People's Money'. It developed a special interest in shipping affairs because it found them particularly inscrutable and a surprisingly high risk for the average investor. Was he being done?

was usually where the journal started its comments, and it concluded that he was in the case of several companies which were examined.

There are several very odd features in the prospectus. Mention has already been made of the Albion Line's half-hearted commitment. The new company gave them a chance to realize their investments in the trade by selling them to the public by way of shares for £200,157 in cash. This money presumably went to support the other shipping interests of Paddy Henderson in the Far East, particularly the Irrawaddy Flotilla Company, which was seen as a more fruitful trading area. However, the chairman and managing director of the Albion Line (Peter Denny and James Galbraith) and a director of Paddy Henderson (John Galloway) were on the board of the new company to oversee the Clyde-New Zealand end of the trade for which they were expecting to earn £10,000 a year for their services as managing agents.

The Shaw Savill partners on the other hand received little in cash (£85,110) for their investments in the trade but were allotted £100,000 in shares and £100,000 in debentures. However, they were compensated by being invited to run the business and to receive three-quarters of the surplus profits after payment of dividends and other charges. Therefore, whilst the Scots took a fixed amount of cash, the English partnership had to make do with payment by results but they were content because they were still in the thick of the trade, had a bigger and more modern fleet, including the famous *Dunedin* and her goodwill, had acquired important new contracts and had invested in political leverage by having a prominent MP as chairman, namely C.T. Ritchie, later President of the Board of Trade and Lord Ritchie of Dundee. They were ready to do battle with the New Zealand Shipping Company on equal, if not superior, terms.

The balance of the 70,000 £10 shares of the new company were applied for twice over by friends, former passengers and colleagues in the trade. Five thousand shares were reserved for New Zealand holders.

Another odd feature in the prospectus is the declaration that the merger of the two fleets of sailing-ships was the upshot of the proved successful carriage of meat in such ships. This type of ship is emphasized in italics. There is no explicit mention of the desperate need to use steamships in future, although both parties to the merger knew very well that it was the thought of the Shipping Company's steamship-building programme which had brought them together in order to stay in the trade.

Without putting too fine a point on it, was the prospectus

*Samuel Plimsoll* – water colour by J. Spurling

*Star of India (ex Euterpe)* restored at San Diego, 1965 – photograph by M.W. Guest

genuine in extolling the virtues of particular sailing-ships for the successful carriage of frozen meat or was it a desperate throw to raise money quickly for providing other means of carriage? Probably no one was too bothered, except the New Zealand Shipping Company. To the public, however, in for a penny, in for a pound was the appeal of investment in the Empire. But *Vanity Fair* was quick to question the sudden new commitment to steamships within two months of the Company's registration and successful share flotation. Orders had been placed, on the strength of the funds now available, for two steamships to be built (*Arawa* and *Tainui*) for Shaw Savill & Albion for £123,000 each and three more steamships were to be made available by White Star (*Ionic*, *Doric* and *Coptic*). Meanwhile the new company was chartering steamships in numbers (mainly to lay a successful claim to the Government mail contract between UK and New Zealand).

The formation of the new company on the basis of the prospectus (Appendix G) caused some cryptic comment on two occasions in *Vanity Fair* which makes entertaining reading now and throws some doubt on the integrity of the whole transaction. Indeed it is extremely doubtful whether the company's flotation on the terms agreed would have been permitted today.

The *Vanity Fair* analyses of the company's prospectus are withering blasts, not without some humour, which speak for themselves. With hindsight, their comments that they considered the prospectus one of the most remarkable undertakings they had ever come across and to be placed at the head of all the great financial efforts of recent years has more the ring of truth now than of satire. Walter Savill was probably rather pleased with that sly comment.

An article on 18 November 1882 and related material are quoted in full so as not to miss any part of their salty flavour.

*[Vanity Fair – 18 November 1882]*

SHAW SAVILL AND ALBION COMPANY LIMITED
    Capital £700,000 in shares of £10 each;
    Debentures to be issued, £180,000

*Directors*:
C.T. Ritchie, MP, Chairman
Walter Savill, of the firm of Shaw Savill & Co } Managing Directors
James W. Temple                               }
Peter Denny, Chairman of the Albion Shipping Company, Ltd
James Galbraith, Managing Director of the Albion Shipping Company Ltd

John Galloway of P. Henderson & Co, Glasgow
James Park, of Park Brothers, London
Edward Pembroke, of Galbraith, Pembroke & Co, London
    Managing Agents for the Clyde and New Zealand Trade – P. Henderson & Co, Glasgow.

This is the warmest thing in the shape of a shipping company we have yet come across, and as we have lately had to deal with Money Wigram & Co and the Monarch Line, the palm of excellence which we accord to this effort should be regarded by Mr Ritchie and his friends as no mean tribute to their constructive ability. There is something of the family party about the business. We observe that Messrs Ritchie, Savill and Temple, directors of the concern, are also on the board of Money Wigram: they were therefore parties to the purchase of the *Norfolk* for account of the shareholders at cost price, and to her sale immediately afterwards for account of the same shareholders at a ruinous loss: they were responsible, with others, for the peculiar manner in which the loss was entered in the balance sheet: in fact, they have proved themselves to be in every way most reliable and safe guides, and entitled in consequence to the gratitude of investors in the past, and their confidence in the future.

With them are coupled Messrs Denny and Galbraith, of whose accomplishments it is perhaps enough to say they valued the Cunard fleet when the owners were kind enough to transfer for a consideration the future earnings of that truly magnificent property to an expectant and, we hope, grateful public.

The prospectus commences with this passage; 'The transport of produce between Great Britain and New Zealand, which for many years has rapidly progressed, has now assumed such dimensions as to convince those most intimately conversant with the trade that the advantages afforded by the extension of joint-stock enterprise are best fitted to meet the present requirements, and to cope with the further development of the traffic.'

We have a powerful microscope, which we always use in studying a prospectus. By its aid we are able to read between the lines, and we often find by this treatment something not apparent to the unassisted eye is brought to light. In this instance we seem to read as follows:

The keen and increasing competition in the New Zealand trade has rendered it impossible for the owners of these two lines of vessels to make a satisfactory profit out of them. They have thought it desirable under the circumstances to clear out: and they feel justified in inviting the co-operation of the public in their efforts to realise their property and to get their finances generally on a sound and pleasant footing. It is felt that people who buy gold mines without knowing whether or not there is gold in them, cannot reasonably object to buying a fleet of ships in full work without knowing whether the work activity pays or not. For this and for other reasons the directors deem it unnecessary to say anything about the profits of the last few years.

It is, we believe, notorious that the New Zealand Shipping Company with its fine fleet, and other rival Companies, have long since been running Shaw Savill & Co very hard; and the cargo taken, as is the case in every branch of shipping, is on the increase. For the public this is perhaps well: for the owners of an antediluvian fleet it is far from well; and the absence of any allusion to the earnings of the thirty one ships of all ages and conditions scheduled in the prospectus does not suggest a state of affairs calculated, if faithfully recorded, to impress the public with the desirability of rushing in to subscribe for shares.

And what is it we find when we study the list of ships so generously offered to the public? One new vessel and thirty old cranks of the aggregate tonnage of 34,672 tons. Amongst them is included that venerable old dowager the *Lady Jocelyn*, aged some thirty years. These ships, including her ladyship, are to be taken by the Company at the modest price of £485,276, equal in average to £14 per ton. This would make the price of the *Lady Jocelyn* £29,932 and what, we ask, will the shipping fraternity say to that? Considering that the partners of Shaw Savill and Co were parties to selling the *Norfolk* to the Royal Mail Co at a price which certainly does not suggest £14 per ton as the value of such vessels as their own, being an average age of thirteen years, we shall be glad to learn upon what principle the valuation has been made. It is nearly double that at which we should value the ships as between a buyer and a seller both anxious to come to terms; and it is more than double the price at which the ships would find buyers on the open market.

On one point the prospectus is ominously silent, and that is on the necessity of appealing to the public at all. The Company, we are told, is to carry on exactly the same business that the separate firms have been carrying on so successfully hitherto, and we are also told that by way of the amalgamation some advantages not specified will be gained. This may be so; but the amalgamation could be made without forming a public company. Shaw Savill & Co and the Albion could put their fleets together and work. 'They've got the ships, they've got the men' – must we add – 'they want the money too.'

There is in fact no reason why the amalgamation, if that is all that is required, should be preceded by the sale of the ships to these parties: and no explanation on this point is vouchsafed: it is true that, in our opinion, none is wanted.

It is intensely funny to read in the prospectus that 'the directors have by their purchase contract made an arrangement with Messrs Shaw Savill & Co which they consider of very great importance to the Company viz: that these gentlemen are to give their services to the Company as managing directors for a period of not less than five years.' One would think this had been a matter of most delicate negotiation, and no doubt this is what the public are intended to believe. Most people however who know anything whatever about shipping would expect that Messrs Shaw Savill & Co would not only give their services for five years to anyone bringing them a cheque of £485,267 for the joint fleets (it ought to have been £485,268 to make exactly the £14 per ton, but as with the man and the starlings it was not worthwhile to overvalue the fleets by one pound) but that they would have given the bearer a cheque on the spot for at least £100,000 commission. The fact is that the New Zealand trade is a most difficult one. For some years Messrs Shaw Savill & Co had the cream of it: they have now come down to the skim milk, and apparently they don't relish the change.

One piece of advice we will offer to all who may feel themselves capable of taking a share in a shipping group: that is to study the list of directors and see whether any of them are engaged in business which might derive an advantage from connection with the Company. In this instance let them ask whether Mr Temple, Director of Wigrams and of Shaw Savill and the Albion, is still the head of a large provision business; and, if so, let them ask themselves whether his presence on the boards of these concerns may not possibly lead to an undue preference for Mr Temple's own provisions over those of other provision dealers. Let them ask whether other Directors happen to be insurance brokers and, if so, whether they are most likely to be unduly favoured in their calling. These are the points to be considered. Cases might be mentioned in which managing directors, agents, insurance brokers and all connected with a shipping business get rich whilst the unfortunate shareholders get nothing.

[*Vanity Fair* – 2 *December 1882*]

Mr C Ritchie MP one of the directors of Money Wigram Ltd and of Shaw Savill and Albion has asked us to publish the following paragraph. We do so without hesitation.

It is needless to say that we never tried to convey any imputation on Mr Ritchie's character as an honest man.

'Representations have been made to us with reference to our recent article on the above Company to the effect that the Company was found practically for the purpose of amalgamating the two businesses of Messrs. Shaw Savill & Co and the Albion Co, and that in the price paid for the ships is included the goodwill of a valuable business. It has also been pointed out to us that in the price of the *Lady Jocelyn* is included the cost of a freezing chamber recently put on board at an expenditure of £6,000. In the same article it was stated that the Directors of Money Wigram & Sons Ltd had shortly after the formation of the Company sold the *Norfolk* at a ruinous loss. It is true that the ship was sold at a large loss, but that was borne by the partners of the late firm and not by the shareholders. The fact of the sale and the loss was stated in the report. We are also requested to state that Mr Temple is in no way connected with a provision business.'

*(Vanity Fair – 9 December 1882]*
[In an article assessing the value of the British Fleet]
As regards iron sailing vessels, we have seen Shaw Savill & Albion value their old ships at £14 per ton. We are advised that new ships can be built for £10 per ton: but they might possibly be of inferior quality: so we will take the middle price of £12 as being about what such vessels as ordinary people own would have cost, and the wooden ships we will take all round as having cost £8 per ton.

*[Vanity Fair – 13 January 1883]*
The Government of New Zealand has taken a new departure. It is advertising for tenders to supply a regular steam communication between this country and the Colony, upon conditions specified. The effect of this novel procedure must be to enhance the value of the goodwill of the venerable fleet of sailing ships recently offered to the public on such favourable terms, and for the purchase of which the capital, as we were informed by the papers, was subscribed twice over.

In its issue of 27 January 1883, *Vanity Fair* was still plugging away at the prospectus as follows:

We called attention in our issue of the 18th Nov. last to this Company. We considered it then to be one of the most remarkable undertakings we had ever come across. Further investigation of the documents connected with it leads us to place it absolutely at the head of all the great financial efforts of recent years. The Emma Mine, perhaps, which, after its known contents had been scooped out, was sold to the British public for a million, was possibly a higher flight of genius; but then it belonged to a different order of things. You can never tell what may be got out of a mine; but there are plenty of people in London who can tell pretty nearly what may be got out of a line of sailing ships engaged in a well-known trade. It is this fact which lent such a brilliant colour to the prospectus. Ships were valued as if they were fancy articles having no fixed market price; or as if, like china vases, their value increased with their age.

Clause 94 deals with the mode in which the accounts are to be made up, by not insisting on the publication of a trading account and thus provides for putting a proper check on the inquisitiveness of shareholders.

Agreement No. 2 transfers the Albion fleet and goodwill to the new Company in consideration of a sum of £200,157, to be paid according to the schedule, as and when the different vessels are handed over; the payment to be cash on delivery, a stipulation which proves that Glasgow has not forfeited its old character for shrewdness. It also provides for the issue of 35,000 shares, on which £35,000 are to be paid, half on application and half on allotment – thus apparently differing both from the prospectus and from Agreement No. 3.

Agreement No. 3 transfers the ships and goodwill of Shaw Savill and Co to the new concern, but under very different conditions from those imposed by the Albion Company. Messrs Shaw Savill and Co are to receive £285,110, but not in cash, by any means. The schedule, which we give below, will show how the payments are to be made. There is none of the rigidity here of the Glasgow gentlemen. 'If,' the London firm seems to say, 'we can't get cash, give us paper; only give us something in hand – shares, debentures, anything you like; if the Company floats we can unload.'

The following is the schedule of Messrs Shaw Savill's ships referred to. We have inserted the dates at which the ships were built, their tonnage, what we believe to be their value per ton, and the total value of each ship worked out on that basis:

SHAW SAVILL'S SHIPS

| Ships | Built in | Tons. | Payment in | | | Total | Actual value per ton | — |
|---|---|---|---|---|---|---|---|---|
| | | | Shares | Debent. | Cash | | | |
| Akaroa | 1881 | 1,298 | £6,370 | £6,400 | £5,402 | £18,172 | £12 | £15,576 |
| Crusader | 1865 | 1,058 | 5,200 | 5,200 | 4,412 | 14,812 | 7 | 7,406 |
| Himalaya | 1863 | 1,018 | 4,950 | 4,900 | 4,262 | 14,112 | 7 | 7,126 |
| Lutterworth | 1863 | 883 | 4,330 | 4,300 | 3,732 | 12,362 | 8 | 7,064 |
| Soukar | 1864 | 1,304 | 6,400 | 6,400 | 5,456 | 18,256 | 7 | 9,128 |
| Trevelyan | 1863 | 1,042 | 5,120 | 5,100 | 4,368 | 14,588 | 7 | 7,294 |
| Zealandia | 1869 | 1,116 | 5,570 | 5,300 | 4,754 | 15,624 | 8 | 8,928 |
| Pleione | 1876 | 1,092 | 5,360 | 5,400 | 4,528 | 15,288 | 9 | 9,828 |
| Langstone | 1869 | 726 | 3,660 | 3,700 | 3,084 | 10,444 | 8 | 5,968 |
| Helen Denny | 1866 | 728 | 3,570 | 3,600 | 3,022 | 10,192 | 8 | 5,824 |
| St. Leonards | 1864 | 1,054 | 5,170 | 5,200 | 4,386 | 14,756 | 7 | 7,378 |
| Euterpe | 1863 | 1,197 | 5,880 | 5,900 | 4,978 | 16,758 | 7 | 8,379 |
| Pleiades | 1869 | 997 | 4,900 | 4,900 | 4,158 | 13,958 | 8 | 7,976 |
| Margaret Galbraith | 1868 | 841 | 4,130 | 4,200 | 3,444 | 11,774 | 7 | 5,887 |
| Lady Jocelyn | 1852 | 2,138 | 10,440 | 10,500 | 8,992 | 29,932 | 5 | 10,690 |
| Glenlora | 1864 | 774 | 3,800 | 3,800 | 3,236 | 10,836 | 7 | 5,418 |
| Hudson | 1869 | 797 | 3,900 | 3,900 | 3,358 | 11,158 | 8 | 6,376 |
| Merope | 1870 | 1,054 | 5,170 | 5,200 | 4,386 | 14,756 | 8 | 8,432 |
| Forfarshire | 1867 | 1,238 | 6,080 | 6,100 | 5,152 | 17,332 | 5 | 6,190 |
| Av. 16 yrs. | | 20,375 | £100,000 | £100,000 | £85,110 | £285,110 | ... | £150,488 |

The Albion fleet is scheduled and valued as follows, and we add our valuations:–

| Ships | Built in | Tons | Price in Cash | | | Actual value per ton | | |
|---|---|---|---|---|---|---|---|---|
| | | | £ | s. | d. | £ | s. | £ |
| Aukland | 1874 | 1,245 | 17,423 | 8 | 0 | 8 | 10 | 10,582 |
| Canterbury | 1874 | 1,245 | 17,434 | 6 | 6 | 8 | 10 | 10,582 |
| Dunedin | 1874 | 1,250 | 17,494 | 16 | 0 | 8 | 10 | 10,625 |
| Invercargill | 1874 | 1,246 | 17,449 | 17 | 0 | 8 | 10 | 10,591 |
| Jessie Readman | 1869 | 962 | 13,467 | 8 | 6 | 8 | 0 | 7,696 |
| Lyttleton | 1878 | 1,111 | 15,551 | 9 | 6 | 10 | 0 | 11,110 |
| Nelson | 1874 | 1,247 | 17,463 | 0 | 6 | 9 | 0 | 11,223 |
| Oamaru | 1874 | 1,306 | 18,281 | 9 | 6 | 9 | 0 | 11,754 |
| Timaru | 1874 | 1,306 | 18,282 | 3 | 0 | 9 | 0 | 11,754 |
| Wellington | 1874 | 1,247 | 17,457 | 11 | 0 | 9 | 0 | 11,223 |
| Westland | 1878 | 1,116 | 15,624 | 0 | 0 | 10 | 10 | 11,710 |
| Wild Deer | 1863 | 1,016 | 14,227 | 10 | 0 | 8 | 0 | 8,128 |
| Tons | | 14,297 | £200,157 | 0 | 0 | | | £126,986 |

We must here observe that the valuations we have affixed to the different ships have been carefully made, and we have reason to believe that they are such as a competent and impartial valuer would confirm. This being so, we are led to some strange conclusions. It is clear that, as nothing is specifically charged in the prospectus for goodwill, whilst at the same time the goodwill is carefully mentioned as one of the considerations given in return for the purchase of the ships, old and young, at £14 per ton, it must follow that the difference between the actual value of the ships and the price at which they are taken over by the Company represents the amount charged to the shareholders for the goodwill in question. Thus we find that, in the case of the Albion Company, the cash payment for the twelve ships is to be £200,157, their actual value being, in our opinion, £126,985, leaving a sum of £73,172, which we must suppose to be paid for the goodwill or the privilege of working this particular business, and this sum divided by the tonnage of the fleet equals about £5 per ton. That Messrs. Galbraith and Galloway should be prepared to pay a good round sum for the privilege of making a handsome income out of the business would be intelligible; but why anyone should be ready to contribute money to help them to do it is not so easy to understand.

In regard to Messrs. Shaw Savill's fleet, we find that our valuation amounts to only £150,488 against £285,110 charged, leaving £144,622 for the goodwill of that remarkable business, and this again would be equal to about £7 per ton on the tonnage of the fleet. And here we are landed in a difficulty. The average age of the Albion fleet is ten years, that of Shaw Savill's sixteen years, and yet the former Company are only to receive £5 per ton goodwill, whilst the latter firm are to receive £7. But, on the other hand, compensation may perhaps be found in the fact that the Albion are to be paid in hard cash on the nail, whilst the others have a good deal of hoping to do.

No one can look down the list of the Shaw Savill fleet without being forcibly struck by the anomalies it presents. The goodwill is calculated separately on every ship, and therefore the older the ship the greater the sum paid for the privilege of possessing her. A veritable Noah's Ark like the *Lady Jocelyn*, worth at the very outside £10,000 is charged to the public at £30,000. Now would any sane man give £20,000 for the profits to be made out of working the ship after he had paid £10,000 for her? The question answers itself. Would anyone give £7000 a-piece for the privilege of buying a lot of these old ships at a valuation? Yet that is what the public have been asked to do, and in the prospectus in which they are so asked there is not from first to last a word indicating the profits of the two businesses separately or combined.

We have been told by the Press that the shares in the Company were applied for twice over; this may be so, but we should like to know something about the applicants. We cannot conceive that the public generally would give more for old ships than they could get new ones built for, or that they would pay for the goodwill of a business the profits of which were not disclosed.

The next point is that, whilst the agreement which fixes Messrs. Galbraith and Galloway's profits is immutable, each of the other agreements relating to the sale of the ships contains the following unique clause:

'The parties to these presents, or the said intended Company when formed, or the directors thereof, shall be at liberty to vary any of the terms in these presents contained at any time by the mutual consent of the vendors, the purchasers, the said intended Company, or *the directors thereof.*'

The meaning of this clause we take to be: 'If we can float this Company and sell these ships, well and good; if we cannot, it will be a case of "As you was," before you said "As you were." ' Only with such a clause as this, what was the use of stipulating for anything at all?

*[Vanity Fair – 3 February 1883]*
*Shaw Savill and Albion Co Ltd*

The following extract from the *Glasgow Herald* of 27 January makes a new departure in the career of the above Company, and seems to suggest that the fine fleet of old sailing ships for which so much was charged might perhaps so far as the New Zealand trade is concerned, have been dispensed with, if not wholly, at least in a great measure.

Important shipbuilding contract – We understand that Messrs P. Henderson & Co, of Glasgow, have arranged with Messrs. William Denny and Brothers, shipbuilders, Dumbarton for the construction of three steamers of 5000 tons register for Shaw Savill and Albion's line from London and New Zealand. These steamers will have large accommodation for cabin and steerage passengers and will be fitted up with refrigerators for conveyance of fresh meat from New Zealand, the first importation of which was successfully made in that Company's sailing ship *Dunedin*.

# 11. 'Set All Plain Sail Again, Mr Mate'

A further odd feature in the Shaw Savill & Albion prospectus was that, despite the merger and the appointment of Walter Savill and James Temple as the new joint managing directors for at least five years (in fact they served in this capacity for much longer), their old business of Shaw Savill & Co could continue provided it did not conflict with the new company's interests.

Rather than allow the seven sailing-ships which had not been taken over by the new company (the *Anazi, Bebington, Chaudière, Edwin Fox, Electra, Elizabeth Graham* and *Hermione*) to remain idle, the two managing directors must have had difficulties in deciding how they should be employed without accusations of divided loyalties – because to them the situation was almost as it was previously. They decided to sell two (the *Bebington* and *Chaudière*) and to continue to put the other five, as necessary, on the New Zealand berths but under the Shaw Savill & Albion name as suitable chartered tonnage for the new company to employ in the trade. They also continued to employ some ships in which they had a stake (e.g. *Hydaspes* and *Halcione*) but which were managed by friends and had not been brought into the merger at all.

Walter Savill and James Temple worked very hard and closely together for about ten more years, until the former resigned on 30 April 1892, leaving his partner to carry on alone as sole managing director of the new public company, though he remained on its board as a director. There was no question of Walter Savill's failing health. At fifty-six he was fine. The truth was that the new manager, John Potter, with the enthusiasm, arrogance and impatience of youth, had little time for the niceties and clubability of the way the London business used to be run by the men who created the business and who were indeed still the bosses. In Walter Savill's eyes, a little of Potter went a long way, despite his obvious abilities, and their relationship so deteriorated under the new scheme of things that Walter Savill and James Temple were soon working six months in the office alternately so that the burden of Potter could be halved.

For three more years, Walter Savill saw the advantage of the operations of his sailing-ships continuing to be managed from the same office as Shaw Savill & Albion in Leadenhall Street, but in 1895 he pricked up his ears when he heard that the City Line of George Smith & Sons was in financial difficulties and was going cheap. It included some fine sailing-ships which he had often chartered and which were engaged in the Australian trade where he knew there were pickings. But the Smith family were looking for a younger man and staggered on until they found him in 1901, in Sir John Ellerman, the rising shipping star in the City, only thirty-nine years old.

When the Smith prospect fell through, Walter decamped from Leadenhall Street to his old haunts in Billiter Street, leaving his partner to cope with Potter. He opened an office at no. 14 and vigorously reactivated his old firm, instead of allowing it to tick along with the new company. He started trading independently again with his old loves, his sailing-ships, of which as a result of the merger he was still left with one survivor (the *Hermione*). He had however, since 1882 bought three others (the *Asterion, City of Brussels* and *Halcione*). He had also built two big steel four-masted barques in 1891-2, the *Lindfield* and *Mayfield*, of nearly 2,300 gross tons. Needless to say, they all flew his old house flag, despite its having been taken over by the new company.

Whilst it had been a good arrangement for him under the terms of the merger to be able to charter his own ships in effect to himself, which he did freely, there was a not unreasonable condition that, if they were employed in this capacity in the New Zealand trade, it had to be at standard charter rates for the trade. When he found his freedom again in 1895, he discovered he could put them to more profitable use elsewhere. For sixteen years, from 1895 until 1910, he traded them and their replacements, together with two ships owned by Captain John Leslie (the *Hinemoa* and *Taranaki*), all over the world picking up bulk cargoes, mainly in South America and Australia. To Walter, it was just like the old days again. He was his own boss, he had his sailing-ships and he was having fun with his City friends, who were still prepared to invest in his restless spirit and to encourage his enterprise. He again had a sparkle in his eye and a jaunty step as he surveyed the rewards available to a man with commercial courage and sense of adventure abroad.

Walter Savill enjoyed playing his hand in the imperial market-place where the pickings were exciting. The ships turned in a modest profit but more important to Walter was his joy at continuing to operate a fleet of sailing ships, whose beauty when in full sail he would not dispute. Whenever he sighted them off the Sussex coast, they gave him a deep sense of security and lasting satisfaction as they bowled along up Channel under a great press of billowing white canvas and taut rigging or fought their way down Channel into the teeth of a sou'westerly, outward bound for the other side of the world.

He was never taken with steamships, although the first ship he had sent to New Zealand in 1858, the *Lord Ashley*, had been one. In 1858 however, he could not afford prejudices. By 1895, he was his own man.

In appearance, Walter was square and of average height. His most distinguished feature was his deep-set, pale blue, piercing eyes under a broad brow, supported by a firm jaw. He dressed quietly. Top hat, wing collar and frock coat were his normal office attire with a white polka-dot tie. He looked a model of rectitude. But how else could he appear in the City of the Victorian age and perform with any confidence and conviction?

His great interests besides his business and family (in decent moderation) were his garden and his horses and carriages. Their livery and smart turn-out were a familiar sight on the sea front at Brighton where he enjoyed watching the passing parade of equine and female fashion. He was well known to the cabbies on the rank with whom he always exchanged a friendly word. He was also no novice on the turf, enjoying the sight of expensive horseflesh and the escorted female form as he weighed up the odds of both.

He became a *bon viveur*, dazzling his friends with his generosity and vitality. But to his family, he had become a very different person as the years of business hardened his thoughts and moods and took up more of his time.

His own fleet of ships over this period is given in Appendix H. It included four spectacular ships of renown and beauty – but probably past their best. First, the great clipper, the *Samuel Plimsoll* which had had the misfortune to catch fire in the Thames in 1899. She was scuttled, raised and repaired before he bought her. He ran her until 1902 when she was so badly dismasted and damaged outward bound to Otago as to be beyond repair. She then became a coal hulk at Melbourne.

Second, the fast *Nelson*, which he had bought from Shaw Savill & Albion in 1896. She held the record for the fastest passage by any ship from Tristan da Cunha to Western Australia – 5,150 nautical miles in nineteen days, reaching speeds of sixteen knots. Some say she ranked supreme with the *Thermopylae*, even though not built or rigged as a clipper. The third beauty was the *Star of Russia* built by Harland & Wolff of Belfast in 1874. She had such a turn of speed that she beat the great *Sobraon* when bound for Melbourne together in 1884 by five full days, logging speeds of over sixteen knots as her fine hull lanced through the water in seventy-five days. And finally the *Belfast*, the fastest ship in the Brocklebank fleet and a fine sea boat.

James Temple, Walter Savill's partner for thirty-four years, died in 1898. Although he had been involved in the business for a long time, plus his own ship's stores business, he left only a small fortune compared with his partner's. The only possible reason for the enormous difference can be explained by his partner's propensity for substantial speculations on the Stock Exchange in overseas investments, supported by profits from his sailing-ships in the next thirteen years before he too succumbed.

Walter was always very careful with money until towards the end of his life when he fell in with some men of great wealth who also lived at Brighton. They formed themselves into a private club called Princes, which met in another part of the building where Walter lived. Here they were at peace, away from their families. They could read the daily papers, discuss the investment scene and eat, drink and enjoy each other's company. It is possibly that in this company Walter came to realize that there was even more money to be made in investment speculation overseas in the Empire than in shipping, or at Lloyd's, where he was an underwriting member.

At any rate, at this later time in his life he invested large sums of money on the Stock Exchange in a few commodities and in overseas railways, particularly in South America and even in his arch business rival – the New Zealand Shipping Company – not surprisingly under a nominee. He was fortunate. They paid off. He became a director of Broken Hill Mines in Australia and helped establish both Sunnygama and Grand Central Tea and Rubber estates in Ceylon, where he was advised by one of his sons, Frank (who was known in Ceylon as 'Bookie Savill' because he found it more interesting and profitable pursuing a sporting and social life in Colombo than on the tea and rubber estates under his management).

In 1910 Walter's health began to fail. He sold out most of his holding in Shaw Savill & Albion to Sir John Ellerman for £70,000. By November he had withdrawn from business altogether. By 1911 it was time even for him to draw stumps, and for others to discover the impressive score of the number of runs that he had amassed on the playing fields of the Empire.

He died on Friday 4 May 1911 at Finches, aged seventy-four. His brother, Ebenezer, died the next day aged eighty in Brighton. At the time of his death, London was *en fête* for the coronation of

King George V on 24 June, but at Lindfield at 2.45 p.m. on 9 May a large circle of private and business friends had arrived to attend the funeral of a country lad who had made good.

To his widow and ten children, Walter had left £1.6 million (over £40 million at 1986 values). He also left very substantial legacies to the Royal Merchant Seamen's Orphanage and to hospitals at Brighton and Putney. There was one particular proviso in his eighteen-page closely typed will. His family lost their inheritance if they ceased to profess the Protestant religion, which was deemed 'to be any Christian religion which protested against the errors of the Church of Rome'. This proviso was not so extraordinary then as it might be now.

Matilda had experienced forty-seven years of married life with Walter. Her marriage had been difficult at times, with her husband's restless energy and determination as he drove his own ship forward in search of some new port, and with the fearful responsibilities of it all. She had found some comfort in Philip, another brother, whose character was more gentle. There were moments when she wondered whether he would have suited her better, as he stood by her at critical times. He did not marry until he was forty-two: his bride was a girl of nineteen.

Matilda lived on at Finches until 13 February 1941, when she died just two years short of her century. Like her mother-in-law, Maria, she had become a great matriarch of her family of ten children and their own children.

Her eldest son, Walter H. Savill, who was to remain a director of Shaw Savill & Albion until 1937, wound up Shaw Savill & Co and sold his father's remaining three sailing-ships (*Lindfield*, *Gladys* and *County of Inverness*) for which there was little profitable demand, although all continued trading under their new owners. The *Lindfield* was sunk by a German submarine in 1916; the *Gladys* was sold for £4,500 and wrecked in 1919 when serving as an auxiliary tanker, and the *County of Inverness* sailed under the Estonian flag for many years.

The portfolio of Walter's securities on his death is an indication of his wide-ranging search for profitable investment and is probably typical of many other Victorian entrepreneurs bent on following the flag. Although there was obviously self-interest in such activities, there was also an awareness of what a convenient and happy duty it was to contribute to Britain's imperial obligations. The call to such service reached a peak of patriotic fervour in 1897 at Queen Victoria's Diamond Jubilee and was sustained at that level until 1914, despite the temporary setback earlier in South Africa.

Walter Savill was very much a man of his time. He had

thoroughly enjoyed being in the thick of all the creative energy and hubbub of the Empire's capital during an era when more adventurous spirits in search of new frontiers across the world rapaciously claimed even more extensions of the Queen's Dominions. He had had plenty of fun, and hoped he had given in return more than a fair measure of happiness and hope to the new families settling in New Zealand.

# 12. *Epilogue*

Shaw Savill & Albion continued to trade on a major scale for another seventy years between the United Kingdom and New Zealand (and Australia) as the senior liner company operating a regular passenger and cargo service with well-found and distinctive ships. It became a household name in those countries. (It had even merited a mention by Rudyard Kipling, a passenger in 1891, in his *Just So Stories*.) Its striking and beautiful house flag was always honoured and was to be seen in the thick of two World Wars in the service of its country. Its employees both at home and afloat set themselves high standards, and generation after generation were to be found prepared to offer the same quality of loyal service as they went about their work.

The Company has had possibly three moments of singularity or greatness which has endeared it to the keepers of Britain's maritime heritage; perhaps also to others.

The first was in 1905 when it had grown sufficiently strong under Walter Savill's guidance and continuing influence to begin its rescue from oblivion of the Aberdeen White Star Line of George Thompson & Co, the former proud owners of as smart and swift a fleet of particularly beautiful green-hulled white-masted clippers as were ever to be found under the Red Ensign and therefore a memory of superlative standards worth preserving – even for the sake of one spectacular member of that fleet, the *Thermopylae* (many still say she was the greatest clipper of them all, when Captain Kemball had her).

The second moment was to stir men's thoughts and to catch the imagination of the British people. It came one gloomy evening in November 1940 when news reached London of a hopeless but gloriously defiant action in the cold North Atlantic in protection of a convoy of ships by Captain Fogarty Fegan RN in command of the *Jervis Bay*, a passenger ship converted into an armed merchant cruiser, against the *Admiral Scheer*, a German battle cruiser. The *Jervis Bay* went down with Captain Fegan and many Company employees. Thirty-three ships of the convoy reached port safely, and a Victoria Cross was awarded posthumously to their gallant deliverer and his ship.

The third moment came in 1954, when the Company's ship *Gothic* had the honour of acting as the Royal Yacht when it carried HM The Queen and HRH The Duke of Edinburgh on their world tour of Australia and New Zealand.

Today the Company is still listed, but like so many old-established British shipping companies it is a mere ghost of its former glory.

Walter Savill's death in 1911 had brought to an end the single-minded efforts of the sixth child of a country builder, brought up by a widowed mother with few resources and given a limited education. Shy of success but a stickler for form, he had gone about his life's work sincerely and methodically. In the space of sixty years, since he had first found employment in the shipping industry in the City he had created, despite the early loss of his senior partner and close friend, a very special enterprise which had made a major contribution to the order of things between Great Britain and New Zealand. He had brought about the meeting of their peoples and influenced and enriched the quality and regulation of their lives. He had also raised their spirits and widened their experiences and horizons. In short, he had helped, in his own way, to change an outpost of the Empire into one of the Queen's Dominions, a status given to New Zealand four years before his death.

His life's work was seen by his City friends and others as a remarkable *tour de force*. He probably saw himself somewhat less heroically, beset more poignantly by fragile thoughts and distant echoes of what should have been – but he would have been content to be counted one of the Queen's men – entrepreneur, visionary and Empire-builder.

> My stem was fair, my bud was green,
>   My blossom sweet did blow;
> The dew fell fresh, the sun rose mild,
>   And made my branches grow.
>           (Robert Burns)

# Appendix A

Extracts from *New Zealand – the land of promise and its resources* by William Stones, first edition, published 1858.

## PREFACE TO THE SEVENTH EDITION

The Essay of Mr Stones, which we now reprint, contains information so much sought after, that the previous Editions have met with a very rapid sale.

We give Mr Stones' original paper unaltered and unabridged, and embrace the opportunity of embodying with it the latest intelligence of the colony's progress, our object being to present to our readers a truthful but concise sketch of 'New Zealand as it is.'

The statistics and general notices which we append are derived from authentic and official sources.

We trust that the present Edition may meet as favorable a reception as its predecessors, and prove useful to those interested in a country which is attracting so large a share of public attention as an emigration field.

SHAW, SAVILL & CO

London, October 1st, 1864.

## HINTS TO EMIGRANTS

New Zealand is situated on the opposite side of the globe to England; hence, to reach it, we must cross the Equator, and pass through the tropical or hottest region of the earth; after which, the voyage advances toward the south, in order to round the Cape of Good Hope, and then sails, for several weeks, in an easterly direction.

Land is seldom seen on the voyage; sometimes, however, the islands of Madeira, the Cape de Verds, the Azores, the small Island of Tristan d'Acunha or St Paul's, and Van Diemen's Land, are approached close enough to be visible.

It will, therefore, be evident that for a short portion of the voyage the emigrant is exposed to extreme heat, after which he is likely to feel the cold weather, particularly if (as some navigators prefer) the ship is made to stand well to the southward, in order to shorten the length of the degrees of longitude, and thereby make a quick passage; in no case, however, does the cold become so intense as in England.

The average duration of the voyage to New Zealand is now about fourteen weeks, a long period of idleness to those who may have been accustomed to regular labour at home, but offering good opportunity for reading, and learning many useful matters connected with the sea.

To lend a willing hand with the sails, to learn something of ships and rigging, steering, reefing, &c., afford amusement, and at the same time enable the attentive emigrant to acquire many valuable notions which may be extremely advantageous to him in a country like New Zealand, where boating and coasting form so large an item in all the transactions of the place.

We should advise the intending emigrant to dispose of all his furniture, because the freight is high; it would be an encumbrance to him on landing, and to move it about would be very expensive, whereas the possession of its money value would at first be most important to him. When in a position to furnish a cottage, the requisites can always be purchased on the spot.

As many books as can be obtained will afford amusement and instruction on the voyage.

The ordinary clothes worn in England will answer every purpose, and a large stock need not be taken, as a very small quantity of luggage is allowed for each passenger, excess being charged with freight.

A good overcoat, or a complete suit of waterproofs, for men, and a warm cloak for women, against wet and cold weather are very desirable, and a pair of good stout ten quarter blankets we should advise, as being a sufficient covering during the voyage, and forming a very acceptable bed in the bush; both for the sea, and in such a warm climate as New Zealand, a mattrass is to be preferred to a bed, being cooler and more wholesome.

The only articles with which an emigrant cannot be overstocked are boots; New Zealand is a rainy country, and there being a great deal of out-door work, boots are destroyed more quickly there than in any other country in the world.

The boots which are the most desirable are watertights with

fastened tongues and eyeleted, not heavy, but strongly made, and bradded or lightly nailed; for the climate is warm, although wet, and therefore boots should not be so heavy as to fatigue the wearer.

Pieces of plain calico and printed cotton may be advantageously taken by females to amuse and occupy their time in the making of apparel during the voyage, and for this purpose a good stock of tapes, needles, and sewing cotton should be provided.

For those who can afford it, a small filter in a wicker guard, a ham or even two, and a few tins of small plain biscuits, will be found acceptable on the voyage.

Attention to cleanliness, and courtesy to one another, will render the voyage pleasant and improving to the health.

Contentment also with the circumstances in which the emigrant is temporarily placed, and a hearty co-operation with the captain, officers and medical attendant will do a great deal to soften down the disagreeables incident to a sea voyage; and if emigrants would occasionally ask themselves what object the officers of the ship can possibly have but the safety, comfort, and well-being of all under their charge, it would change the little grumbles into a cordial sympathy and cheerful acquiescence in those regulations which are absolutely essential to the health of the whole body.

On arrival, we earnestly advise the acceptance of immediate employment, even if it should not exactly be what is desired; it puts the emigrant in heart, it saves expenditure, it gives hope and prevents repining and homesickness, and settles one at once; and last, and most important, establishes the emigrant in the good opinion of the Colonists, who, above all things, detest *lazy* people. At first, an engagement should only be for a short period, until the 'new chum' knows the place and people.

Do not carry any cash with you, but obtain a letter of credit for same from a bank which has branches in New Zealand, or from some respectable ship-broker who grants such instruments, taking an order payable in the Colony, sending the duplicate by another ship: on arrival, leave as much as possible on interest at a bank in the colony for six months, and do not be tempted to draw it out or embark in any speculation of your own, but endeavour to work for wages, and at the end of that time you will be better able to judge what to do with yourself and your money, than the writer to advise you – so farewell and God speed.


## HINTS ABOUT SHIPS, &c.

In the early days of New Zealand colonization, the voyage was looked upon generally as something of a formidable and momentous nature, and in most Emigrants' Manuals elaborate recommendations were to be met with, as to choice of ship, captain, &c, with a view to the attainment of safety and comfort in the transit. At the present day, there happily exists little occasion for any such preliminary investigations.

The advancement of science has done much to smooth the path of the intended voyager to a very great extent. Not only are the ships now in the trade of superior construction, combining strength and roominess, with the highest speed, but a number of improvements have from time to time been introduced, by means of which a considerable lessening has taken place of the discomforts necessarily attendant on a sea life to the inexperienced.

Modern appliances secure thorough ventilation and light; the preserved provisions are prepared in a much greater style of excellence than formerly, thereby affording a varied and wholesome diet for all classes, whilst a most valuable invention now exists and is applied in all large vessels to distil fresh water from salt, and to supply a practically unlimited quantity of that precious article for the whole voyage.

Moreover, enlightened views on the subject of navigation have shortened the passage considerably, and, instead of the four or five months which were formerly consumed on the way, the run is now frequently made in less than three.

A very strict supervision is also exercised by the Government over all emigrant ships. The duties of Government Surveyor for London devolve upon Captain Lean RN &c, assisted by a numerous staff of naval officers. This gentleman has occupied his present post for many years, the duties of which he has discharged in a manner which has secured for him the high respect of all with whom he has been brought into contact.

To the patient attention which he bestows upon all matters where the real interests of the emigrants are concerned, may be largely attributed the fact that emigration business from London has hitherto been so free from reproach.

It will be seen, therefore, that beyond taking the simple precaution, in the first instance, of ascertaining that the parties with whom he treats, and who contract to forward him to his destination, are well known and of good standing, the emigrant need not give himself much trouble about the vessel in which he has to take the voyage.

We would only advise him by all means to take passage in a ship going direct to the settlement wherein he intends locating himself, and for the rest, to trust to the practical experience of the Ship

Brokers guaranteeing him, as far as human foresight goes, a safe and pleasant conveyance.

The emigrant will sometimes perceive, in Ship Brokers' advertisements, a great deal of credit assumed for the providing of medical comforts, and a variety of other alluring luxuries. The fact is, that the Government compel these things to be provided, and in such cases a necessity is exaggerated into a virtue. There is no very great amount of difficulty in making comfortable provision for emigrants on board ship. Practical experience and honesty of purpose are all that are wanted. Every man naturally prefers his own particular interest, and therefore if we are asked to recommend any particular Line of Packets we naturally recommend our own.

## THE PASSENGERS' LINE OF PACKETS

During the six years which have elapsed since the establishment of this line it has been our privilege to convey to New Zealand a very much larger number of persons than have ever been despatched during the same period by any of our neighbours.

We would specially direct attention to the facts, that we have obtained contracts from all the Provincial Governments for the conduct of their public emigration, and that with hardly an exception all the returning colonists take passage by our ships. We hold this as the most emphatic evidence that the condition in which our passengers are landed must have favourably impressed all persons in the colony – both private and official – with the liberality of our arrangements.

We are also happy to record the fact, that out of some hundreds of ships which we have despatched, conveying many thousands of passengers, we have never met with a serious calamity to the ship, nor epidemic among the passengers. We mention this in no spirit of self-laudation, but as evidence that the voyage is one fraught with little danger, and that the necessary precautions for ensuring safety are not neglected on our part.

Our future aim will be to profit by our large experience, and to introduce, as we have hitherto done, every modern improvement which may present itself from time to time, as calculated to increase the safety and comfort of passengers, and to secure for ourselves a continuance of the great public confidence which we have the privilege to enjoy.

We would add on this head, that there is a marked advantage to passengers in doing business with a firm largely embarked in the trade, inasmuch as they have the security afforded by the interests at stake in doing the work well, and moreover, the benefit of experience, as well as the very great advantages which a line such as ours possesses in making all the arrangements for provisioning and general equipment with greater facility and in a more efficient manner, than can be done in the ease of ships despatched less frequently.

We subjoin a list of rates of passage and general hints as to passenger arrangements.

One feature to which we would advert, as distinguishing our ships from those of other Lines, is the finding of the cabin table. It has hitherto been the practice to place chief cabin passengers upon a restricted scale of dietary. By many persons this was found to be objectionable in practice, and we have abolished it, substituting an unrestricted cabin table, as in the first class Ocean Steamers.

We also make live stock and fresh provisions generally a more permanent item in the daily fare. The increase of expense is very considerable, but we are satisfied that it will materially contribute to comfort, and that we shall reap the benefit in the long run. Indeed it is to this circumstance we attribute the fact, that our line has been selected by a very large proportion of returning colonists, whose experience of restricted dietaries upon previous voyages has not been of a nature to induce them to repeat the experiment.

We are often asked by second and third class passengers, whether it is desirable for them to take a few extra provisions for their own use? The dietary scale for them will be found adequate fully to supply all absolute necessities; but where circumstances admit of it, a few additional luxuries will be a great relief from sea fare, which, at the best, is monotonous. We would advise those who can afford it, to take with them a small quantity of jams and jellies, ordinary fancy biscuits, a little sago, or arrowroot, and such like things, which can be packed into small compass, and are prepared for use without much trouble. Preserved milk is also a valuable though somewhat expensive luxury. There is one modern preparation of it in the shape of a powder, a small bottle of which makes a quart of milk, at a cost of a shilling. It possesses an advantage over milk preserved in a liquid state, inasmuch as it need not be all used at once. Where there are children, it will be found a very salutary change.

With regard to the necessary outfit, authorities upon this point agree in giving the following as the minimum quantity which an emigrant should take, viz:

Mattrasses (which should be new, if possible, and of the following dimensions: For men, 6 feet by 20 inches; Women, 5 feet 9 inches by 18 inches; Married Couples, 6 feet by 3 feet; Children, according to size), Bolsters, Blankets, and Counterpanes, Canvas Bags to contain Linen, &c.; Knives, Forks, Spoons, Metal Plates, Hook Pots, Drinking Mugs, Water Can, &c. Also, necessary clothing as under, viz:

### FOR MALES

6 Shirts.
6 Pair Stockings.
2 Warm Flannel or Guernsey Shirts.
2 Pair New Shoes.
2 Complete Suits Strong Exterior Clothing.

### FOR FEMALES

6 Shifts.
2 Warm and Strong Flannel Petticoats.
6 Pair Stockings.
2 Pair Strong Shoes.
2 Strong Gowns, one of which must be warm.

### FOR CHILDREN

7 Shirts or Shifts.
4 Warm Flannel Waistcoats.
1 Warm Cloak or Outside Coat.
6 Pair Stockings.
2 Pair Strong Shoes.
2 Complete Suits of Exterior Clothing, and a sufficient supply of covering for the head. Also, 3 sheets for each berth, and 4 towels and 2 lbs. Marine Soap for each person.

The cost of this will not exceed four or five pounds. Of course, where a passenger can afford it, there is no limit to the extent according to which he can provide himself. It is a great mistake, however, to think that a very large stock of clothing is *indispensable* for the voyage. Passing through the heat of the tropics, and often exposed to cold at the southward of the Cape of Good Hope, the passenger should of course be provided against both extremes. Both this can be done without preparation of either an elaborate or expensive character. We should advise all passengers to obtain the sea-going portion of their outfit from some one of the many respectable outfitters in *London*. These houses have much practical experience, and can give sound and reliable advice.

We will only further add that being in constant communication with friends and correspondents in the colony, and being daily brought into contact with persons who have returned from thence, we have access to the newest and most authentic information. It at all times affords us pleasure to communicate that information, and any inquiries which may be addressed to us will always meet with prompt reply.

SHAW, SAVILL & Co

Agents for the Passengers' Line of Packets, 34 Leadenhall Street, London EC.

## RATES OF PASSAGE AND GENERAL ARRANGEMENTS
(Provisions included)

Chief Cabin Fare – Poop Cabins according
    to accommodation ................. 45 to 75 guineas each.
           Stern Cabins by special arrangement.
Second Cabin Fare – Enclosed Cabins .............. £25 each
Steerage – Enclosed Berths, separate Cabins for
    Married Couples ....................... £20 & 18 each
    Open Berths ................... £15 & upwards each
    Children under 12 years to pay one-half Passage Money.
       Infants under 1 year no charge.

*Chief Cabin Passengers supplied with an unlimited table,*
*including Live Stock.*

*Scale of Dietary for Each Adult Passenger Per Week*

| Articles | Second Cabin | Steerage |
| --- | --- | --- |
| Preserved Meats | 2 lb | 1 lb |
| Soup and Bouilli | $\frac{1}{2}$ lb | — |
| York Ham | $\frac{1}{2}$ lb | — |
| Fish | $\frac{1}{4}$ lb | — |
| Prime India Beef | 1 lb | $1\frac{1}{4}$ lb |
| Irish Mess Pork | $1\frac{1}{2}$ lb | 1 lb |
| Biscuit | $4\frac{1}{4}$ lb | $3\frac{1}{2}$ lb |
| Flour | $4\frac{1}{4}$ lb | 3 lb |
| Rice | 1 lb | $\frac{1}{2}$ lb |
| Barley | $\frac{1}{2}$ lb | — |
| Peas | $\frac{1}{2}$ pint | $\frac{1}{2}$ pint |
| Oatmeal | $\frac{1}{2}$ pint | 1 pint |
| Sugar, Raw | 1 lb | 1 lb |
| Lime Juice | 6 oz | 6 oz |
| Tea | $1\frac{1}{2}$ oz | $1\frac{1}{2}$ oz |
| Coffee | 3 oz | 2 oz |
| Butter | $\frac{1}{2}$ lb | 6 oz |
| Cheese | $\frac{1}{4}$ lb | — |
| Currants, or | $\frac{1}{4}$ lb | — |

| | | |
|---|---|---|
| Raisins, Valencia | $\frac{1}{2}$ lb | $\frac{1}{2}$ lb |
| Suet | 6 oz | 6 oz |
| Pickles | $\frac{1}{4}$ pint | $\frac{1}{4}$ pint |
| Mustard | $\frac{1}{2}$ oz | $\frac{1}{2}$ oz |
| Pepper | $\frac{1}{4}$ oz | $\frac{1}{4}$ oz |
| Salt | 2 oz | 2 oz |
| Potatoes fresh, or | $3\frac{1}{2}$ lb | 2 lb |
| Ditto preserved | $\frac{1}{2}$ lb | $\frac{1}{2}$ lb |
| Water | 21 quarts | 21 quarts |

For all children and infants an equivalent quantity of sago, flour, rice, raisins, suet and sugar will be substituted for salt meat, if required.

Provisions of the best quality are put on board according to the above scale for 22 weeks, together with an abundant supply of extra stores, as medical comforts for passengers generally.

The arrangements of these vessels are based upon long experience. Every improvement which, from time to time, suggests itself as conducive to the comfort of Passengers (without losing sight of economy in the rates of Passage) will be promptly adopted.

### SHIP'S REGULATIONS

Passage Money – Each Passenger is required to pay a deposit of one-half of the passage money on securing his berth, which deposit will be forfeited in case of non-embarkation. The other half to be paid, prior to embarkation, at the Office of Shaw, Savill & Co. On remitting deposit, particulars of *Name, Age, Country, and Occupation* of each Passenger must also be given.

Cabins are appropriated in rotation as the deposits are paid.

Luggage – Chief Cabin and Second Cabin Passengers carry half a ton, and other passengers quarter of a ton measurement of Luggage only, *free of charge*; any excess to be charged for at the current rate of freight. What linen, &c., is required for the first week or two should be packed in a handy bag, and should be clearly marked 'Cabin.' – Luggage forwarded from the country for shipment must be carriage paid. The name of the Passenger and the Port of his destination should be *painted* on each case or package; and then each should have a card tacked on bearing the direction: 'To be delivered at the East India Docks, per the Ship –.' All extra Passengers' Luggage and Goods should be at the Docks seven days before the sailing of the ship. The Dock charges on Luggage amount to about 2s. per box or package, according to size, which must be paid before the ship sails, otherwise the goods will not be shipped. Passengers must superintend the shipment of their own baggage, and they must take charge of it when on board, as the ship will not be responsible for its loss, damage, or detention, under any circumstances.

*N.B. – The Luggage packages most necessary to have in the Cabin should be marked 'Cabin;' and those most likely to be 'Wanted on the Voyage,' should bear these words, so that they may be stowed in the Hold, where access can be had from time to time.*

Embarkation – Passengers embark at Gravesend the day following the Ship's leaving the Docks.

Liquors – Wines, Beer, &c., of the best quality, are provided at the following prices: Port or Sherry Wines, 4s. per bottle; Ale or Porter. 1s. per bottle; Brandy, 5s. per bottle; Spirits, for Chief Cabin Passengers only, 3s per bottle; but for the better preservation of order in the Ship, the quantity so supplied will be under the regulation of the Commander. No private supply allowed to be taken into the cabins.

Chief Cabin Passengers provide their own furniture, bed places, and whatever else they may think requisite within their private Cabins. The owners of the Ship supply everything that is required for the table, viz., – plate, linen, glass, attendance, &c.

Second Cabin and Steerage Passengers have berths built for them, but find their own bedding, and other fittings they may require. They must also provide themselves with the following utensils, viz. – knives and forks, table and tea-spoons, one or two deep metal plates and dishes, a hook teapot, cups and saucers, or tin drinking vessels, and a water-can. The Provisions are daily prepared by the Cook of the Ship, but passengers must in other respects attend to their own arrangements for messing. They must be provided with a proper supply of Clothing and other necessaries for the voyage. Second Cabin Passengers receive only partial attendance in cleaning the Cabin.

The Agents effect Insurances on Baggage and Passage Money.

# Appendix B

## Ships Owned and Managed by Shaw, Savill and Co 1858-82

| Name | Gross Reg. Tons | Year Built | Builder | Hull | Rig | Year Bought | Age when Bought | Total Service Years a | Year lost or sold | Age when lost or sold |
|---|---|---|---|---|---|---|---|---|---|---|
| Adamant | 815 | 1858 | Hull | Iron | Barque | 1873 | 15 | 9 | 1882 | 24 |
| Akaroa | 1,334 | 1881 | Osbourne, Sunderland | Iron | Barque | 1881 | — | 23 | 1904 | 23 |
| Anazi | 468 | 1865 | Turnbull, Portsmouth | Comp. | Barque | 1873 | 8 | 13 | 1886 | 21 |
| Avalanche | 1,210 | 1874 | Hall, Aberdeen | Iron | Ship | 1874 | — | 3 | 1877 | 3 |
| Ballarat | 685 | 1852 | Duthie, Aberdeen | Wood | Barque | 1871 | 19 | 2(9) | 1873 | 21 |
| Bebington | 941 | 1859 | Hickson, Belfast | Iron | Barque | 1875 | 16 | 8(11) | 1883 | 24 |
| Bulwark | 1,332 | 1862 | King, New Brunswick | Wood | Ship | 1872 | 10 | 9 | 1881 | 19 |
| Caduceus | 1,116 | 1854 | Fletcher, London | Wood | Barque | 1869 | 15 | 4(6) | 1873 | 19 |
| Charlotte Gladstone | 1,304 | 1865 | Fisher, New Brunswick | Wood | Ship | 1869 | 4 | 4 | 1873 | 8 |
| Chaudière | 470 | 1863 | Doxford, Sunderland | Comp. | Barque | 1873 | 10 | 10(11) | 1883 | 20 |
| Chile | 768 | 1856 | London | Iron | Ship | 1868 | 12 | 12(19) | 1880 | 24 |
| Cospatrick | 1,200 | 1856 | Moulmein, Burma | Wood | Ship | 1873 | 17 | 1(1) | 1874 | 18 |
| Cossipore | 834 | 1851 | Dundee | Wood | Ship | 1865 | 14 | 1 | 1866 | 15 |
| Crusader | 1,058 | 1865 | Connell, Glasgow | Iron | Ship | 1869 | 4 | 29 | 1898 | 33* |
| Dover Castle | 1,003 | 1858 | Sunderland | Wood | Ship | 1871 | 13 | 10 | 1881 | 23 |
| Edward P. Bouverie | 997 | 1864 | Hall, Aberdeen | Comp. | Ship | 1872 | 8 | 5 | 1877 | 13 |
| Edwin Fox | 836 | 1853 | Calcutta | Wood | Barque | 1873 | 20 | 11 | 1884 | 31 |
| Electra | 668 | 1866 | Hall, Aberdeen | Comp. | Ship | 1881 | 15 | 6(19) | 1887 | 21 |
| Elizabeth Graham | 616 | 1869 | Harkness, Middlesbrough | Comp. | Barque | 1873 | 4 | 12 | 1885 | 16 |

| Name | Gross Reg. Tons | Year Built | Builder | Hull | Rig | Year Bought | Age when Bought | Total Service Years a | Year lost or sold | Age when lost or sold |
|---|---|---|---|---|---|---|---|---|---|---|
| Euterpe (now Star of India) | 1,197 | 1863 | Gibson, Macdonald Isle of Man | Iron | Ship | 1871 | 8 | 28 | 1899 | 36* |
| Forfarshire | 1,238 | 1867 | Morison, Sunderland | Comp. | Ship | 1873 | 6 | 22(23) | 1895 | 28 |
| Glenlora | 774 | 1864 | Vernon, Liverpool | Iron | Barque | 1873 | 9 | 25 | 1898 | 34* |
| Golden Sea | 1,418 | 1864 | Oliver, Quebec | Wood | Ship | 1874 | 10 | 6 | 1880 | 16 |
| Helen Denny | 728 | 1866 | Duncan, Port Glasgow | Iron | Ship | 1872 | 6 | 24 | 1896 | 30* |
| Hermione | 1,176 | 1876 | Hall, Aberdeen | Iron | Ship | 1876 | — | 30 | 1906 | 30 |
| Himalaya | 1,008 | 1863 | Pile, Sunderland | Iron | Ship | 1874 | 11 | 23(26) | 1897 | 34 |
| Hudson | 848 | 1869 | Pearse, Stockton | Iron | Ship | 1873 | 4 | 25(26) | 1898 | 29* |
| Lady Jocelyn | 2,138 | 1852 | Mare, London | Iron | Ship | 1882 | 30 | 17(30) | 1899 | 47* |
| Langstone | 746 | 1869 | Pile, Sunderland | Iron | Ship | 1873 | 4 | 22 | 1895 | 26 |
| Lutterworth | 915 | 1868 | Denton Gray, H'pool | Iron | Barque | 1879 | 11 | 27(34) | 1906 | 38 |
| Margaret Galbraith | 889 | 1868 | Duncan Port Glasgow | Iron | Ship | 1876 | 8 | 24 | 1900 | 32 |
| Matoaka | 1,323 | 1853 | New Brunswick | Wood | Ship | 1867 | 14 | 2(10) | 1869 | 16 |
| Mermaid | 1,321 | 1853 | St Johns, Newfoundland | Wood | Ship | 1868 | 15 | 1(8) | 1869 | 16 |
| Merope | 1,082 | 1870 | Oswald, Sunderland | Comp. | Ship | 1870 | — | 20 | 1890 | 20 |
| Monarch | 1,415 | 1844 | Green, London | Wood | Ship | 1866 | 22 | 7 | 1873 | 29 |
| Pleiades | 1,020 | 1869 | Macmillan, Dumbarton | Iron | Ship | 1872 | 3 | 27 | 1899 | 30 |
| Pleione | 1,139 | 1876 | Stephen, Glasgow | Iron | Ship | 1876 | — | 23 | 1899 | 23* |
| Queen Bee | 726 | 1859 | Briggs, Sunderland | Wood | Ship | 1873 | 14 | 4(11) | 1877 | 18 |
| Robert Henderson | 552 | 1857 | Aberdeen | Wood | Ship | 1871 | 14 | 1(3) | 1872 | 15 |
| St Leonards | 1,054 | 1864 | Pile, Sunderland | Iron | Ship | 1871 | 7 | 12 | 1883 | 19 |
| Schieballion | 602 | 1809 | Brown, Dundee | Iron | Barque | 1874 | 5 | 5(9) | 1879 | 10 |
| Soukar | 1,304 | 1864 | Reid, Port Glasgow | Iron | Ship | 1874 | 10 | 25(26) | 1899 | 35* |
| Stratballan | 548 | 1857 | Dundee | Wood | Barque | 1866 | 9 | 2(3) | 1868 | 11 |

| Name | Gross Reg. Tons | Year Built | Builder | Hull | Rig | Year Bought | Age when Bought | Total Service Years a | Year lost or sold | Age when lost or sold |
|---|---|---|---|---|---|---|---|---|---|---|
| Trevelyan | 1,042 | 1863 | Pile, Sunderland | Iron | Ship | 1873 | 10 | 15 | 1888 | 25 |
| Wild Duck | 735 | 1859 | Robinson, Sunderland | Wood | Ship | 1867 | 8 | 7(15) | 1874 | 15 |
| Zealandia | 1,165 | 1869 | Connell, Glasgow | Iron | Ship | 1869 | — | 34 | 1903 | 34 |

a Includes subsequent service with Shaw Savill & Albion and again with Shaw, Savill & Co.
( ) includes years employed on charter prior to purchase.
Comp. Composite build, wood planking on an iron frame.
% over forty-five years when finally broken up or lost.

# Appendix C

## *Emigration of 800 Nonconformists to New Zealand*

Extract from the *Illustrated London News* 7 June 1862

The London Docks were thronged at an early hour on Thursday week by an immense concourse of persons assembled to witness the departure of the first instalment, about eight hundred persons, chiefly members of different Nonconformist bodies, who are emigrating to the new colony of Albertland, in New Zealand. Availing themselves of the liberal offer of the New Zealand Government to grant forty acres of land to every emigrant paying his passage to the colony, with a proportionate grant in addition for each member of his family, Mr W.R. Brame and a number of friends have organised an emigration on an extensive scale. In a comparatively brief period over a thousand persons have been duly registered. Only such persons were selected as possessed a certain amount of capital or were proficient in some valuable mechanical avocation, or were in other points calculated to prove profitable to the new colony. Should the pioneers report favourably we may expect their new settlement to become highly popular. The colony of Albertland to which they proceed is situated on the banks of a beautiful river named the Ornawharo, fifty or sixty miles from Auckland, a district of the fertility of which the most encouraging reports are given by competent authorities.

The *Matilda Wattenbach*, a British-built clipper-ship of 1000 tons, belonging to Messrs Wattenbach, Heilgers and Co of Mincing Lane; and the *Hanover*, a ship of the same class and tonnage, and owned by George Marshall and Co, were specially selected from Messrs Shaw and Savill's well-known passenger line of packets, and will be followed by the *William Miles*, 1250 tons, on the 10th of July. The *Ida Ziegler*, also belonging to Messrs Wattenbach,

Heilgers and Co, follows the *William Miles* in the course of July. On board the *Matilda Wattenbach* there were about 350 passengers, including the Rev. S. Edgar, Mr W.R. Brame, the originator of the movement, and the committee of management for 'the new settlement.' On board the *Hanover* there were about 280 passengers.

At ten o'clock the company began to assemble in a spacious booth erected for the purpose within the dock premises, where a public 'farewell demonstration' was held, under the presidency of Mr Harper Twelvetrees. At half-past eleven a hymn was sung, in which the vast crowd united, and they were accompanied by a powerful brass band. The Chairman then delivered a brief address, bidding the emigrants 'God speed,' wishing them a pleasant voyage and a happy realisation of their fondest hopes in the land of their adoption, where he trusted they would found a prosperous and important community.

The Rev. Thomas Penrose followed with a remarkably opportune farewell address, replete with sound advice, judicious cautions, seasonable admonitions, and abounding with the heartiest good wishes for their future wellbeing.

The Rev. W. Landells next spoke. He reminded the emigrants of the responsibilities of their position, and counselled them to prepare for many unexpected difficulties and discouragements which they would have to encounter, and to acquit themselves as men. He considered that they were setting out with prospects of the most hopeful description. He spoke in the most complimentary terms of the merits of Mr Brame, the founder of the movement, and especially of the Rev. Mr Edgar, who goes out with the colonists in the capacity of pastor.

At this point the band, which had gone round the docks for the purpose of assembling the friends, returned, and the company collected now amounted to nearly 15,000 persons. The greatest interest was excited in the movement. The docks have not for many a day been startled from their dull propriety by such a spectacle as was then witnessed. The leave-takings were of the most exciting and sometimes painful description. The band played 'Auld Lang Syne,' and its plaintive strains drew tears from the eyes of many who had till then remained apparently unmoved.

Affectionate addresses were delivered by Mr Heaton and the Rev. Mr Edgar, and the company proceeded on board the two magnifcent ships, which then left the docks, the band playing the National Anthem. Salutes were fired, and the vessels were taken in tow by powerful steam-tugs amidst deafening applause from the immense multitude assembled to bid their friends farewell. A large

Departure of the *Matilda Wattenbach*, 30 May 1862.
Walter Savill is the figure in front of the mast

number of friends proceeded with the emigrants on board as far as Gravesend, which they reached shortly after four o'clock.

Mr Ball MP addressed the emigrants on board, and spoke in the most encouraging terms of the prospects which were before them. He said he had two sons who had spent many years in the colony, and had been remarkably successful. The soil was fertile, and there were no serpents or dangerous wild beasts which infested other quarters of the globe. The climate was good, and the temperature was equable. There were no extremes of cold to be feared. They had only to dig and to plant the potato, for instance, and the fruitful soil would return them in some cases tenfold, in some cases twentyfold, and in other cases even a hundredfold. If they carried out their Christian principles in their conduct towards the natives they would find a cordial response to all their kindness. Mr Jesse Hobson also delivered an address full of sympathy and encouragement. He counselled the emigrants to expect many disappointments; but he assured them that, if their hopes were not fully realised in the precise way in which they expected, they would often be fulfilled in a manner not less advantageous to them. He eloquently placed before them their grave responsibilities as emigrants proceeding to a new country, the physical and the moral character of which would largely depend upon the way in which they discharged those duties they were expected to fulfil; and he concluded by a few words of counsel and encouragement. After a few words from the Rev. Mr Millard, of Maze-pond, the visitors left the ships, which had now reached Gravesend, and they returned to town by rail.

# Appendix D

## Summary of London to New Zealand Sailings, 1858–82

| Year | Auckland | Napier/ Hawke Bay | Wellington | Taranaki | Nelson | Canterbury | Otago | Southland | Total No. of Sailings | Total Reg. Tons | Average Tons | Average Passage Days a |
|---|---|---|---|---|---|---|---|---|---|---|---|---|
| 1858 | 3 | — | 1(1) | | 2 | (2) | 3 | — | 9 | 4,007 | 445 | 123 |
| 1859 | 7 | (1) | 6(1) | (4) | 4(1) | 4(2) | 4(2) | — | 25 | 13,587 | 543 | 124 |
| 1860 | 7 | — | 4(1) | (4) | 4 | 3 | 3 | — | 21 | 12,748 | 607 | 114 |
| 1861 | 9 | (1) | 6(1) | (5) | 6 | 5 | 7 | — | 33 | 19,910 | 603 | 119 |
| 1862 | 13 | (3) | 8 | (2) | 5 | 7 | 7 | 1 | 45 | 31,404 | 698 | 118 |
| 1863 | 16 | 1(3) | 10 | (1) | 8 | 14(1) | 11(1) | 6 | 70 | 55,956 | 799 | 116[d] |
| 1864 | 24 | 1 | 7 | | 6 | 9(1) | 15[b](3) | 3 | 62 | 50,975 | 822 | 114 |
| 1865 | 16 | 2(1) | 10 | (2) | 7 | 10 | 12[c] | — | 56 | 47,352 | 846 | 115[d] |
| 1866 | 14 | 2 | 13 | (2) | 8 | 14 | 11 | 2 | 68 | 49,893 | 734 | 118 |
| 1867 | 10 | — | 9 | | 7 | 9 | 15 | 1 | 50 | 36,744 | 735 | 109[d] |
| 1868 | 10 | 2 | 11 | | 6 | 7 | 14(1) | 2[e] | 50 | 37,837 | 757 | 111 |
| 1869 | 15[e] | 1 | 9 | | 6 | 10 | 12 | 1[e] | 57 | 41,449 | 727 | 109 |
| 1870 | 12 | (1) | 8 | | 5 | 8 | 15 | — | 44 | 36,972 | 840 | 103 |
| 1871 | 10 | (1) | 6 | 1[f] | 5 | 10(2) | 10(1) | (1) | 42 | 32,329 | 770 | 101 |
| 1872 | 17[g] | 2(1) | 13[h] | (1[f]) | 5 | 11(2) | 10 | — | 64 | 54,449 | 864 | 110[d] |
| 1873 | 14 | (1) | 15 | (1[f]) | 5 | 15 | 16(1) | — | 67 | 59,585 | 889 | 106[d] |
| 1874 | 15 | 6 | 11(2) | 1 | 7 | 16(2) | 18 | 1[e](5) | 73 | 69,565 | 953 | 102 |
| 1875 | 12 | 2(2) | 11(1) | 2 | 5(2) | 12 | 16[e](2) | 1(2) | 63 | 62,861 | 998 | 106 |
| 1876 | 11 | 1(4) (2[i]) | 10(1) | | 6 | 12 | 18 | 1(3) | 51 | 42,686 | 837 | 105 |
| 1877 | 9 | (5) | 12 | | 5 | 11 | 10 | (1) | 51 | 46,663 | 915 | 100 |
| 1878 | 13 | 1(4) (1[i]) | 17 | (1) | 4(1) | 16 | 14 | 3(2) | 71 | 68,093 | 959 | 106 |
| 1879 | 12 | 2(2) | 14(2) | | 3 | 11(1) | 17(3) | (2) | 60 | 58,756 | 979 | 104 |
| 1880 | 12[f](1) | (3) | 10(1) | 1 | 3 | 13 | 18 | 1(2) | 54 | 54,437 | 1,008 | 99 |
| 1881 | 12[i](1) | (3[i]) | 13(1) | | 4 | 11(1) | 15[e](8) | 2(1) | 57 | 57,030 | 1,000 | 101 |
| 1882 | 15 | (3) | 14 | | 3 | 14 | 16[h] | 5(1) | 67 | 62,348 | 931 | 103 |
| Total Calls | 310(21%) | 65(5%) | 260(18%) | 28(2%) | 133(9%) | 266(18%) | 335(23%) | 51(4%) | 1310 | | | |

Total Calls 1448

*Notes:*
[a] = From Gravesend according to the firm's records
[b] = Including one voyage direct to Timaru
[c] = Including one voyage direct to Oamaru
[d] = Exceptionally long voyage(s) in this year
[e] = Including one departure from Liverpool
[f] = Wanganui
[g] = Including one departure from Glasgow
[h] = Including one departure from Middlesbrough
[i] = Poverty Bay
[j] = Including one voyage direct to Tauranga

Non-arrivals have been excluded from average passage days
Figures in brackets denote second ports of call.
Canterbury = *Lyttelton*
Otago = Dunedin and Port Chalmers, with a few second port calls at Oamaru and Timaru.
Southland = Bluff and Invercargill
Taranaki = New Plymouth, Wanganui

# Appendix E

## Typical Sailings and Experiences of Ships Despatched by Shaw Savill in 1858, 1874 and 1880

These records have been extracted from the Sailings Books of the firm, where they are entered in Victorian copperplate writing, giving the bare essentials of each voyage on line after line and page after page of the heavy ledgers. They must be allowed to speak for themselves. They are considered typical of their kind. One has to look elsewhere to discover whether a particular voyage was a greater or lesser chapter of disasters than the one before or after it. The unmitigated misery of it all was the only common denominator.

The books do not include ships advertised to be on the berth and later switched or withdrawn for various reasons. There were a few false alarms.

The days on passage are from the date the ship sailed from Gravesend until she anchored or berthed at her destination port. There were many ways of squeezing a few days off the passage time when recounting the experiences of a voyage, but port to port rather than landfall to landfall or pilot to pilot or other devious measurements has been taken here as the most realistic (even if the ship was unfortunate enough to have to put back for repairs or shelter). Records of passage times are notoriously unreliable unless one can be sure that like is being compared with like.

Tonnage was another area where some licence appeared conventional, whether to allay the fears of potential passengers or to minimize harbour dues. The registered tonnage was always amended whenever alterations to the ship were made, even of a minor nature such as an additional deckhouse or when such permanent ballast as cement was stowed. And the Merchant

Shipping Acts of 1856 and 1867 introduced new measurement rules. Nevertheless, to the untrained eye, the registered tonnage figure for a particular ship chosen to be quoted from time to time did appear irregular, depending on whether it was advantageous in the circumstances to quote the measurement of weight (tons burthen) or the measurement of space (gross register tons) or some nice round figure such as a thousand, or whether or not owners had opted for new measurement rules.

1858

TO NEW ZEALAND

| No. | Name | Reg. Tons | Destination | Sailed from Gravesend | Arrived | Days |
|---|---|---|---|---|---|---|
| 1. | ss *Lord Ashley* | 287 | Auckland | 19 May | 14 Oct. | 148 |
| 2. | *Chieftain*(a) | 382 | Nelson & Canterbury | 23 May | 19 Oct. | 149 |
| 3. | ss *Lord Worsley* | 282 | Otago & Wellington | 2 June(b) | 4 Oct. | 122 |
| 4. | *Avalanche* | 692 | Auckland | 24 June | 27 Sept.(c) | 95 |
| 5. | *Lady Alice*(d) | 419 | Nelson | 6 Sept. | 15 Jan. | 131 |
| 6. | *Gloucester* | 591 | Otago & Canterbury | 13 Sept.(e) | 26 Dec. | 104 |
| 7. | *Kinnaird* | 555 | Wellington | 9 Oct.(f) | 6 Feb. | 120 |
| 8. | *Tamora* | 419 | Otago | 17 Nov.(g) | 8 March | 111 |
| 9. | *Lochnagar* | 380 | Auckland | 1 Dec. | 5 April | 125 |

ELSEWHERE

| No. | Name | Reg. Tons | Destination | Sailed from Gravesend | Arrived | Days |
|---|---|---|---|---|---|---|
| 1. | *Prince Alfred* | 931 | Port Philip (Melbourne) | 22 Aug. | 4 Dec. | 104 |
| 2. | *Thames City* | 557 | Victoria (Vancouver) | 10 Oct.(h) | 12 April | 184 |

*1858*

(a) On passage to New Zealand, the first officer became drunk and was locked up after assaulting the Commander.
(b) Later wrecked on 1 September 1862 on a hostile shore near New Plymouth. The local Maoris gallantly gave passengers and their luggage a safe escort and transport to New Plymouth.
(c) The news of the *Avalanche*'s safe arrival was not known in London until 21 December 1858, some six months after sailing.
(d) Maiden voyage.
(e) Sailed with 98 passengers.
(f) Sailed with 83 passengers.
(g) Delayed 15 days at Cape de Verde Islands repairing gale damage.
(h) One of five vessels that took out a contingent of Royal Engineers and their supplies to establish and maintain law and order in British Columbia at the onset of the Gold Rush.

1874

TO NEW ZEALAND

| No. | Name | Reg. Tons | Destination | Sailed from Gravesend | Arrived | Days |
|---|---|---|---|---|---|---|
| 1. | *John Bull* | 484 | Nelson | 4 Jan. | 18 April | 104 |
| 2. | *Portland* | 872 | Canterbury | 4 Jan. | 12 April | 95 |
| 3. | *Durham* | 998 | Otago | 14 Jan. | 16 April | 92 |
| 4. | *Jubilee* | 764 | Auckland | 20 Jan. | 15 May | 115 |
| 5. | *Golden Sea* | 1,418 | Wellington & Canterbury | 23 Jan.(a) | 30 April | 97 |
| 6. | *Undine* | 796 | Otago | 31 Jan. | 24 April | 83 |
| 7. | *Fratelli Gaggino* | 644 | Canterbury | 8 Feb. | 12 June | 124 |
| 8. | ss *Atrato* | 2,051 | Otago & Canterbury | 10 Feb.(b) | 8 June | 118 |
| 9. | *Schieballion* | 602 | Napier | 11 Feb. | 26 May | 104 |
| 10. | *La Hogue* | 1,331 | Wellington | 20 Feb(c) | 26 May | 95 |
| 11. | *Huntly Castle* | 623 | Auckland | 22 Feb.(d) | 28 May | 95 |
| 12. | *La Paix* | 449 | Nelson | 2 March | 29 June | 119 |
| 13. | *Buckinghamshire* | 1,446 | Otago | 8 March | 1 June | 85 |
| 14. | *City of Agra*(e) | 1,073 | Canterbury | 10 March | 27 May | 78 |
| 15. | *Syren* | 299 | Canterbury & Timaru | 15 March | 31 July | 138 |
| 16. | *Halcione* | 843 | Napier | 24 March(f) | 4 July | 102 |
| 17. | *Weymouth* | 829 | Wellington | 28 March | 17 July | 111 |
| 18. | *Stonehouse* | 1,163 | Canterbury | 28 March | 24 June | 88 |
| 19. | *Countess of Kintore* | 737 | Auckland | 30 March | 15 July | 107 |
| 20. | *Devana* | 795 | Otago | 13 April | 16 July | 94 |
| 21. | *Hereford* | 1,439 | Canterbury | 18 April | 14 July | 87 |
| 22. | *Carrick Castle* | 879 | Bluff Harbour Liverpool | 18 April | 13 July | 86 |
| 23. | *Euterpe* | 1,197 | Wellington | 28 April | 30 Aug. | 124 |
| 24. | *Adamant* | 815 | Nelson | 28 April(g) | 8 Aug | 102 |
| 25. | *Miltiades*(h) | 1,452 | Auckland | 3 May | 23 July | 81 |
| 26. | *Taunton* | 688 | Canterbury | 8 May | 4 Sept | 119 |
| 27. | *Sam Mendel* | 1,034 | Otago | 9 May | 23 July(i) | 75 |
| 28. | *City of Auckland* | 779 | Auckland | 19 May | 2 Sept. | 106 |
| 29. | *St Leonards* | 1,054 | Wellington | 3 June | 2 Sept. | 91 |
| 30. | *Pasithea* | 587 | Nelson | 6 June | 10 Oct. | 126 |
| 31. | *Oxford* | 1,282 | Auckland | 9 June | 8 Sept. | 91 |
| 32. | *Cathcart* | 1,387 | Canterbury | 11 June(j) | 29 Aug. | 79 |
| 33. | *Haddon Hall* | 1,416 | Otago | 13 June | 16 Sept. | 95 |
| 34. | *Merope* | 1,054 | Canterbury | 20 June | 27 Sept. | 99 |
| 35. | *Queen Bee* | 726 | Napier | 20 June | 16 Oct.(k) | 118 |
| 36. | *The Douglas* | 1,428 | Wellington | 3 July | 22 Oct. | 111 |
| 37. | *Celestial Queen* | 843 | Otago | 8 July(l) | 3 Nov. | 118 |
| 38. | *Zealandia* | 1,116 | Auckland & Otago | 10 July | 15 Oct. | 97 |
| 39. | *Elizabeth Graham* | 598 | Canterbury | 16 July | 7 Nov. | 114 |
| 40. | *Chile* | 768 | Nelson | 22 July | 26 Oct | 96 |
| 41. | *Helen Denny* | 728 | Napier & Wellington | 24 July | 22 Oct. | 90 |
| 42. | *Bebington* | 889 | Napier & Bluff | 28 July(m) | 21 Nov. | 116 |
| 43. | *Calypso* | 1,013 | Otago | 4 Aug.(n) | 25 Oct. | 82 |
| 44. | *Hydaspes* | 2,093 | Auckland | 11 Aug. | 6 Nov. | 87 |
| 45. | *Edward P. Bouverie* | 997 | Canterbury & Southland | 15 Aug. | 25 Nov. | 102 |
| 46. | *May Queen* | 733 | Otago | 19 Aug. | 15 Nov. | 88 |

| No. | Name | Reg. Tons | Destination | Sailed from Gravesend | Arrived | Days |
|-----|------|-----------|-------------|-----------------------|---------|------|
| 47. | *Soukar* | 1,304 | Wellington | 22 Aug.(o) | 2 Dec. | 102 |
| 48. | *Pleiades* | 997 | Canterbury | 29 Aug. | 16 Dec. | 109 |
| 49. | *Florence* | 841 | Otago | 6 Sept. | 30 Dec. | 115 |
| 50. | *Cospatrick* | 1,200 | Auckland | 11 Sept. | (p) | |
| 51. | *Langstone* | 746 | Wellington | 13 Sept. | 25 Dec. | 103 |
| 52. | *W.E. Gladstone* | 534 | Nelson | 19 Sept. | 4 Jan. | 107 |
| 53. | *Crusader* | 1,058 | Canterbury | 19 Sept. | 31 Dec. | 103 |
| 54. | *Glenlora* | 774 | Auckland | 26 Sept(q) | 5 Jan. | 101 |
| 55. | *Janet Cowan* | 1,278 | Otago | 9 Oct. | 4 Jan. | 87 |
| 56. | *Warwick* | 1,005 | Auckland | 11 Oct. | 22 Jan. | 103 |
| 57. | *Alice* | 627 | Canterbury & Southland | 11 Oct.(r) | 4 Feb. | 116 |
| 58. | *Avalanche* | 1,161 | Taranaki & Wellington | 22 Oct.(s) | 21 Jan. | 91 |
| 59. | *Lady Jocelyn* | 2,138 | Canterbury | 28 Oct. | 21 Jan. | 85 |
| 60. | *Anazi* | 468 | Auckland | 29 Oct. | 19 Feb. | 113 |
| 61. | *Michael Angelo* | 1,174 | Nelson & Bluff | 31 Oct.(t) | 22 Jan. | 83 |
| 62. | *City of Vienna* | 1,000 | Otago | 5 Nov. | 2 Feb. | 89 |
| 63. | *Esk* | 496 | Wellington | 12 Nov. | 4 March | 112 |
| 64. | *Hudson* | 797 | Napier | 20 Nov. | 12 Feb. | 84 |
| 65. | *Gareloch* | 1,177 | Otago | 23 Nov. | 12 Feb. | 81 |
| 66. | *Ada* | 686 | Auckland | 23 Nov. | 11 March | 108 |
| 67. | *India* | 912 | Auckland & Bluff | 25 Nov. | 4 March(u) | 99 |
| 68. | *Edwin Fox* | 836 | Wellington | 2 Dec.(v) | 18 April | 137 |
| 69. | *Ocean Beauty* | 578 | Canterbury | 3 Dec. | 24 March | 111 |
| 70. | *Kedron* | 373 | Otago | Liverpool 5 Dec. | 20 April | 136 |
| 71. | *Mallowdale* | 1,290 | Otago | 17 Dec. | 9 March | 82 |
| 72. | *Shooting Star* | 461 | Auckland | 24 Dec. | 17 May(w) | 144 |
| 73. | *Sunbeam* | 442 | Wellington | 24 Dec. | 23 April | 120 |

ELSEWHERE

| | Name | Reg. Tons | Destination | Sailed from Gravesend | Arrived | Days |
|-|------|-----------|-------------|-----------------------|---------|------|
| | *Bulwark* | 1,332 | Bombay | Liverpool 31 July | 25 Nov. | 117 |

*1874*

(a)  Sailed with 368 passengers. Eight deaths from scarlet fever during the voyage.
(b)  Only third steamship departure since the *Lord Ashley* in 1858. Sailed with 762 passengers (280 children, of whom 33 died). Put into Plymouth for repairs. Only 64 days from Plymouth to Otago.
(c)  Sailed with about 500 passengers. A large comfortable Blackwall frigate. Every cabin with its own light, grand saloon and generally a very superior ship. Massive figurehead. Popular Commander.
(d)  Sailed with only 26 passengers.
(e)  A well-heeled ship giving a fast passage.
(f)  Commander died at sea.
(g)  Sailed with 337 passengers. A very overcrowded voyage. Not the first of Shaw Savill's vessels in this condition. Three crew knocked overboard when shipping a gangway; one drowned.

(h) A great clipper. Stranded off Auckland Harbour, having missed stays but soon towed off.
(i) A fast passage in good weather.
(j) Sailed with 481 passengers. Cargo broached by crew. Commander fired pistol at crew, wounding some. Sore heads led to mutiny. Three months hard labour on arrival for four culprits.
(k) Took four months to secure sufficient homeward cargo.
(l) Detained in English Channel for ten days by bad weather.
(m) One crew member found dead, clinging to a spar aloft.
(n) Maiden voyage.
(o) Sailed with 600 passengers.
(p) Burnt at sea.
(q) The third of 26 voyages to New Zealand.
(r) Put back for repairs after collision in Channel: sailed finally on 7 November.
(s) Maiden voyage of a Company ship.
(t) Commander died at sea.
(u) Sailed with 183 passengers. Cargo broached, crew drunk and further visits to the Magistrate's Court at Auckland. Commander also fined for wilful interference with the Pilot in the discharge of his duties.
(v) Lost anchor in a gale: put back. In collision: again put back after a narrow shave with rocks off Deal. Sailed finally on 27 December.
(w) Arrived crippled. Two births during the voyage.

## 1880

### TO NEW ZEALAND

| No. | Name | Reg. Tons | Destination | Sailed from Gravesend | Arrived | Days |
|---|---|---|---|---|---|---|
| 1. | City of Quebec | 708 | Auckland | 3 Jan. | 18 April(a) | 106 |
| 2. | City of Florence | 1,200 | Otago | 3 Jan. | 12 April | 100 |
| 3. | Edwin Fox | 836 | Canterbury | 8 Jan.(b) | 3 May | 116 |
| 4. | Himalaya | 1,008 | Wellington | 7 Feb. | 17 May | 100 |
| 5. | John Bull | 484 | Auckland | 8 Feb. | 20 May | 102 |
| 6. | Trevelyan | 1,042 | Canterbury | 8 Feb. | 13 May | 95 |
| 7. | Rialto | 1,166 | Otago | 9 Feb. | 18 May | 99 |
| 8. | Chaudière | 470 | Nelson | 4 March | 1 July | 119 |
| 9. | Chile | 768 | Auckland | 6 March | 19 June | 105 |
| 10. | Ben Venue | 999 | Wellington | 6 March(c) | 9 June | 95 |
| 11. | Dunbritton | 1,471 | Otago | 12 March(d) | 12 June | 92 |
| 12. | Hudson | 797 | Canterbury | 16 March | 23 June | 99 |
| 13. | Mallowdale | 1,290 | Otago | 13 April | 12 July | 90 |
| 14. | Famenoth | 983 | Auckland | 16 April | 17 July | 92 |
| 15. | ss Norfolk | 2,027 | Canterbury & Wellington | 17 April | 12 June | 56 |
| 16. | Merope | 1,054 | Wellington | 19 April | 16 July | 88 |
| 17. | Helen Denny | 728 | Canterbury | 28 April | 19 July | 82(e) |
| 18. | Invercargill | 1,246 | Otago | 11 May | 30 July | 80 |
| 19. | Langstone | 746 | Auckland | 17 May | 22 Aug. | 97 |
| 20. | St. Leonards | 1,054 | Wellington | 23 May | 22 Aug. | 91 |
| 21. | Halcione | 843 | Canterbury | 30 May | 29 Aug. | 91 |
| 22. | City of Sparta | 1,193 | Otago | 10 June | 5 Sept. | 87 |
| 23. | Lochnagar | 468 | Auckland | 12 June | 16 Sept. | 96(f) |
| 24. | Wave Queen | 853 | Wellington & Napier | 19 June | 6 Oct. | 109 |
| 25. | Durham | 998 | Otago | 26 June | 2 Oct. | 98 |
| 26. | Crusader | 1,058 | Canterbury | 3 July | 7 Oct. | 96 |
| 27. | Lutterworth | 883 | Auckland | 7 July | 21 Oct. | 106 |

| No. | Name | Reg. Tons | Destination | Sailed from Gravesend | Arrived | Days |
|---|---|---|---|---|---|---|
| 28. | Zealandia | 1,116 | Otago | 19 July | 21 Oct. | 94 |
| 29 | Jessie Readman | 962 | Canterbury & Bluff | 25 July | 22 Oct. | 89 |
| 30. | Hermione | 1,120 | Wellington | 27 July | 30 Oct. | 95 |
| 31. | Glenlora | 774 | Auckland & Napier | 3 Aug. | 29 Oct. | 87 |
| 32. | Timaru | 1,306 | Otago | 14 Aug. | 11 Nov.(g) | 89 |
| 33. | Pleione | 1,092 | Wellington | 15 Aug. | 28 Nov | 105 |
| 34. | May Queen | 733 | Canterbury & Bluff | 22 Aug. | 3 Dec. | 103 |
| 35. | Anazi | 468 | Nelson | 28 Aug. | 27 Dec. | 121 |
| 36. | Dunloe | 674 | Auckland | 29 Aug. | 13 Dec. | 106 |
| 37. | Taranaki | 1,126 | Otago | 11 Sept. | 13 Dec. | 93 |
| 38. | Antares | 821 | Wellington | 16 Sept. | 12 Jan. | 118 |
| 39. | ss Durham | 1,638 | Canterbury | 18 Sept. | 22 Nov. | 65 |
| 40. | Lady Jocelyn | 2,138 | Tauranga & Auckland | 28 Sept. | 4 Jan.(h) | 98 |
| 41. | Auckland | 1,245 | Otago | 13 Oct. | 5 Jan. | 84 |
| 42. | Pleiades | 997 | Canterbury | 15 Oct.(i) | 17 Jan. | 94 |
| 43. | Euterpe | 1,197 | Wellington | 25 Oct. | 8 Feb. | 106 |
| 44. | Margaret Galbraith | 841 | Auckland | 29 Oct. | 25 Jan. | 88 |
| 45. | Wellington | 1,247 | Otago | 4 Nov. | 23 Jan. | 80 |
| 46. | Elizabeth Graham | 598 | Canterbury | 6 Nov. | 7 March | 122 |
| 47. | Electra | 668 | Nelson & Napier | 6 Nov. | 26 Feb. | 112 |
| 48. | Adamant | 815 | New Plymouth | 20 Nov. | 7 April | 139 |
| 49. | Alastor | 824 | Wellington | 29 Nov. | 3 April | 126 |
| 50. | Oamaru | 1,306 | Otago | 1 Dec. | 1 March | 91 |
| 51. | Oxford | 1,282 | Auckland | 4 Dec. | 2 April | 119 |
| 52. | Marlborough | 1,124 | Canterbury | 12 Dec. | 18 March | 97 |
| 53. | Westland | 1,116 | Otago | 22 Dec.(j) | 25 March | 94 |
| 54. | Edwin Fox | 836 | Bluff | 25 Dec.(k) | 23 May | 150 |

| No. | Name | Reg. Tons | Destination | Sailed from Greenock* | Arrived | Days |
|---|---|---|---|---|---|---|
| 1. | William Davie | 841 | Otago | 21 Jan. | 13 May | 113 |
| 2. | Abernyte | 700 | Otago | 3 March | 12 June | 101 |
| 3. | Otago | 993 | Otago | 30 April | 29 July | 90 |
| 4. | Rodell Bay | 1,080 | Wellington | 6 May | 14 Aug. | 100 |
| 5. | Lyttelton | 1,111 | Otago | 9 June | 6 Sept | 89 |
| 6. | Stirlingshire | 1,178 | Wellington | 11 June | 13 Sept. | 94 |
| 7. | Wild Deer | 1,016 | Otago | 15 July | 15 Oct. | 92 |
| 8. | Hannah Landles | 1,271 | Wellington | 6 Aug. | 15 Nov. | 101 |
| 9. | Dunedin | 1,250 | Otago | 24 Aug. | 24 Nov. | 92 |
| 10. | West Riding | 913 | Canterbury | 28 Aug. | 13 Dec. | 107 |
| 11. | Nelson | 1,247 | Otago | 29 Sept. | 25 Dec. | 87 |
| 12. | Isle of Erin | 889 | Wellington | 6 Oct. | 26 Jan. | 112 |
| 13. | Wigtonshire | 899 | Wellington | 30 Oct. | 7 Feb. | 100 |
| 14. | Canterbury | 1,245 | Otago | 3 Nov | 20 Jan. | 78 |
| 15. | Firth of Lorn | 833 | Canterbury | 9 Nov. | 19 March | 131 |
| 16. | William Davie | 841 | Otago | 9 Dec. | 22 March | 104 |

* Joint service with the Albion Line.

ELSEWHERE

| No. | Name | Reg. Tons | Destination | Sailed from Gravesend | Arrived | Days |
|---|---|---|---|---|---|---|
| 1. | *Warwick* | 1,005 | Brisbane | 20 March | 5 July | 107 |
| 2. | *Soukar* | 1,304 | Sydney | 2 July | 24 Oct.(l) | 114 |
| 3. | *Hydaspes* | 2,093 | Melbourne | 17 July | | |
| 4. | *Forfarshire* | 1,238 | San Francisco Newport | 19 July | 18 Dec. | 152 |
| 5. | *Bebington* | 889 | Melbourne | 13 Nov. | 24 March | 131 |

(a)  Fine weather all the way.
(b)  Sailed with 109 passengers. Iron rations for most of the voyage and wet berths.
(c)  Overran her destination and whilst retracing steps nearly came to grief on the Snares after seas had made a clean sweep of decks and smashed steering gear.
(d)  Sailed with 72 passengers.
(e)  The fastest voyage of this popular ship, despite a pasting.
(f)  When dragging anchors in gale at Gisborne Roadstead whilst loading homeward bound, Commander squared away and beached her high and dry – remaining there for several weeks before refloating herself.
(g)  Gales, decks awash, mountainous seas.
(h)  The first immigrant ship to call direct at Tauranga. A splendid sight this large clipper made as she made her landfall off the estuary and stood off awaiting a tow, which proved to be some adventure (including a broken tow rope and an emergency anchoring) during the difficult negotiation of the S-bend in the river. The tow cost £40, which was dear.
(i)  Sighted and boarded a derelict with bulwarks awash, masts gone and no sign of life. Two crew washed overboard and one apprentice fell from aloft. All drowned.
(j)  Two crew washed overboard and one apprentice fell from aloft. All drowned.
(k)  Second voyage in one year but could she go much slower?
(l)  Sunk next day in collision with ss *Centurion* five miles off Dungeness. All saved but all effects lost. Accident took place at 5 p.m. in dense fog whilst being towed down Channel.

# Appendix F

## *Postscript to the Sinking of the* Avalanche *and* Forest: *Extracts from Lloyd's List (1877)*

*Portland 12th September 10.05 am. Avalanche* been in collision and foundered off Portland; nearly all passengers and crew drowned. Further particulars when obtained. At present only John Sherrington, Third Officer, and two seamen found.

Another telegram – from John Sherrington, above report referred to, *Avalanche* foundered, nearly all crew and passengers drowned.

*Weymouth 12th September.* The Third Officer, J.C. Sherrington, one of the survivors of the *Avalanche*, reports as follows:

On Tuesday 11th September, about 9.00 pm, the weather being very dark, wind south-west blowing a stiff breeze, the ship being about fifteen miles south by west from Portland under short sail with both lights burning brightly, sailing by the wind, Second Mate's watch on deck, Channel Pilot in charge heard the man at the lookout forward report a light which was followed by the Pilot calling out 'Hard up!' to the man at the helm, and 'Port your helm' to the stranger, in the meantime taking the spanker and endeavouring to square cross jack yard. At this time I was in my bunk: jumped out and rushed on deck when I heard Second Officer say to the Chief Officer 'Come on deck, I think there will be another smash'. The first thing seen was the jibboom of the stranger coming through the main rigging and striking main mast, breaking jibboom in two. I got as far as quarter hatch when I felt myself lifted up and pitched head foremost down the hatch, falling on a number of passengers. A sudden rush of wind indicated that the ship was filling. The stranger had by this time struck the *Avalanche* a second time above the main mast; I sung out to the passengers to get on deck and save themselves if possible: rushed onto the poop and saw the Captain standing by the break: caught hold of him and told him to save himself as the ship was sinking; let him go when I, as the bows of the ship were coming down a third time, sung out to him to catch hold; this time the *Avalanche* was struck in the fore part of the mizzen rigging. In the rising of the stranger I caught hold of a chain and was dragged up clear of the *Avalanche* and as she was going down the fourth time jumped on to the foc'sle and went to the port side and saw the *Avalanche* almost gone, her decks being under water. The passengers and crew had by this time gone forward, the stern being under water and after most heartrending screams she gradually disappeared.

*Weymouth 17th September.* The wreck of the *Forest* is lying about four miles south and half east of the Shambles lightship. The whole of the stern is out of the water rising to a height of between 40 and 50 feet, while a large proportion of her bright metallic keel lies exposed to view. On this the sea is breaking but without affecting the stability of the hull. The *Forest* lies on her counter bottom upwards but not a spar of any description is to be seen. The Master of the *Commodore* had had a sounding taken of the depth of water in which the hull lies and found it to be twenty-seven fathoms so that according to her length she should be touching the ground. As she has not shifted a great deal since Sunday it is thought her bow is embedded in the sand on account of her ballast having all gone forward. Whatever the cause there must be a tremendous weight forward to keep her in the position in which she now remains. A more dangerous obstruction to navigation cannot be imagined than this great towering hull rising like a rock out of the sea and if it is not speedily removed there is no doubt serious consequences will result to shipping. Revenue cutter was cruising round her this morning and on the counter of the wreck was one of the cutter's men who seemed to be trying to establish a communication between the two. This was at last obtained but no sooner had the rope become taut and a strain put upon it than it parted. It is said that seven steamers passed nearly close to the wreck on Saturday night and that a barque was not far from coming into collision with the hull. To show how directly it lies in the highway of ships coming up and down the Channel it is mentioned that even during the short the *Premier* was going out several full rigged ships passed the hull.

It is said that a telegram was received from the Admiralty ordering one of the torpedo boats to be despatched tomorrow and blow up the hull.

Later, it is reported that a telegram was received from the Admiralty in reply to a message forwarded to the First Lord stating that although the ship will be blown up it is not likely to be by the use of torpedoes.

*Weymouth 18th September.* Early this morning Her Majesty's Ship *Defence*, lying in the Portland roads, got up steam and at 8 o'clock left for the wreck of the *Forest* accompanied by the steam launches of the *Warrior* and the *Thunderer*, and the steam pinnace of the *Black Prince*. The wreck was still lying about five miles from the Shambles and there was no noticeable alteration in her position or appearance. The *Defence* took up position about a quarter of a mile from the wreck at 11 o'clock and fired a shell that passed through the quarter just under the poop and out of the other side when it exploded in the air enveloping the wreck in smoke. When this had cleared away the hull was seen unmoved but she had two small holes in her quarter some six feet above the water. A rum puncheon charged with some 300 lbs of gunpowder or cotton was then loaded with extra weight and lowered down to the wreck from the steam launch of the *Warrior*. This operation was protracted and during all this time men were engaged in the wreck chopping through her quarters above the shell hole. About half-past-one Admiral Dowell arrived in his steam barge from the *Black Prince*. At 1.40 men were taken from the wreck and five minutes afterwards the contents of the puncheon were exploded from the stern of the *Warrior*'s launch. A magnificent cascade of water ascending some fifty feet and a few bits of timber set afloat were however the only result, the mine appearing to have been out of position – that is over, and not under, the wreck. The Admiral steamed back to Portland. The two launches attached three red kegs apparently containing about 100 lbs of gunpowder to the keep of the *Forest* having connected them with a battery on board the *Black Prince*'s pinnace. At 5 o'clock the charge was fired. The only result again was the rising a few feet into the air and mass of water. Half an hour afterwards steam was made for Portland roads and the sinking the hull is as far as ever from being accomplished. The *Forest* lies as yesterday in a most dangerous position.

Later, tomorrow it is stated that three mines of 300 lbs each will be placed under the ship and success is considered as certain. Divers cannot be used as the tide runs too strongly at this place.

*Weymouth 23rd September.* The attempts made by the boat sent from Her Majesty's Ship *Defence* to blow up the hull of the *Forest* having been proved ineffectual it was decided to endeavour to tow it into deep water for the purpose of destroying it. The reason it is said why these attempts have hitherto been unsuccessful is because the vessel was so firmly embedded into the sand that it was impossible to get any explosive materials under her deck whereas if she was in deep water this would be easy to accomplish. On Saturday therefore Her Majesty's Ship *Defence* and the Trinity boat *Galatea* steamed to the hull and succeeded by the evening in dragging it from its position off the Shambles and towing it in the direction of mid Channel so no doubt on Monday will be blown to pieces.

Later, the destruction of the *Forest* has been successfully accomplished and she is blown to pieces. This morning the *Defence* and *Galatea* were observed some miles off towing huge fragments of the wreck in the direction of Portland roads so at last the Channel is free of the dangerous obstruction which has impeded navigation for the last ten days.

# SHAW SAVILL AND ALBION COMPANY, LIMITED.

Incorporated under the Companies Acts 1862 to 1880, whereby the liability of Shareholders is limited to the amount of their Shares.

## CAPITAL, £700,000.
### In 70,000 Shares of £10 each.

First issue 35,000 Shares of £10 each (inclusive of 10,000 fully paid up Shares to be allotted to Walter Savill and James William Temple as Vendors), payable 10s. per Share on Application, 10s. on Allotment. The balance of this issue will be called up at intervals, as required, during the first year. One month's notice of each call being given.

5000 Shares reserved for the Colony of New Zealand.

The Company will also issue Debentures for £180,000, bearing interest at the rate of £5 per cent. per annum.

### Directors.

C. T. RITCHIE, M.P., *Chairman.*

WALTER SAVILL,
JAMES WM. TEMPLE, } of the Firm
OF SHAW SAVILL AND COMPANY,
*Managing Directors.*

PETER DENNY, CHAIRMAN OF THE ALBION SHIPPING CO., LIMITED.

JAMES GALBRAITH, MANAGING DIRECTOR OF THE ALBION SHIPPING CO., LIMITED.

JOHN GALLOWAY, of P. HENDERSON & Co., Glasgow.

JAMES PARK, of PARK BROTHERS, London.

EDWARD PEMBROKE, of GALBRAITH, PEMBROKE & Co., London.

### Managing Agents FOR THE CLYDE AND NEW ZEALAND TRADE.
P. HENDERSON & CO., Glasgow.

### Agents in New Zealand.

1. AUCKLAND—
   CRUICKSHANK & Co.
   OWEN & GRAHAM.
   L. D. NATHAN & Co.
2. WELLINGTON—
   LEVIN & Co.
   W. & G. TURNBULL & Co.
   EDWD. PEARCE.
3. CANTERBURY—
   DALGETY & Co.
   EDWARDS, BENNETT & Co.
   J. INGLIS.
4. OTAGO—
   NATIONAL MORTGAGE AND AGENCY Co. OF NEW ZEALAND, LIMITED.
   DALGETY & Co.
   BRITISH AND NEW ZEALAND MORTGAGE AND AGENCY Co., LIMITED.

5. BLUFF HARBOUR—
   AITKEN, CROSS & Co.
   McPHERSON & Co.
   WM. PAISLEY & Co.

6. NAPIER—
   KINROSS & Co.
   MURRAY, ROBERTS & Co.

7. NELSON—
   SCLANDERS & Co.
   J. H. COCK & Co.

8. NEW PLYMOUTH—
   JOHN GILMOUR.

9. POVERTY BAY—
   GRAHAM, PITT & BENNETT.

### Bankers.
LONDON & WESTMINSTER BANK, LIMITED, Lothbury, London.
THE CLYDESDALE BANK, LIMITED, Glasgow, Edinburgh, Aberdeen.

### Brokers.
LONDON—MACNICOLL & ROGERS, 35, Gresham House, E.C.
GLASGOW—{ KERR, ANDERSONS, MUIR & MAIN,
{ JOHN MILLER & J. H. FERGUSON.
EDINBURGH—BELL, BEGG & COWAN.

### Solicitors.
INGLEDEW & INCE, St. Benet Chambers, Fenchurch Street, E.C.

### Auditors.
TURQUAND, YOUNGS & CO.

### Manager in London.
JOHN GREENWAY.

### Secretary.
GEORGE D. TURNER.

### Offices.
34, LEADENHALL STREET, LONDON, E.C., AND 15, ST. VINCENT PLACE, GLASGOW.

# PROSPECTUS.

THE transport of produce between Great Britain and New Zealand, which for many years has rapidly progressed, has now assumed such dimensions as to convince those most intimately conversant with the trade that the advantages afforded by the extension of joint-stock enterprise are best fitted to meet the present requirements and to cope with the further development of this traffic, which, it is expected, will be largely increased by the exportation of fresh meat from the colony, the conveyance of which in perfect condition by *sailing ships*, under refrigerating processes, has recently been successfully demonstrated.

With this view the oldest shipowning firms in the New Zealand trade—Messrs. Shaw Savill & Co., of London, and the Albion Shipping Company, Limited, of Glasgow—have agreed, under certain conditions, to transfer their business to a new Company to be called "Shaw Savill and Albion Company, Limited."

The vessels to be taken over by the new Company, from the combined fleets of Messrs. Shaw Savill & Co. and the Albion Shipping Company, Limited, on the completion of the respective voyages on which they may be engaged on the 1st of January, 1883, when the business of the Company will commence, are as follows:

### LIST OF FLEET.

| | | | | |
|---|---|---|---|---|
| Akaroa | . 1298 Tons. | | Lyttelton | . 1111 Tons. |
| Auckland | . 1245 „ | | Margaret Galbraith | . 811 „ |
| Canterbury | . 1245 „ | | Merope | . 1051 „ |
| Crusader | . 1058 „ | | Nelson | . 1247 „ |
| Dunedin | . 1250 „ | | Oamaru | . 1306 „ |
| Euterpe | . 1197 „ | | Pleiades | . 997 „ |
| Forfarshire | . 1238 „ | | Pleione | . 1092 „ |
| Glenlora | . 774 „ | | Saint Leonards | . 1051 „ |
| Helen Denny | . 728 „ | | Soukar | . 1301 „ |
| Himalaya | . 1008 „ | | Timaru | . 1306 „ |
| Hudson | . 797 „ | | Trevelyan | . 1042 „ |
| Invercargill | . 1246 „ | | Wellington | . 1247 „ |
| Jessie Readman | . 962 „ | | Westland | . 1116 „ |
| Lady Jocelyn | . 2138 „ | | Wild Deer | . 1016 „ |
| Langstone | . 746 „ | | Zealandia | . 1116 „ |
| Lutterworth | . 883 „ | | | |

These are all first-class iron vessels, with the exception of the "Forfarshire," "Merope," and "Wild Deer," which are composite. The "Lady Jocelyn" and "Dunedin" are fitted with the Bell-Coleman refrigerating apparatus, and are together capable of carrying 15,000 sheep in their freezing rooms.

Particulars of the provisional contracts entered into are given, by which the Company will acquire the combined business of the two firms, and the ships specified, for the sum of £485,267.

Messrs. Walter Savill and James William Temple have agreed to take 10,000 fully paid-up Shares, of the nominal value of £10 each, and £100,000 in debentures, in part payment of the purchase-money due to them for their ships and the goodwill of their business.

The Directors have by their purchase-contract made an arrangement with Messrs. Shaw Savill and Co., which they consider of very great importance to the Company, viz., that these gentlemen are to give their services to the Company as Managing Directors for a period of not less than five years; and during that time are to receive as sole remuneration for their

3

services three fourths of the surplus profits made by the Company, after payment of a dividend of ten per cent. to the Shareholders, the interest on the debentures, and after writing off five per cent. to a depreciation fund against the amount from time to time standing to the debit of the Company in respect of the amount paid the vendors for their ships and the goodwill of their business.

Messrs. Shaw Savill & Co. and the Albion Shipping Company, Limited, are represented at the different ports in New Zealand by agents of well-known standing and influential position, whose services it is intended to continue for this Company.

The Directors of the Company will undertake precisely the same description of business as that heretofore carried on so successfully by Messrs. Shaw Savill & Co., and the Albion Shipping Company, Limited; and they believe with an increased amount of profit arising from the support of a large body of colonial and other shareholders who are expected to become interested in the undertaking.

The agreements entered into are as follows :

(1.) An Agreement, dated the 6th day of November, 1882, between Walter Savill and James William Temple, trading as Shaw, Savill & Co., of the one part, and John Greenway, as Trustee for and on behalf of this Company then in course of formation, of the other part.

(2.) An Agreement, dated the 6th day of November, 1882, between James Galbraith, on behalf of the Albion Shipping Company, Limited, of the one part, and John Greenway, as Trustee for and on behalf of this Company, then in course of formation, of the other part.

(3.) An Agreement, dated the 6th day of November, 1882, between P. Henderson & Co., of Glasgow, Managing Agents for the Albion Shipping Company, Limited, of the one part, and John Greenway, as Trustee for and on behalf of this Company then in course of formation, of the other part.

The above Agreements, together with the Memorandum and Articles of Association of the Company, can be inspected at the Offices of the Solicitors to the Company.

Copies of this Prospectus may be obtained on application to the Bankers and Brokers, Solicitors, or Secretary of the Company; and applications for Shares should be made on the form accompanying this prospectus, and where no allotment is made the amount paid on application will be returned in full.

*10th November,* 1882.

# Appendix H

## Ships Owned and Managed by Shaw Savill & Co after 1882

| Name | Gross Reg. Tons | Year Built | Builder | Hull | Rig | Year Bought | Age when Bought | Total Service Years | Year lost or sold | Age when lost or sold |
|---|---|---|---|---|---|---|---|---|---|---|
| Anazi* | | | | | | | | | | |
| Annesley | 1,696 | 1876 | Richardson, Stockton | Iron | Barque | 1902 | 26 | 9 | 1911 | 35 |
| Asterion | 528 | 1869 | Iliff, Sunderland | Iron | Barque | 1887 | 18 | 12 | 1899 | 30 |
| Bebington | | | | | | | | | | |
| Belfast | 1,957 | 1874 | Harland & Wolff, Belfast | Iron | Barque | 1892 | 18 | 18 | 1910 | 36 |
| City of Brussels | 991 | 1863 | Connell, Glasgow | Iron | Barque | 1892 | 29 | 12 | 1904 | 41 |
| Chaudière* | | | | | | | | | | |
| County of Inverness | 1,716 | 1877 | Barclay Curle, Glasgow | Iron | Ship | 1900 | 23 | 11 | 1911 | 34 |
| Edwin Fox* | | | | | | | | | | |
| Electra* | | | | | | | | | | |
| Elizabeth Graham* | | | | | | | | | | |
| Gladys | 1,363 | 1891 | Hill, Bristol | Steel | Barque | 1898 | 7 | 14 | 1912 | 21 |
| Halcione | 878 | 1869 | Steele, Greenock | Iron | Ship | 1887 | 18 | 9 | 1896 | 27 |
| Hermione* | | | | | | | | | | |
| Lindfield | 2,280 | 1891 | Russell, Greenock | Steel | Barque | 1891 | — | 20 | 1911 | 20 |
| Mayfield | 2,285 | 1892 | Russell, Greenock | Steel | Barque | 1892 | — | 13 | 1905 | 13 |
| Nelson | 1,310 | 1874 | Duncan, Port Glasgow | Iron | Ship | 1896 | 22 | 11 | 1907 | 33 |
| Samuel Plimsoll | 1,524 | 1873 | Hood, Aberdeen | Iron | Ship | 1900 | 27 | 3 | 1903 | 30 |
| Star of Russia | 1,981 | 1874 | Harland & Wolff, Belfast | Iron | Ship | 1898 | 24 | 1 | 1899 | 25 |

* see Appendix B for particulars.
Elizabeth Graham one of the very few ships refloated after stranding (in 1884) on the Seven Stones Reef, Scilly Islands.

# Bibliography

Andrews, G., *Veteran Ships of Australia and New Zealand* (Reed, New Zealand, 1976)

Appleton, Marjorie, *They Came to New Zealand* (Methuen, London, 1958)

Archibald, E.H.H., *Travellers by Sea* (HMSO, 1962)

Bott, A., *The Sailing Ships of the New Zealand Shipping Company* (Batsford, London, 1972)

Bouquet, Michael, *South Eastern Sail* (David & Charles, 1972)

Bowen, F.C., *Flag of the Southern Cross* (Shaw Savill and Albion, London 1939 and 1947)

*Sailing Ships of the London River* (Sampson Low, London)

Brett, Sir Henry, *White Wings* (Brett, New Zealand, 1924-8)

Bryant, Sir Arthur, *100 Years under the Southern Cross* (London, 1963)

Crawford, J.C., *Travels in New Zealand and Australia* (Trubner, London, 1880)

de Kerbrech, R.P., *Shaw, Savill & Albion – The Post-War Fortunes of a Shipping Empire* (Conway Maritime Press, London, 1986)

Domville-Fife, C.W., *Epics of the Square-Rigged Ships* (Seeley, Service, London, 1958)

Glue, W.A., *The New Zealand Ensign* (Government Printers, Wellington, 1965)

Greenhill, B. and Gifford, A., *The Merchant Sailing Ship* (David & Charles, UK, 1970)

Hillary, J.H., *Westland* (Acorn, UK, 1979)

Ingram, C.W.N. and Wheatley, P.O., *New Zealand Shipwrecks* (Reed, New Zealand, 1936)

Laird, Dorothy, *Paddy Henderson* (Outram, Glasgow, 1961)

Lloyd's Lists

Lloyd's Registers of Shipping

Lubbock, B., *The Colonial Clippers* (Brown, Glasgow, 1919)

*The Blackwall Frigates* (Brown, Glasgow, 1924)

*Sail* (Blue Peter, UK, 1927)

*The Last of the Windjammers* (Brown, Glasgow, 1927)

*The Romance of the Clipper Ships* (Hennel Locke, London, 1948)

Maber, John M., *North Star to Southern Cross* (Stephenson, UK, 1967)
MacGregor, D.R., *Fast Sailing Ships* (Nautical, UK, 1973)
  *Square Rigged Sailing Ships* (Argus Books, UK, 1977)
  *Merchant Sailing Ships, 1850-1875* (Conway Maritime Press, London, 1984)
  *The Tea Clippers: Their History and Development 1833-1875* (Conway Maritime Press, London, 1984)
MacMullen, J., *Star of India* (Howel-North, 1961)
*Making New Zealand* (New Zealand Department of Internal Affairs, 1940)
Parsons, R., *Sail in the South* (Hale, London, 1975)
Pearse, A.W., *Windward Ho* (Andrew, Sydney, 1932)
Saint, A. *Richard Norman Shaw* (Yale, London, 1983)
Seaman, L.C.B., *Victorian England* (Methuen, London, 1973)
Shaw, F.H., *Famous Shipwrecks* (Elkin Mathews, London, 1930)
Sinclair, Keith, *A History of New Zealand* (Penguin Books, UK, 1984)
Stewart, I.G., *The Ships that Serve New Zealand* (Reed, New Zealand, 1964)
Sutton, J., *Lords of the East* (Conway Maritime Press, London, 1981)
Thomson, M.G., *A Pakeha's Recollections* (Reed, New Zealand, 1944)
*Vanity Fair*
Villiers, Alan, *The War with Cape Horn* (Hodder & Stoughton, London, 1971)
  *Voyaging with the Wind* (HMSO, 1975)
Waters, S.D., *Clipper Ship to Motor Liner* (New Zealand Shipping Co. London, 1939)
  *Shaw Savill Line* (Whitcombe & Tombs, New Zealand, 1961)
Watson, J., *Savills, A Family and a Firm 1652-1977* – the land agents (Hutchinson Benham, London 1977)
Wilkinson, J.D., *Early New Zealand Steamers* (Maritime Historical Publications, New Zealand, 1966)
Winchester, C., *Shipping Wonders of the World* (Amalgamated Press, London, 1937)
Wood, W., *Survivors' Tales of Famous Shipwrecks* (EP Publishing, UK, 1974)

### Libraries and Museums

HM Customs and Excise archives, London
New Zealand House, London
The Canterbury Museum, Christchurch
The Central Reference Library, London
The *Illustrated London News* Picture Library, London
The National Maritime Museum, London
The Royal Commonwealth Society, London
The Victoria and Albert Museum, London

# Index